Liz Curtis Higgs

Loved by God

Trusting His Promises
& Experiencing His Blessings

A Bible Study Workbook

SAMPSON RESOURCES

CONTENTS

What others are saying about Liz Curtis Higgs and *Loved by God*

"*Loved by God* is a must for every women's ministry!"
Debbie Stuart, Director of Women's Ministry
Prestonwood Baptist Church, Dallas, TX

"What a master storyteller Liz is. She makes the Bible come alive."
Amie Price, Women's Ministries
RiverTree Christian Church, Massillon, OH

"*Loved by God* is an inspiring Bible study. You'll be blessed.
And I love the workbook!"
Melissa Shaver, Director of Women's Ministries
The Heights Baptist Church, Richardson, TX

"I am constantly amazed at Liz's biblical depth, understanding, and the
tremendous way she shares it. Truly, she has been anointed of God."
Evelyn Blount, Executive Director
South Carolina Women's Missionary Union

"*Loved by God* will touch your heart and encourage your spirit."
Kay Daigle, Women's Ministry Director
Northwest Bible Church, Dallas, TX

"Liz was a hit with our audience! She is a gift to my life!"
Gloria Gaither, Praise Gathering, Indianapolis, IN

"We have laughed and cried and been encouraged that God loves us."
Debra Lavin, President, Alliance Women
First Alliance Church, Erie, PA

"Liz is a true master at touching the hearts of people. She's fantastic!"
Judy Russell, wife of Bob Russell, Senior Minister
Southeast Christian Church, Louisville, KY

Welcome to the Family!

God's Plans for Us Are Bigger Than We Can Imagine

GENESIS 25:19-28

Welcome to the Family!

O h, dear sister, what a thrilling journey awaits us!

I am honored to lead the way as we study the lives of Jacob and Esau, Leah and Rachel and discover what it truly means to be loved by God. If you've ever doubted God's love for you or felt unworthy of his blessings, you've come to the right place.

We'll soon learn that Jacob used every trick in the book to achieve success on his own terms before his past caught up with him…and still God stood by him: "Yet I have loved Jacob" (Malachi 1:2). Leah, meanwhile, tried her best to earn Jacob's undivided devotion, yet received God's unconditional love instead when he blessed her with children: "When the LORD saw that Leah was not loved, he opened her womb…" (Genesis 29:31).

What a heart-changing difference this story has made in my own walk with God! Imagine what God will do in your life as you open his timeless Word and watch it come alive.

Do yourself a favor and complete your lessons each day—I promise it won't take very long—using whatever Bible you most enjoy. My primary translation is the New International Version (NIV). I'd encourage you to locate other translations in your favorite bookstore or online to enhance your understanding of each passage.

There are optional questions, marked with a ♥ that will add to your growth and understanding. Wise is the woman who finds a few extra minutes to explore those questions…and *forgiven* is the woman whose busy life won't allow that additional study just now. At the end of each day's lesson appears a prayer, which I've intentionally left open-ended. Please take a moment to add your own heartfelt words for our loving, listening God to hear.

In your small-group time, share the principles you've learned and the ways they apply to your daily life. After all, the truths found in the Bible are meant not only to be studied but also to be put into action. Women at various stages of spiritual growth will be seated around you. Why not encourage the "younger" women and draw strength from those who have known God's love longer so that it becomes a meaningful time for every participant?

Come walk with me, friend, as we embark on a journey together that will change your life forever!

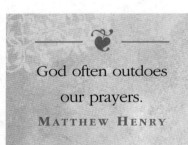

God often outdoes
our prayers.
MATTHEW HENRY

God's Plans for Us Are Bigger Than We Can Imagine

Today's lesson: Genesis 25:19-28

Major events:

■ Jacob and Esau are born to Isaac and Rebekah after many struggles.

■ Each parent chooses a favorite, pitting the brothers against each other.

Isaac wasn't praying selfishly. He was concerned about God's plan for fulfilling His covenant and blessing the whole world through the promised Messiah.

WARREN WIERSBE

Video Notes

Insights:

Sibling Rivalry

God Honors His Promises,
Even When We Don't

GENESIS 25:27-34; 26:34-35; 27:1-29

Sibling Rivalry

God Honors His Promises, Even When We Don't

Read Genesis 25:27-34; 26:34-35; 27:1-29.

Major events:

■ Esau sells his birthright to Jacob for a bowl of stew and later marries poorly.

■ Rebekah disguises Jacob, who proceeds to steal Esau's blessing.

■ Isaac unintentionally blesses his younger son, Jacob.

This week's verse to remember:

"God is no mere human! He doesn't tell lies or change his mind. God always keeps his promises." (Numbers 23:19, CEV)

his week we'll find out what sort of young men these two brothers became, shaped and molded as they were by their older parents, each of whom picked a favorite son. Dangerous practice, that. Had the boys been identical twins, we might have seen more similarities, not only in their looks, but in their personalities and preferences as well. Instead, they become as different as night and day, as dark and light, as hairy and smooth.

Jacob had more than smooth skin, though; he had a smooth way of handling his brother to get what he wanted. A manipulative parent may (unintentionally) teach a child the value of persuasive speech and clever finagling.

You'll soon see that the drama in these scenes is of a domestic nature. Not big, parting-of-the-Red-Sea stuff. Just family gatherings around a meal. But gatherings marked by deception. Three centuries before the birth of Christ, Demosthenes wrote, "Nothing is more easy than to deceive one's self." Deception and self-deception are at the heart of this week's lesson.

When we study the family of Isaac and Rebekah, we may shake our heads and say, "Dysfunctional with a capital *D!*" Rebekah and Jacob fell into the traps of self-deception and rationalization, dragging Isaac and Esau along for a bumpy ride and permanently changing all their lives in the process. And if we're not careful, we can do the same.

Day One: A Bold Bargain

Read Genesis 25:27-28.

1. Both Rebekah and Isaac were on hand to raise their sons, yet it seems they did not parent in the same fashion. Whom did each parent favor and why?

_____

_____

2. If you've seen parental favoritism in a family, how did that preferential treatment affect the child's...

relationship with the other parent?

_____

_____

relationship(s) with his or her sibling(s)?

_____

_____

relationship with God (if apparent)?

_____

_____

> *They personified two ways of life typical for Palestine, which at that time was more wooded: that of the hunter and that of the shepherd.*
> GERHARD VON RAD

3. If you have children, do you relate to them in the same ways? Even if you have twins, do you find yourself relating to one better than the other?

_____

How can you understand one child better than another and yet not show favoritism?

_____

_____

While we wouldn't condone favoritism, what does a parent do when a child has special needs, is chronically ill, or has suffered a trauma? How can you give special attention to one child, when necessary, without favoring that child?

_____

_____

_____

4. What do the following verses teach us about our responsibilities as parents—or as anyone who has influence over the lives of children?

Deuteronomy 5:29 _____

Deuteronomy 11:18-21 _____

Ephesians 6:4 _____

Read Genesis 25:29-34.

5. In this short but dramatic scene, what trade does Jacob suggest, and why is it audacious?

_____

_____

6. The birthright "applied to certain advantages, privileges, and responsibilities of firstborn baby boys....The *advantages* and privileges were that this baby became the object of special affection and would legally receive a double portion of his father's estate. The *responsibilities* were that he was expected to assume the spiritual leadership of the family. He was also required to provide food, clothing, and other necessities for his mother until her death and all unmarried sisters until their marriage." To better understand the cultural significance of this role, look up these other instances of the "firstborn." What does each tell us about the significance of the firstborn?

Deuteronomy 15:19 _____

Deuteronomy 21:15-17 _____

Luke 2:23 _____

Hebrews 1:6 (To whom is this specifically referring?)_____

Revelation 1:5 _____

7. Let's look first at Jacob's role in this exchange. A matter of mere seconds separated his birth from Esau's, yet in that culture those seconds would make all the difference in what he inherited and his role in the family. How might Jacob have justified bargaining with Esau for the birthright?

_____

_____

Do you think he wanted the earthly blessings, or do you think he was aware of God's promise to his mother and he was just "helping God" fulfill the promise? Why do you think this? Refer to Genesis 25:19-28.

_____

_____

8. Although the concept of the blessings of birthright may seem foreign to you, have you ever been in a work situation where someone else got the promotion, the raise, the perks, or the praise even though you were just as deserving? Which of the following best describes your reaction?

❑ It's not fair, and I'm going to do something about it!

❑ I resent it, and it makes me angry, but I have to put up a good front.

❑ If that's the way it's going to be, I'll never again go the extra mile for this company!

❑ It's not fair, but maybe it'll be my turn next.

❑ I'm disappointed, but I'm going to trust God with this.

If you were to face that situation again someday, how might you handle it differently?

_____

_____

9. Jacob's own grandfather Abraham (formerly called Abram) tried to help God fulfill his promises to him. What promise did God make to Abram (Genesis 15:1-5)?

_____

_____

How did Abraham and Sarah try to fulfill God's promise themselves (Genesis 16:1-4a)?

_____

_____

What consequences were there (Genesis 16:4b-16)?

_____

Why did Abraham laugh when God restated his promise to bless Abraham (Genesis 17:15-17)?

_____

_____

How was God's promise fulfilled (Genesis 21:1-3)? Why do you suppose God waited this long to fulfill his promise to Abraham?

_____

_____

Surely Jacob knew the story of his father's birth. What lesson should he have learned from Isaac?

_____

_____

10. Have you ever seen a bit of Jacob in yourself—"helping God out"? What was the result?

_____

_____

_____

_____

Prayer

Father, when I look at Abraham, Isaac, Rebekah, and Jacob, I can so easily see their flaws and wonder why they did such foolish things. Help me to examine myself as well and see the flaws and sins I overlook or maybe even dismiss as insignificant. Shine the light of your truth on my life, and forgive me when I try to fulfill your promises on my own…

Day Two: Older but Not Wiser

Read Genesis 25:29-34.

1. Now let's examine Esau's role in this drama. What kind of condition is Esau in when Jacob proposes this bargain? Do you think his statement in verse 32 is an exaggeration or the truth? Why?

_____

_____

2. What is he willing to give up for the sake of a meal?

_____

_____

3. Based on the description of the birthright in yesterday's question 6, what do you think might have influenced Esau to give up his birthright?

_____

_____

> ❦
>
> He was defrauded
> of that which he
> was incapable of
> appreciating.
>
> RALPH H. ELLIOTT

4. When you look at Esau in this scene, being led astray by his appetite, what words come to mind to describe his behavior?

_____

5. We don't have to look very far to find examples of modern-day people who gave away things of lasting value—relationships, integrity, their self-esteem, their souls—to satisfy an appetite for money, pleasure, fame. Have you ever had tendencies toward Esau's temperament (on a very bad day, perhaps!)? Describe an example in your own life when you went for short-term gain instead of long-term benefit.

_____

_____

What were the consequences?

_____

_____

What lesson did you learn?

_____

_____

6. We can have a godly appetite as well. Make a note of your discoveries in each of the following verses.

Psalm 107:8-9 _____

Luke 6:21 _____

John 6:35 _____

7. Esau's actions in 25:34 are described in Hebrew with four short verbs in succession, a very unusual construction in that language. In your translation, what are those four actions?

_____

What conclusions could we draw from this stark description of Esau's behavior?

_____

_____

8. The last line of verse 34 neatly summarizes this sibling's struggle. How did Esau feel about his birthright?

_____

This is the only place in all of Genesis where this Hebrew word, translated as "despised" in the New International Version, is used. To compare, check out the following verses, and you'll see the thing that is despised has great value. In each case, what valuable "thing" is held in contempt and treated as worthless (all three of which involved King David)?

1 Samuel 17:42 _____

2 Samuel 6:16 _____

2 Samuel 12:9 _____

How would you restate that last sentence of Genesis 25:34 in your own words?

_____

9. In a sad irony, Esau himself would be despised for his actions. What does Hebrews 12:15-17 say about Esau?

_____

_____

Read Genesis 26:34-35.

10. Commentator John Hartley suggests the boys were in their late teens when the scene with the red stew took place, but by the end of the next chapter, Genesis 26:34, many years have passed. How old is Esau here, and whom has he married?

_____

Most parents are pleased when their sons marry, but what was the reaction of Isaac and Rebekah?

_____

_____

The problem is not that there were two wives but that they were Hittites; they were from a tribe of Canaanites. Earlier, in Genesis 24:1-4, Abraham had made sure that his son Isaac didn't marry a Canaanite. Why did both of these families not want their sons to marry Canaanites? Read Deuteronomy 7:1-4

_____

_____

Although God's command in Deuteronomy 7:1-4 was recorded many years after this story, what clue does it give into the problem of marrying Canaanites?

_____

_____

In what way do Esau's actions in Genesis 26:34 fit with his actions in chapter 25?

_____

_____

11. After looking at these passages regarding Esau, how would you sum up his nature? If we learn by example, what is the strongest lesson he has taught you?

_____

_____

_____

Prayer

Father, when I read the sad and stark words that Esau was rejected and could bring about no change of mind even though he sought the blessing with tears, I am so grateful that the same doesn't have to be said of me. Thank you that you do not reject me, that when I seek you in tears over my mistakes, you do not turn me away. Help me never to take for granted, or to treat casually, the blessing of being your child…

Day Three: An Aging Father, a Scheming Mother

Read Genesis 27:1-10.

1. As was the custom, Isaac prepared to give his firstborn son, Esau, his blessing. What two facts do we learn about Isaac at the start of this scene? Both play an important part in the story!

_____

_____

This week's verse to remember:
"God is no mere human! He doesn't tell lies or change his mind. God always keeps his promises." (Numbers 23:19, CEV)

2. Despite Esau's marriage to two Hittite brides, how does Isaac appear to feel about Esau? What do you base this on?

_____

_____

3. When Isaac calls him, Esau immediately responds, "Here I am." Perhaps he had an inkling of what was coming. Genesis 27:2 is an opening statement any hearer of the time would have understood to be nigh to legal terminology. What two statements does Isaac make?

_____

_____

4. In Genesis 27:3-4, what two tasks does Isaac give Esau to do?

_____

_____

And what will Isaac do for him in return?

_____

What similarities do you see between this plan and Esau and Jacob's exchange over the stew?

_____

_____

5. While Esau hunts for venison, Rebekah hunts for a solution. Why is she so determined that Jacob receive the blessing instead? What could it be compared to today?

_____

_____

_____

6. The word "blessing" appears twelve times in this chapter alone. It *really* mattered! And it still matters today. Although we may long for a blessing from our earthly parents, it is the blessing of our heavenly Father that matters most. What can we learn about those blessings from the following verses?

John 1:16 _____

Galatians 3:13-14_____

Ephesians 1:3 _____

7. Carefully compare Isaac's words to Esau (Genesis 27:4) with Rebekah's retelling of those same words to Jacob (Genesis 27:7). What *significant* difference do you see in Rebekah's version? Why does she add those words, do you think?

_____

_____

8. Rebekah's actions beg the question, "On whose behalf is she doing this: the Lord's, her son Jacob's, or her own?" See if can you make a case for any or for all three.

For the Lord: _____

For Jacob: _____

For herself: _____

9. Much like Jacob earlier, Rebekah takes God's promise into her own hands and devises a plan to fulfill it. In what way is her plan even more cunning than Jacob's clever bartering with the lentil soup?

_____

_____

_____

10. Although Rebekah *may* have had good motives, she certainly engaged in some dubious behavior. Which of her following behaviors do you see at work in your own life?

❏ eavesdropping on a private conversation

❏ exploiting someone else's weaknesses for her own gain

❏ invoking the Lord's name to strengthen her words

❏ assuming she knows what's best for her grown child and directing his actions

❏ taking the fulfillment of God's promise into her own hands

What one step could you take to begin changing this tendency?

_____

Day Four: A Hairy Plan

Read Genesis 27:8-17.

1. Genesis 27:8 indicates that Rebekah had a plan. Does she give Jacob the option of *not* obeying her? What does that tell us about their relationship, even though he is very much a grown man at this point?

_____

_____

> *This week's verse to remember:*
> "God is no mere human! He doesn't tell lies or change his mind. God always keeps his promises."
> (Numbers 23:19, CEV)

2. In Genesis 27:9, Rebekah repeats once more the request that Isaac made of Esau as she stated it in Genesis 27:7, this time with a *subtle* difference. What is it?

_____

_____

Why do you think she would have dared try so risky a substitution?

_____

_____

3. Now Jacob responds to his mother's wild plan. What is Jacob worried about?

_____

What does he *not* express concern about (all those practical questions you and I might have asked!)?

_____

_____

4. His mother's initial response in Genesis 27:13 is shocking. What does she say?

_____

_____

Oh, Rebekah! Look up Genesis 4:9-12 for a sense of what it meant to be cursed by God. According to those verses, who was cursed and why?

_____

_____

And how does that cursed young man respond in Genesis 4:13?

_____

_____

Why would Rebekah have made such an outrageous statement?

_____

_____

> She operates behind the scenes, but she controls the action.
> CHRISTIANA DE GROOT

5. The following verses remind us to keep our motives and actions pure. Look up each passage and jot down what it says to you about deceiving others:

Proverbs 14:8 _____

Proverbs 24:28_____

Romans 16:17-18_____

2 Corinthians 4:1-2 _____

6. Although we might not plan as elaborate a deception as Rebekah's, what are some more subtle ways we intentionally deceive other people?

_____

_____

7. We are also cautioned by Scripture not to deceive ourselves. What do the following verses teach you about self-deception?

1 Corinthians 3:18-20 _____

James 1:22-25_____

1 John 1:8 _____

8. Which situation is harder for you to watch: one person deliberately deceiving another, or someone foolishly deceiving himself? Why is that?

_____

_____

Which is the easier trap for you to fall into? Why?

_____

_____

9. We tend to treat some levels of deception and lies as minor sins. Flattery, white lies, pulling the wool over someone's eyes—surely they don't rank with murder and adultery! But read John 8:44. Restate in your own words how much God hates lying.

_____

_____

By contrast, how does Paul describe the children of God in Ephesians 5:8-10?

_____

_____

10. Is there any place in your life where deception or a lie has taken root—perhaps even a self-deception? What change do you need to make?

_____

_____

_____

Prayer

Father, I want to rid my life of any desire to deceive others or myself. Help me to take the truth as seriously as you do. Please guide my thoughts, my words, my actions so that the father of lies cannot gain any foothold in me. I want to be solely your child, a child of light…

Day Five: Blessings for the Deceiver

Read Genesis 27:18-29.

1. Rebekah is left to wring her hands while Jacob puts their deceitful plan in motion. In the dialogue between the aging father and scheming son, what questions or concerns does Isaac raise?

_____

_____

This week's verse to remember:

"God is no mere human! He doesn't tell lies or change his mind. God always keeps his promises." (Numbers 23:19, CEV)

2. Now count how many lies Jacob tells, as recorded in these few verses. List as many as you can find (there are often two in a single sentence!).

_____

_____

_____

3. Read Genesis 27:20 again. One biblical commentator, Meredith Kline, said of that verse, "The deceiver...spoke more truth than he realized." What might Dr. Kline mean by that?

_____

_____

And what might this verse tell us about Jacob and his relationship with God at this point?

_____

_____

4. Skim through Genesis 27:18-26. How many times does Isaac use the words "my son" in your translation? _____ Surprised at the number? What might be the significance of Isaac's repetition of these words?

_____

_____

In the passages that you have read this week, who is the only person that Rebekah calls "my son"? What interaction does she have with Esau in these passages?

_____

_____

5. His meat and wine consumed, Isaac puts Jacob to the test once again. In the NIV, Genesis 27:26 is the first time the word "kiss" appears in the Bible. Why do you suppose Isaac requests a kiss? How might Proverbs 24:26 help answer this question?

_____

_____

> An abundant measure of [rain] was especially precious in a country where the rain is confined to two seasons of the year.
>
> JAMES G. MURPHY

What New Testament example does this remind you of involving a kiss, an identity, and a betrayal?

_____

6. Genesis 27:28-29 recounts Isaac's brief but powerful blessing of Jacob. Jot down all the blessing includes.

_____

_____

_____

How does Isaac's blessing parallel God's promise to Rebekah stated in Genesis 25:23?

_____

_____

Which of the four statements that God made to Rebekah was already starting to be fulfilled?

_____

7. Think back over the events we've covered this week. How would you sum up this dysfunctional family? Whom did you relate to the most?

❏ the doting, gullible Isaac

❏ the dramatic, manipulative Rebekah

❏ the clever, deceitful Jacob

❏ the short-sighted, impulsive Esau

What lesson can you learn from that person?

_____

_____

8. From what you have seen of Jacob's behavior thus far, what has Jacob done to earn or deserve the blessings and favor of God?

_____

Why at this point in the story is God still in the process of honoring his promise to make Jacob's descendants a great nation?

_____

♥ 9. The biblical writers described God's faithfulness toward his people with many different word pictures. What different aspect of his faithfulness does each of the following images convey?

Psalm 121:3-4_____

Isaiah 49:14-16 _____

Jeremiah 33:19-21 _____

Hebrews 6:16-19 _____

Which image speaks to your heart the most? Why?

_____

_____

10. Select one of God's promises you find in Scripture that you want to trust more. Then state it in your own words and personalize what that promise means to you.

Because God's Word says in _____ that he _____,

then I can trust him to_____.

If the story stopped right here, we'd have quite a mess on our hands. And there are more lies and deceit to come! But God's will *will* prevail, and his promises will not fail.

After Your Group Discussion...

The main principles or truths I learned this week are...

I want to apply these truths to my life by...

Prayer

Father, thank you that I have not come to the end of the story—not theirs and not mine. Help me to learn from their lives and from your Word. Help me to trust that you keep your promises even when I don't, that you bless me even though I am not worthy, that you love me even when I am unlovable. I praise you for being the one and only constant in life...

Video Notes

Insights:

Running from God

God Knows All About Prodigal Children

GENESIS 27:30–28:9

Running from God

God Knows All About Prodigal Children

Read Genesis 27:30–28:9.

Major events:

■ Esau returns in time to learn that Jacob has received his father's blessing.

■ Furious, Esau threatens to kill Jacob after their father dies.

■ Rebekah tells Jacob to run for his life to her brother Laban in Haran.

■ Isaac urges Jacob to seek a wife among his cousins in Haran.

■ Esau makes yet another blunder, choosing another wife.

This week's verse to remember:
"The unfailing love of the LORD never ends! By his mercies we have been kept from complete destruction. Great is his faithfulness; his mercies begin afresh each day." (Lamentations 3:22-23, NLT)

Everyone has known—and some of us have *been*—a prodigal. The original meaning of "prodigal" stems from the notion of "wasteful extravagance," describing a person who carelessly handles something of great value. Because of the New Testament story of the prodigal son (Luke 15:11-32), the word has also come to mean someone who has thrown away the blessings of God with both hands, only to regret his foolishness later and return home with his hat (and little else) in his hands. Without question, Jesus' listeners would have thought of Jacob and Esau when they first heard the parable of a father and his two sons.

This week in our study, Isaac, who is now old and blind, thinks he has just passed on the blessing to his firstborn son, Esau. But both he and Esau are in for a shock. Rebekah's scheme has succeeded, and now there are consequences. Everyone in the family will pay a price, and we will see that sometimes there are no "do overs." What is spoken must be carried out. It would be a sad story indeed were it not for the promises and plans of God, which while not in the foreground of this week's events, nonetheless play the most critical role.

Since descriptions of motives and emotions are often in short supply in

Scripture, we must look carefully at *what* is said and done and *how* it's said and done. Rebekah's behavior as a mature woman differs significantly from that of the young bride of Genesis 24. And while Jacob seems to hide not only his smooth skin but his feelings as well, Isaac and Esau hold nothing back emotionally in their painful scene together after Isaac has blessed Jacob.

Clyde Francisco, in *The Broadman Bible Commentary: Genesis,* wrote, "It is almost as impossible to call back a spoken word to one's children as it is to summon a soul from the dead." As a parent, I hear that one loud and clear, and I pray my words will bless *both* my children equally and equip them to lead godly lives. One former prodigal in the family—me!—is more than enough.

Day One: A Matter of Minutes

Read Genesis 27:30-33.

1. This scene turns on a single verse: Genesis 27:30. Once again in Jacob's and Esau's lives, timing makes all the difference. Who benefits and who loses this time?

_____

2. Note that all three men—Isaac, Jacob, Esau—are not only named in the verse, but their relationship to one another is also included—father, brothers. What purpose do you suppose all that identification serves?

_____

_____

3. Esau asks Isaac to sit up, just as his brother did earlier. The Hebrew word, *qum,* which appears in verse 31, literally means "to arise, to begin something." What is Esau eager for his father to do?

_____

_____

Given Esau's previously cavalier attitude toward his birthright, how do you explain this keen desire he now shows for the blessing?

_____

_____

4. Instead, his father asks a question. How does this question differ from the one he earlier asked Jacob, back in verse 18? Do you think there is any significance in the difference? If so, explain.

_____

_____

WEEK TWO

5. In response, Esau identifies himself in what three ways?

_____

_____

How had Jacob responded when asked a similar question by Isaac?

_____

_____

6. The two scenes of Jacob and Esau each asking their father for his blessing have been very similar to this point. Why does Isaac respond differently to Esau's answer than he did to Jacob's?

_____

_____

7. When the truth sinks in, Isaac—a quiet, reserved man—does something rather startling…what?

_____

What emotions do you see contributing to that physical response?

_____

8. If anger is one of these possible emotions, whom might Isaac be angry with and why?

_____

_____

9. In these days of "road rage" and "air rage," we're well aware of the power of anger. What do the following passages teach us about handling anger?

Psalm 37:7-9 _____

Proverbs 29:11_____

Ecclesiastes 7:9_____

Ephesians 4:26-27_____

Based on these verses—or others you've considered in the past—state in your own words how you would like to handle anger differently than you have before.

_____

_____

_____

> The tree was shaken, but it did not fall. He knew that God's will had been done.
> CLYDE FRANCISCO

10. Sometimes, if we're honest with ourselves, the one we're angry with is God. Perhaps Psalm 77 is one that we can relate to at such times.

According to verses 1-7, how does the psalmist feel about God at the moment?

_____

_____

According to verses 11-12, what does the psalmist choose to think about?

_____

_____

What effect would this likely have on him?

_____

_____

What traits of God does he focus on in verses 13-15?

_____

_____

The next time you are angry with God, what acts or traits of God could you focus on to gain a better perspective in the situation?

_____

_____

_____

Prayer

Heavenly Father, I confess that so often my focus is on me and what I want, and I get angry when I'm lied to or betrayed. Help me replace my anger with patience, my judgment with forgiveness, my selfishness with generosity. Teach me to extend to others the same mercy I so desperately need from you. Help me accept your will for my life and the lives of those I love…

<table>
<tr><td>

Day Two: Bitter Tears

</td></tr>
</table>

Read Genesis 27:34-40.

1. For the second time this day, someone has come to Isaac, claiming to be Esau, the firstborn. Esau's reaction is immediate and emotional, but Warren Wiersbe suggests that "Esau's tears were not tears of repentance...they were tears of regret." What in the text would support this commentator's statement?

_____

_____

> *This week's verse to remember:*
> "The unfailing love of the LORD never ends! By his mercies we have been kept from complete destruction. Great is his faithfulness; his mercies begin afresh each day." (Lamentations 3:22-23, NLT)

2. In today's world where words are spoken lightly and contracts are often broken, it's hard to understand why this mix-up couldn't be "fixed." However, in that culture such words were binding. Perhaps James G. Murphy offers the best explanation: "The paternal benediction flowed not from the bias of the parent, but from the Spirit of God guiding his will, and therefore when so pronounced could not be revoked." In what way does each person appear to be ignoring God's role in fulfilling his promise to bless the younger son?

   a. Isaac _____

   b. Rebekah _____

   c. Jacob _____

   d. Esau _____

3. Centuries later, Esau's sad tale was still being told. How does Hebrews 12:17 describe Esau's situation?

   _____

4. Whom does Isaac blame for the misplaced blessing?

   _____

   Various translations describe Jacob's actions as being done "treacherously" (NEB), "with subtlety" (KJV), and "with crafty cunning and treacherous deceit" (AMP). This one cuts to the chase: "Your brother tricked me" (CEV). In your opinion, to what extent was Isaac's statement accurate?

   _____

   _____

5. Not surprisingly, Esau also blames Jacob, whose name means "supplanter" or "deceiver." Yet what evidence of self-deception do you detect in Esau's accusation?

   _____

   _____

6. Three times Esau asks his father for a blessing. With Esau's tragic plight fresh in your mind, read Luke 13:23-30. What comparisons do you see between Esau's story in Genesis 27 and Jesus' teaching in Luke 13, looking at the following verses especially?

Luke 13:25 _____

Luke 13:28 _____

Luke 13:30 _____

7. Isaac does bless Esau, but his words aren't what Esau must have been hoping for. Compare Esau's blessing with Jacob's.

Jacob's blessing	*Esau's blessing*
a. _____	a. _____
b. _____	b. _____
c. _____	c. _____
d. _____	d. _____
e. _____	e. _____

What positive note, if any, do you find in Esau's blessing?

_____

_____

8. To see how Esau's blessing was fulfilled—how his descendants, the Edomites, interacted with Jacob's descendants, the Israelites—note what you learn in the following verses.

Genesis 36:6 _____

Numbers 20:14-21 _____

2 Kings 8:20-22 _____

The history of Edom was a perpetual struggle against the supremacy of Israel.

JAMES MURPHY

Prayer

Merciful Father, I don't want to be like Esau. I don't want to trivialize your blessings or blame others for my mistakes. I don't want to come to my senses too late about what truly is important. Please open my eyes and soften my heart toward you so that my tears are tears of repentance, not regret…

WEEK TWO

Day Three: Out for Revenge

Read Genesis 27:41-45.

1. After asking Isaac three times to bless him, Esau finally receives a dubious blessing. What is his response to his lesser blessing?

_____

Why would Esau choose to wait to act until his father dies?

_____

_____

This week's verse to remember:
"The unfailing love of the LORD never ends! By his mercies we have been kept from complete destruction. Great is his faithfulness; his mercies begin afresh each day." (Lamentations 3:22-23, NLT)

2. We learn that some unnamed source reports Esau's plans to Rebekah. Why do you suppose Rebekah was told instead of Isaac or instead of Jacob himself? What else might that tell us about Rebekah?

_____

_____

3. Rebekah warns Jacob with this statement: "Your brother Esau is consoling himself with the thought of killing you" (NIV). By focusing on killing Jacob, what more important issues is Esau ignoring?

_____

_____

How do we sometimes take comfort in negative emotions such as anger or revenge?

_____

_____

_____

What other emotions might anger or revenge mask—emotions that are harder to deal with?

_____

4. If you have ever comforted yourself with a desire for revenge—even if you didn't seriously plan to act on it—what was the result?

_____

_____

Who paid the greatest price—you or the object of your revenge? Why?

_____

_____

At any point did you turn to God for counsel or direction? If so, what was the result?

_____

_____

If you had allowed God to handle things completely, how might that have changed the situation?

_____

_____

5. No doubt Esau was convinced he had the right to take revenge. Yet what do the following verses teach us about vengeance?

Leviticus 19:18 _____

Nahum 1:2-3 _____

Romans 12:19-21 _____

6. Rebekah, meanwhile, is doing what she does best: giving orders, manipulating the situation. What three orders does she give Jacob?

a. _____

b. _____

c. _____

Haran was not a mere jog down the block but a trip of four to five hundred miles. What does this plan indicate?

_____

_____

7. In the first half of verse 45, Rebekah makes it clear who is to blame for Esau's anger. What do we learn about Rebekah from her comments?

_____

_____

8. Rebekah appears to justify her plans for Jacob with her final statement in verse 45. What possible meanings does this statement have?

_____

_____

9. We do not hear directly from God in the scenes we've studied this week, yet we can see him working through the events to accomplish his will. In what ways do you see his love or faithfulness or mercy in action?

_____

_____

_____

10. Describe a time in which you didn't see God working in your life until long after the fact. When you did have the benefit of hindsight, how did it affect your faith?

_____

_____

_____

> Her tactics are questionable, but she was not so much siding with her son against her husband as carrying out God's will for the family.
> **CHRISTIANA DE GROOT**

WEEK TWO

Prayer

Father, I can relate to Esau here; I don't want cheaters to win. Help me remember that it's not my job to see that other people get what they "deserve." Help me overcome my desire to get even or to get revenge. I sincerely want to let go of negative feelings that will only poison me…

Day Four: A Family Split

Read Genesis 27:46–28:4.

1. When Rebekah tells Jacob to flee to Laban's house, she says it is for his protection. However, her clever, cunning nature reveals itself fully in the next scene with Isaac. What did you *expect* Rebekah to tell Isaac?

_____

_____

And what does she bring up instead?

_____

_____

Why do you think she chose this tactic?

_____

_____

This week's verse to remember:
"The unfailing love of the LORD never ends! By his mercies we have been kept from complete destruction. Great is his faithfulness; his mercies begin afresh each day." (Lamentations 3:22-23, NLT)

2. Rebekah apparently knows her husband very well. Isaac's response to her dramatic comments is precisely what she wants: Jacob safely on his way to Laban's house. Even though Jacob's safety may be her first concern, why is it important that Jacob not marry a Canaanite woman? (Look back to Day Two, question 10, of the first week, if necessary.)

_____

_____

Although Isaac and Rebekah were grieved by Esau's Hittite wives, we have no indication that they tried to stop him from marrying women from a foreign nation. What might this indicate?

_____

_____

3. Isaac, you'll remember, had no choice regarding whom he would marry; Abraham sent a servant to find God's best choice for Isaac. In the story we are studying, who was in a position to choose Jacob's wife? Put a check mark in the appropriate column for each person:

	Has a choice	Has no choice
Jacob	❏	❏
Laban	❏	❏
Laban's daughters	❏	❏

Who really is in control of this future marriage situation? How did you come to your conclusion?

_____

_____

The Old Testament term for the church or congregation ["community of peoples," NIV] makes its first appearance.

DEREK KIDNER

4. Although Isaac doesn't invoke God's name when he commands Jacob to marry one of Laban's daughters, in the very next lines Isaac calls upon God to bless Jacob. What two blessings does he ask for Jacob in this final blessing?

a. _____

b. _____

Do you see any hesitancy on Isaac's part to bless Jacob? Or any mention of his son's deception? Why might that be the case?

_____

_____

5. Remember when Rebekah boldly said, "My son, let the curse fall on me," in Genesis 27:13? A curse of sorts is indeed about to fall on her, though she will not realize it for some time: After Jacob leaves for Paddan Aram, we have no record in Scripture that Rebekah ever saw her beloved son again. But she is not the only one to suffer loss this tragic day. Note below the losses each member of the family experiences:

Isaac_____

Rebekah _____

Jacob_____

Esau _____

6. In Luke 15:11-32, Jesus tells the story of the "prodigal son." In some ways both Esau and Jacob could be described as prodigal sons.

a. In what way could it apply to Esau?

_____

b. In what way could it apply to Jacob?

_____

7. Was there ever a time in your life when you were a prodigal child? If so, what were the circumstances?

_____

_____

What brought you back "home"?

_____

_____

How has that experience affected your life since?

_____

_____

Prayer

Heavenly Father, when I think about your unfailing love, I am amazed that you continue to love me even when I sin and turn my back on you or just become apathetic. I am amazed that in your mercy you continue to welcome me back. I am amazed at your faithfulness, that you never give up on me. That you would lavish all this on human beings—on me—is beyond my comprehension…

Day Five: Misguided Steps

Before we look at the last passage of Scripture for the week, let's step back and consider the bigger picture for a moment.

1. God made it clear in Genesis 25:23 that "the older will serve the younger," but do you think *this* was how God intended that truth to be lived out—with lies, deception, threats of murder, revenge, escape, and soon a hasty wedding to an unsuspecting bride? How would you explain God's willingness to work with such an untidy mess?

_____

_____

This week's verse to remember:

"The unfailing love of the LORD never ends! By his mercies we have been kept from complete destruction. Great is his faithfulness; his mercies begin afresh each day." (Lamentations 3:22-23, NLT)

What insights does Psalm 130:1-8 provide?

_____

_____

_____

♥ 2. Consider Matthew Henry's explanation: "God left [Rebekah] to herself, to take this indirect course, that he might have the glory of bringing good out of evil, and of serving his own purposes by the sins and follies of men, and that we might have the satisfaction of knowing that, though there is so much wickedness and deceit in the world, God governs it according to his will, to his own praise."

How would you restate his thoughts in your own words?

_____

_____

_____

How would you answer someone who said just the opposite—that the presence of so much wickedness in the world shows that God isn't governing it?

_____

_____

_____

What scriptures would you use to support your stance?

_____

_____

Note that Matthew Henry says God brings good out of evil so that "he might have the glory." Which are you more apt to do—praise God when good overcomes or doubt him when evil rules the day?

_____

_____

What intentional step could you take this very day to increase your praise?

_____

_____

3. The following verses describe what happens when we follow our own plans. Make a note of what each one says to you about the folly of plans made apart from God.

Isaiah 29:15-16 _____

Isaiah 30:1 _____

Jeremiah 18:11-12 _____

4. These verses address the good plans of God. What hope do you find in each one?

Psalm 33:10-11 _____

Proverbs 16:3 _____

Proverbs 19:21 _____

Jeremiah 29:11-13 _____

Read Genesis 28:5-9.

5. Jacob is sent on his way by his parents. Look carefully at all the names and places mentioned in Genesis 28:5. What is the significance of all this detailed information?

_____

_____

6. We have our last visit with Esau in these verses. Talk about irony! What does Esau learn about Jacob?

_____

_____

What does Esau realize about his father?

_____

_____

How does he address this oversight?

_____

_____

> Esau's response to this news was further evidence that he despised everything spiritual, for he went out and took another wife.
> **WARREN WIERSBE**

What do you think he was trying to achieve?

_____

_____

As we learn in Genesis 17:20-21, what was the good news–bad news about Ishmael and his descendants?

_____

_____

Prayer

All-powerful Father, I praise you for who you are—perfect love. I praise you that every good and perfect gift comes from your hand. I praise you that your glory can be seen in everything from the tiniest atom to the vastness of space. Open my eyes to see your goodness even in the smallest details and the darkest circumstances…

After Your Group Discussion…

As we close out this second week of study, what principles or insights or lessons were the most meaningful to you?

Name at least one change you would like to make as a result of your study this week (perhaps a change in attitude, or a habit you want to break, or a discipline you want to develop…).

Video Notes

Insights:

A Dream Come True

God's Love Knows No Bounds

GENESIS 28:10–22

A Dream Come True

God's Love Knows No Bounds

Read Genesis 28:10-22.

Major events:

■ On his journey Jacob dreams of a ladder of angels, stretching to heaven.

■ Jacob receives a blessing from God as well as a promise: "I am with you."

This week's verse to remember:

"God Himself has said, "I will not in any way fail you nor give you up nor leave you without support. I will not, I will not, I will not in any degree leave you helpless nor forsake nor let you down!"

(Hebrews 13:5, AMP)

h, brother! We left Esau threatening to kill Jacob and Jacob preparing to run. Just as he couldn't have anticipated how that day would change his life, little does Jacob know what greater things the night will hold for him: a vivid encounter with a ladder full of angels and a Word from on high, from the God of Abraham and the God of Isaac, from a God who declares, "I am with you."

Can this be true? Almighty God, the ruler of the universe, is willing, even eager, to be with Jacob the deceiver, to watch over him wherever he goes? That's grace at work—nothing short of it. A perfect God reaching down from heaven to rescue an imperfect man. To guard and guide, protect and provide.

"But Jacob doesn't deserve you, Lord!" my petulant self whines. "He did nothing to honor your name; in fact, he woefully misused it." Careful, Liz. If God's grace were extended only to the deserving, *none* of us would qualify, for "no one is good—except God alone" (Luke 18:19). Instead, God "gives grace to the humble" (1 Peter 5:5), and "in him we have redemption through his blood, the forgiveness of sins" (Ephesians 1:7).

What a relief that is for us all! And what a revelation it must have been to Jacob to hear the voice of the Divine saying, "I will not leave you." It's an exciting turn in the biblical story—and an encouraging word of hope for those who love his name.

Day One: Divine Communication

Read Genesis 28:10-12.

1. Do you find any mention of traveling companions for Jacob? What might that suggest about his journey?

_____

_____

2. Despite all he has been through, Jacob falls asleep and dreams…and what a dream he has! This is not the only instance in Scripture where God spoke to someone through a dream. According to Job 33:14-18, what sort of messages does God at times convey?

_____

_____

3. There are other Old Testament "dreamers" we might consider. Look up the following passages and note *who* is dreaming, what God's *purpose* is, and what the *results* were:

	The dreamer	God's purpose	The result of the dream
Genesis 20:3-7	_____	_____	_____
Genesis 37:5-8	_____	_____	_____
1 Kings 3:5-15	_____	_____	_____

4. Back to Jacob. Take a moment to sketch out (yes, *draw!*) his dream as described in Genesis 28:12. Not to worry if you have zero artistic ability. I simply want you to get a clear picture of his vision in your mind by committing it to paper. (Hint: It probably wasn't a ladder with rungs but more like the sloping side of a ziggurat. Think Mayan pyramid.)

5. Jesus describes a similar "stream of messengers" in John 1:51. What might be the significance of the angels ascending and descending?

_____

_____

6. A band of angels coming down from heaven is not a common occurrence in either the Old or New Testament. What is their purpose in each of the following examples?

a. Luke 2:8-14_____

b. Matthew 4:1-11_____

c. Matthew 24:29-31_____

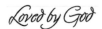

What does this suggest about Jacob, since God sent him a vision of angels as well?

_____

_____

> There could not have been a time when he needed more divine encouragement than now, nor a moment when he expected it less.
>
> CLYDE FRANCISCO

7. Throughout Scripture, God "came down" to appear before his people. David gives a vivid description of God coming down from heaven in Psalm 18:6-15. Note below how David describes his experience, and then compare it to Jacob's vision.

	David	Jacob
What was happening in David's/Jacob's life at the time?	_____	_____
God appeared at whose initiative?	_____	_____
What was God's purpose?	_____	_____
In what form did the heavenly being appear?	_____	_____
What was David's/Jacob's relationship with God like at the time?	_____	_____

What does this tell you about God?

_____

_____

8. Read Isaiah 64:3-9, where the prophet Isaiah gives an impassioned plea for God to come down to his people.

a. What does he say God's appearing would be like?

_____

b. What would happen to sinners?

_____

c. To what does he compare man's righteous acts?

_____

d. To what was he literally referring?

_____

e. What hope do these verses offer?

_____

9. When you look at God's interaction with Jacob and David and others, what stands out most to you about the nature of God as he interacts with mankind?

_____

_____

_____

Prayer

Heavenly Father, when I realize that the best thing I will ever do in my life is no better than a dirty rag to you, I know that on my own I am totally unworthy of being saved. Thank you for coming down to earth in human form so I could be saved from my sins. And thank you for sending your Holy Spirit to remain with me and to guide me…

Day Two: God's Promise and Presence

Read Genesis 28:13-16.

1. God speaks directly to Jacob in his dream and begins by identifying himself. Specifically, how does God do so?

_____

_____

2. Speaking of Abraham and Isaac, God had spoken to them, too. List under each man the statements and promises God made to him.

   Abraham (Genesis 15:7)

   _____

   _____

   _____

   _____

   Isaac (Genesis 26:23-24)

   _____

   _____

   _____

   _____

   Jacob (Genesis 28:13-15)

   _____

   _____

   _____

   _____

   Which statements and promises do they have in common?

   _____

   _____

   Which promises are given just to Jacob?

   _____

   _____

   Can you sense the excitement building as God continues to work out his plan to fulfill the promise he made first to Abraham!

> **This week's verse to remember:**
> "God Himself has said, "I will not in any way fail you nor give you up nor leave you without support. I will not, I will not, I will not in any degree leave you helpless nor forsake nor let you down!" (Hebrews 13:5, AMP)

3. That very phrase—"I am the LORD"—appears in the NIV 158 times, all in the Old Testament. It is apparent that God reached down to his people again and again, trying to get their attention, extending his unmerited grace. It is also apparent that both he and his name were to be taken seriously. What do the following verses reveal?

Exodus 20:1-7 _____

Isaiah 42:8 _____

Isaiah 43:11-13 _____

Isaiah 45:5-7 _____

This is how Exodus 20:7 reads in the Amplified Version: "You shall not use or repeat the name of the Lord your God in vain [that is, lightly or frivolously, in false affirmations or profanely]; for the Lord will not hold him guiltless who takes His name in vain."

Do you need to exercise greater care in using the Lord's name? In what ways?

_____

_____

_____

4. How do God's promises to Jacob in Genesis 28:13-14 compare to Isaac's last words to Jacob in Genesis 28:3-4?

_____

_____

_____

5. Perhaps the greatest promise God makes to Jacob is found in Genesis 28:15a. Write out the first part of that verse below. Just as God spoke those words to Jacob four thousand years ago, God speaks those same words to those who love him today:

_____

_____

How does that word from God comfort or encourage you in your present circumstances?

_____

_____

_____

In what unique way is this promise given to Christians, according to John 14:15-17?

_____

_____

This is the greatest promise God can make to anyone.

JOHN HARTLEY

6. Note one way in which each of the following passages assures you that God is with you at all times:

Psalm 23:4 _____

Psalm 42:8 _____

Psalm 118:6-7_____

Psalm 139:7-12 _____

7. In what ways does it encourage to you to know that God is *always* with you?

_____

_____

When are you most eager to have him with you?

_____

_____

When, if ever, are you uncomfortable thinking, "God is here with me"?

_____

_____

8. The first thing that popped into Jacob's mind when he awoke from his dream was not breakfast or the long journey ahead; he thought of God. What was his statement?

_____

_____

Perhaps you're reminded of the praise chorus "Surely the presence of the LORD is in this place." The phrase "presence of the LORD" appears 34 times in the NIV translation of the Old Testament. His presence was something to be sought, yet reverently feared. Recall an incident when you were especially aware of the presence of the Lord. What brought about that awareness?

_____

_____

_____

How might you enter into his presence on a daily, even hourly, basis?

_____

_____

_____

Prayer

Holy Father, how lightly I take your presence at times. Help me to take comfort in you as my "Abba, Father," who loves and protects and guides me, but also to revere you as the only God, a holy God, and the Creator of the universe. Please guard my words and my thoughts so that I never treat your name or your presence with anything less than awe-filled respect…

WEEK THREE

Day Three: Sacred Sites

Read Genesis 28:16-17.

1. As we studied yesterday, when Jacob wakes up, he realizes that this was no ordinary dream and that he has been in the presence of God. According to verse 17, what was his immediate reaction?

_____

_____

This week's verse to remember:

"God Himself has said, 'I will not in any way fail you nor give you up nor leave you without support. I will not, I will not, I will not in any degree leave you helpless nor forsake nor let you down!'" (Hebrews 13:5, AMP)

The *Holman Bible Dictionary* explains: "When God appears to a person, the person experiences the reality of God's holiness. This self-disclosure of God points to the vast distinction between humans and God, to the mysterious characteristic of God that at the same time attracts and repels." Why would God's holiness both attract and repel us?

_____

_____

2. The "fear of the Lord" has little to do with anxiety but a great deal to do with reverence and respect and honor. Below, you will find just a few of the verses in the NIV translation that include "the fear of the LORD." Note what each one teaches you:

Psalm 19:9 _____

Proverbs 1:7 _____

Proverbs 14:27 _____

Proverbs 16:6 _____

Proverbs 23:17 _____

3. The phrase "the fear of the Lord" appears just once in the NIV New Testament, referring to the first-century church. How is that body of believers described in Acts 9:31, and why might fearing God have contributed to their "time of peace"?

_____

_____

4. The presence of the Lord and the fear of the Lord frequently go hand in hand. Ironically, God or his messenger often says, "Fear not." This is not to dissuade people from respecting and honoring God but rather an invitation to trust him. Note in the following passages to whom these words were spoken and what God was asking each to do.

Deuteronomy 31:7-8 _____

Jeremiah 1:1-8 _____

5. Jacob's next words—"How awesome is this place!" (NIV)—sound more contemporary than patriarchal to me! Unfortunately, "awesome" has been overused until it almost has no power to convey its true significance anymore. But we can be sure Jacob didn't use this word lightly. He recognized that God's presence had changed the very ground on which he stood. Sound familiar? What happened in the following instances?

Exodus 3:1-5 _____

Leviticus 16:1-2 _____

6. As stated in 2 Corinthians 6:16-18, God now dwells among us. We, too, should be changed by his presence. Personalize this passage by writing it out below and inserting your name as if God were saying it directly to you. I'll get you started.

_____ is the temple of the living God. As I have said, "I will live with

_____ and walk with her, and… _____

_____

Because we have this promise of God dwelling with us, how does Paul say it should change our lives (2 Corinthians 7:1)?

_____

_____

7. With a final look at Genesis 28:17, we see that Jacob declares he has seen the "gate of heaven." This is the only place that exact phrase appears in the NIV, but you'll find other important "gates" described in the New Testament. Note what the two passages below reveal about Jesus Christ, our own "gate of heaven."

John 10:9_____

Matthew 7:13-14 _____

8. If "only a few" find that gate, how can you be certain you have walked through the "right gate," the one that leads to eternal life?

_____

_____

What insights do the following verses give?

Romans 10:9-10 _____

1 John 5:12-13 _____

9. In your own words explain how we should "fear the Lord." Can you think of a parallel situation or a metaphor that might help an unbeliever understand the difference between a "healthy" and "unhealthy" fear of the Lord?

_____

_____

_____

How will a right fear of the Lord affect our relationship with him?

_____

_____

> In pagan belief a site was sacred from primordial time, but in Scripture a site never became endowed with sacredness; a particular place was holy only as long as God chose to reveal himself there.
>
> JOHN HARTLEY

Prayer

Awesome Father, to be honest, it frightens me to think that you dwell with me. My words, my thoughts, my actions aren't holy, aren't pure. Help me have a more constant awareness of your presence *in* me and *with* me so that your goodness may show *through* me…

Day Four: More Than a Name Change

Read Genesis 28:18-21.

1. After this incredible night in which God has spoken to him, Jacob turns his pillow into a pillar. What was the significance?

_____

_____

Why does he pour oil on it? What insight does Exodus 30:23-29 provide?

_____

_____

2. He also changes the name of that sacred place to Bethel, or *Beth-El,* which in Hebrew means "House of God." We don't put as much significance in names today, but in Jacob's time names were chosen not to sound good but to reveal the nature of who or what was being named. (Remember Hairy and Heel?) And *changing* a name signified a transformation in character or destiny. Although Jacob is changing the name of the *place,* what transformation is occurring in *him?* What indicates this?

_____

_____

The biblical concept of naming was rooted in the ancient world's understanding that a name expressed essence. To know the name of a person was to know that person's total character and nature.

HOLMAN BIBLE DICTIONARY

I like the British tradition of naming one's home—Rose Cottage, Bridgeview, Abbeyside. Consider giving your home a name to express the essence of what you would like your family, friends, neighbors—your Creator—to find there. What name would you give it?

_____

What changes would you make in your home to bring about the transformation?

_____

_____

3. *Bethel* appears dozens of times in Scripture after Jacob renamed it, in some cases parenthetically—Genesis 35:6 says "Luz (that is, Bethel)" and Joshua 16:2 reads "Bethel (that is, Luz)." Check out the following two verses from Genesis 35. Although this scene falls beyond the time boundary of our study, note how God describes what happened at Bethel and then how Jacob views that event.

God in Genesis 35:1 _____

Jacob in Genesis 35:2-3_____

How does Genesis 28:20-21 verify that Jacob is a changed man by this time?

_____

_____

_____

_____

4. Not only did Bethel represent "God's house" to Jacob, it was also where he made a vow to God. What five expectations does Jacob place on God?

a. _____

b. _____

c. _____

d. _____

e. _____

Does this sound presumptuous to you? I am taken aback by Jacob's words, and then I realize how I tend to do the same thing. God offers me heaven and eternal life with him, and I say, "That's great, but I'd be more interested in following you if you made things easier for me here on earth—a little more money, a little less trouble, and no suffering, please. And, by all means, don't ask me to be a missionary!" Oh, I may not say it that candidly, but my actions do. What about you? What stipulations are you putting on God before you are willing to wholeheartedly follow him?

_____

_____

_____

5. How has God already promised each of these things directly or indirectly to Jacob?

_____

_____

What do these statements from Jacob indicate about him?

_____

_____

6. What does Jacob promise to do in return?

_____

_____

7. Jacob vows to do even more than that, as we'll see in a moment, but this is the most momentous promise Jacob makes to God. In truth, it is the most life-changing commitment any of us can make before God. Write out Jacob's brief statement below in your own words. Then read it aloud as though God were present in the room with you…because he is!

_____

_____

_____

8. What does it mean to you, to claim God as *your* God? How could you demonstrate that commitment to him on a daily basis?

_____

_____

_____

Prayer

Gracious Father, your generosity toward me is pure grace. I deserve nothing, yet my prayers are more often filled with requests than praise and thanksgiving. So I stop right now and praise you for your grace and thank you for having already given me everything that is important— salvation through your Son, Jesus Christ…

Day Five: Jacob's Promises and Offerings

Read Genesis 28:22.

1. Jacob goes on to make two more promises to God. What are they?

_____

_____

---

2. This is not the first time the giving of a tenth, or tithe, is mentioned in the Bible. For that story, read Genesis 14:18-23. To whom did Abram (before God changed his name to Abraham) spontaneously present a tithe, and why?

_____

_____

3. Moses will later record the tithe as law in Leviticus. According to the following verses, what is to be tithed to God?

Leviticus 27:30 _____

Leviticus 27:32 _____

4. The people of God grew careless about their giving (sound familiar?), so God spoke to them through the prophet Malachi. Read Malachi 3:6-12, and then answer the following questions.

What does God accuse his people of doing?

_____

_____

What does God tell them to do instead?

_____

_____

And what promises does God make if they do so?

_____

_____

5. Fast-forward to the New Testament. Let's see if God tells us how much we are to give as believers of Jesus Christ. What do the following verses suggest we are to give to God?

1 Corinthians 16:1-2 _____

2 Corinthians 9:7 _____

6. How might you explain the fact that the words *tenth* and *tithe* do not appear in these verses?

_____

_____

What insight does Matthew 23:23 give to the answer?

_____

_____

7. If your present level of giving to God doesn't correspond with the New Testament directives Paul wrote to the Corinthians, what specific steps do you need to take to become a more *generous* giver?

_____

_____

And what steps do you need to take to become a more *cheerful* giver?

_____

_____

♥ What scriptures other than those already mentioned could serve as a good reminder to you as you plan your giving?

_____

_____

_____

> By making such a contribution a person concretely expressed God's lordship over all one's property.
> **JOHN HARTLEY**

After Your Group Discussion…

After nearly three full weeks of study, we finally see a major turnaround starting in Jacob! As you have studied Jacob's character to this point, and God's interaction with him, what principle stands out most in your mind?

Having studied these verses this week, what changes do you want to apply in your life?

Prayer

Father, help me willingly, even joyfully release my "things" to you. Even though I realize they become a burden sometimes, I don't give them up easily. Help me experience the joy of accepting that everything belongs to you— including my money, my time, my life…

WEEK THREE

Video Notes

Insights:

Blinded by Love

Man Looks at the Outward Appearance; God Looks at the Heart

GENESIS 29:1–20

Blinded by Love

Man Looks at the Outward Appearance;
God Looks at the Heart

Read Genesis 29:1-20.

Major events:

■ Jacob questions the local shepherds at a well and asks about his Uncle Laban.

■ Jacob meets his cousin Rachel, waters her sheep, and follows her home.

■ Jacob strikes a bargain for the hand of his beloved Rachel.

> **This week's verse to remember:**
> "Guide my steps by your word, so I will not be overcome by any evil. Rescue me from the oppression of evil people; then I can obey your commandments. Look down on me with love; teach me all your principles." (Psalm 119:133-135, NLT)

Jacob's journey east continues, and what a l-o-n-g trek it is, although not a day of it is described in Scripture. The climax of the trip takes place at a well with three flocks of sheep on hand, some taciturn shepherds, and a certain shepherdess by the name of Rachel. Before the scene ends with tears and a kiss, Jacob will surprise his onlookers with a feat of strength worthy of Samson wooing Delilah.

Rachel runs to tell her father the good news that a relative has arrived, and Laban hurries to meet his nephew. Is it just me, or is this a more energetic branch of the family? Poor Isaac has to be told, "Sit up! Sit up!" while effusive Laban is on his feet and making tracks.

This week we'll consider Laban's warm welcome and what expectations he might have concerning his visiting nephew, and we'll look at Jacob's quick assimilation into the home of his relatives. The word for Jacob is *willing:* willing to work, willing to marry, willing to wait, willing to work some more. His Aramean uncle, grateful for the free labor, is in no hurry to see Jacob pick up his heels and move back home with one of Laban's daughters in tow.

Oh, did we mention the daughters? This week we'll get to know them, at least by name: Leah, the older one with unusual eyes (are they "weak" or "tender" or "sparkling"?), and Rachel, the younger sister, who is "beautiful of form and face" (NASB). Guess which one Jacob decides he loves? And guess what outrageous bride-price the smitten man is willing to pay?

Laban is elated, although he hides it well. "Stay," Laban says, and Jacob does. Time flies. Months are mere minutes. In a single verse, seven years pass. Jacob has fulfilled his duty as a laborer; now he would fulfill his role as a husband.

Day One: Journey's End

Read Genesis 29:1-9.

1. Leaving Bethel behind, Jacob presses east toward Paddan Aram. Verse 1 literally covers nearly five hundred miles! Why do you think that long, arduous journey was not described in detail for us in Scripture? (There are no right or wrong answers here; just give it some thought.)

   _____

   _____

2. Based on God's promises and Jacob's vows at Bethel that we studied last week, what do we know *for certain* about Jacob's journey?

   _____

   _____

3 As Jacob approaches Haran, he comes to a well in the field. Who and what are waiting at the well?

   _____

   What do we learn about the well itself?

   _____

   What possible reason(s) might you offer for Jacob's stopping here first rather than pressing on to his uncle's home?

   _____

   _____

4. To help you step inside Jacob's sandals for a moment, recall a specific time in your adulthood when you were the "new face in town"—in a new neighborhood, a new job, a new church. Any awkward, first-time situation will do. What strategy did *you* use to introduce and ingratiate yourself to that group of strangers?

   _____

   _____

5. In Jacob's brief conversation with the shepherds, he asks simple questions, and they give him *very* brief answers. In your translation, what does Jacob *call* the men? _____. Why might he have done so?

_____

_____

Do they initially offer him any information beyond what he asks of them? _____ What might that indicate?

_____

_____

6. Then the shepherds provide some useful information without being asked. What do they tell Jacob?

_____

_____

Is it good news or bad news…and why?

_____

_____

7. Jacob responds to their announcement with a surprising suggestion, particularly for a visiting stranger. What does he tell them to do?

_____

_____

Various biblical commentators are quite certain why Jacob asked them to do this. Given only the information we have in the text, what do *you* think Jacob was up to?

_____

_____

Is Jacob back to his old, deceptive ways? Why or why not?

_____

_____

8. The shepherds tell him two things must happen before their sheep will be watered:

_____

_____

But as they're talking, Jacob's attention is no longer focused on the shepherds, the sheep, or the well. Who shows up?

_____

> He tries to rid the scene of onlookers even before he has a clue to Rachel's incandescent beauty.
>
> ROSE SALBERG KAM

What do we learn about this newcomer in that single verse?

_____

_____

9. Even in this short episode, we see God at work guiding Jacob and being "with him." Note below at least four indications you see of God's handiwork in these events.

a. _____

b. _____

c. _____

d. _____

10. How is God turning Jacob's desperate situation—running for his life—into a blessing?

_____

_____

_____

Prayer

Merciful Father, how I love to know you are guiding my steps! What peace and comfort that brings. I praise you for those times when I can see your guiding hand. Help me trust you more in those times when I'm uncertain. As the psalmist said, I ask you to guide me through your Word so that I won't be overcome by evil...

Day Two: Jacob Meets His Love

Read Genesis 29:10-11.

1. We have no record of what Jacob said to the new arrival…only what he did. How would you explain this remarkable feat?

_____

_____

This week's verse to remember:
"Guide my steps by your word, so I will not be overcome by any evil. Rescue me from the oppression of evil people; then I can obey your commandments. Look down on me with love; teach me all your principles." (Psalm 119:133-135, NLT)

2. We have more surprises in store! Verse 11 describes a rather emotional display on Jacob's part. In the Old Testament close relatives would kiss upon greeting or departing from each other as a sign of acceptance, but what else might have prompted this kiss?

_____

_____

Why do you think Jacob wept?

_____

_____

3. There is no shame in a man weeping. According to Scripture, many of God's bravest, strongest men wept. Who is crying in the following verses, and why?

	Who wept…	…and why?
Genesis 43:30	_____	_____
		_____
1 Samuel 30:3-4	_____	_____
		_____
Jeremiah 9:1	_____	_____
		_____
Matthew 26:75	_____	_____
		_____
John 11:32-36	_____	_____
		_____

In rolling the stone from the well by himself, Jacob was risking the wrath of the whole community.
CLYDE FRANCISCO

4. Repentance often produces tears. What does 2 Chronicles 34:27 tell us about how God responds to our humble tears?

_____

_____

5. Perhaps Jacob was simply overcome with God's faithfulness in bringing him safely to Paddan Aram. What do the following verses teach us about the faithfulness of God?

Deuteronomy 7:9 _____

_____

Psalm 86:15 _____

_____

Psalm 119:89-90 _____

_____

Isaiah 25:1 _____

6. Have you ever been overwhelmed by the *faithfulness* of God, even to the point of weeping? Describe such a time in your life and how that memory encourages you to remain faithful to God.

_____

_____

_____

_____

Prayer

Father, I thank you for tears of joy—when my heart is so full that I can't hold them back— and I ask you to keep my heart tender. I want to rejoice with those who rejoice and weep with those who weep. I especially want my heart to be tender to your nudging so that I am quick to repent when I sin...

WEEK FOUR

Day Three: Jacob Meets His Match

Read Genesis 29:12-15.

1. Freshly kissed, Rachel starts running, and her father, Laban, starts hurrying. What reasons could you offer for Rachel's eagerness to share the news of her cousin's arrival?

_____

_____

_____

And what of her father, Laban? List some reasons why he might be in a hurry to see his nephew.

_____

_____

_____

Read Genesis 24:28-31, which describes Abraham's messenger selecting Rebekah for Isaac. What clue to Laban's character and motivation does this meeting provide?

_____

_____

2. Laban welcomed Jacob with open arms. In what ways did Laban demonstrate his enthusiasm?

_____

_____

3. What might "all these things" (NIV) that Jacob told his Uncle Laban include? It is clear that he volunteered the information. How much of his story do you think Jacob told Laban, and what makes you say that?

_____

_____

_____

Paraphrase the following verses in one sentence each. How could heeding these admonitions have served Jacob well that day?

Proverbs 17:28 _____

_____

_____

_____

_____

This week's verse to remember:
"Guide my steps by your word, so I will not be overcome by any evil. Rescue me from the oppression of evil people; then I can obey your commandments. Look down on me with love; teach me all your principles." (Psalm 119:133-135, NLT)

Tradition has it that when Laban ran out to greet Jacob, embracing and kissing him, it was solely to discover the money and gems he felt certain that this beloved member of Abraham's household would come bearing as gifts.

BARBARA L. RONSON

Proverbs 21:23 _____

_____

_____

_____

_____

Proverbs 29:20 _____

_____

_____

_____

_____

3. Most of us could profit from these verses as well. Which of the following is the greatest temptation for you?

❑ giving advice too freely

❑ dominating conversations

❑ interrupting others rather than patiently listening

❑ flattering others

❑ cutting others off if you disagree

❑ speaking rashly in anger

❑ being quick to divulge others' sins

❑ revealing too much to people before you know they can be trusted

❑ stretching the truth

Memorize one of the three proverbs mentioned in question 3—or a verse like James 1:19—and commit to work this week on improving in this area. Consider asking a trusted friend or family member to help by holding you accountable to your resolution to guard your tongue and speak with discretion.

4. It's clear that Jacob stays with Laban and works for a full month. Since Jacob's skills include shepherding and Laban clearly owns sheep, we can assume caring for them might have been Jacob's job. How much does Laban pay Jacob for his labors?

_____

Read Deuteronomy 24:14-15 to discover how God said workers were to be paid. *Note:* Although the events recorded in Deuteronomy came several hundred years after those in Genesis, it's important to remember that (1) the Pentateuch (the first five books of the Bible) were all written around 1400 B.C. and (2) Deuteronomy includes laws of the people that were commonly accepted and had been in place for centuries.

What did God direct employers to do? Why?

_____

_____

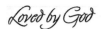

Given the directive in these verses, how do you view the situation at hand? Is Jacob being generous with his time—a month of free labor—or is Laban being stingy with his funds? Offer a plausible explanation for Jacob's working thirty days without pay.

_____

_____

_____

6. Jot down Laban's request as stated in verse 15:

_____

_____

This is the first place in the NIV where we find the word "wages." It will appear seven times in Genesis, each time involving these same two men. How might a similar discussion between Jacob and Laban many years later, as recorded in Genesis 30:27-30, reveal how each man honored his commitment concerning work and wages? Also read Genesis 29:16-30 for your answer.

_____

_____

7. Jacob, himself a deceiver, perhaps does not realize at this point what Laban's true motives are and what his plans are for Jacob. What evidence do we see of Jacob's relying on God as he lives with and works for Laban?

_____

_____

After the powerful experience Jacob had at Bethel, how do you explain his current self-reliance?

_____

_____

Day Four: Beauty Seen and Unseen

Read Genesis 29:16-17.

1. On the heels of the word "wages" comes the introduction of Laban's two daughters. No coincidence, this. Without reading ahead or peeking at any study notes your Bible might contain, write down everything you know (or think you know!) about these two famous sisters. No right or wrong here; this is a matter of perceptions and preconceived notions.

Leah   Rachel

_____   _____

_____   _____

_____   _____

2. "Older" and "younger"—now *that* should ring a bell. Esau and Jacob were born only seconds apart. Are we told how many months or years separate the two sisters?

_____

If you have siblings, what observations could you share about those who are close in age—say, one to three years—and those who are farther apart?

_____

_____

_____

3. The girls are described with only a handful of words. First, let's look at Leah. What does the Word of God say about Leah, the older sister?

_____

_____

Clearly this information matters to the story, or it would not have been included. But *why* did it matter? What might that tell us about Leah—physically, emotionally, spiritually? How might the condition of her eyes affect her appearance, her domestic skills, her ability to be a wife and mother? Jot down everything that specific attribute might indicate about Leah.

_____

_____

_____

4. When we met Esau and Jacob at their births, Esau was indeed described physically. When we met the twins again as young men, in Genesis 25:27, what was the emphasis?

_____

_____

Do you see a similar dichotomy still in place four thousand years later? How do we frequently define women? How do we often define men? Why do you believe this is done?

_____

_____

5. According to the following verses, how does God view people? Restate each passage briefly in your own words and personalize it. (The first one is done as an example.) Try reading the passages in more than one version to see which wording is most meaningful to you.

a. 1 Samuel 16:7—People will judge me by how I look, but the Lord sees my thoughts and my intentions.

b. Proverbs 31:30 _____

_____

c. Isaiah 66:2 _____

_____

d. 1 Peter 3:3-4 _____

_____

If you are in a small group, have members share various translations and their own "paraphrases."

♥ 6. We don't know much about Jesus' physical appearance when he was on earth, but Isaiah 53:2-3 gives us a clue. How does the passage describe Jesus' appearance?

_____

_____

_____

Considering that Jesus could have come in any likeness God desired, why do you think he chose this one?

_____

7. Now let's take a closer look at Rachel. When she first arrives on the scene with her sheep, Rachel's comely looks are not described, though Jacob certainly does respond positively to seeing her. But the later verses leave no question about her appearance. How does your translation describe Rachel?

_____

_____

With the use of the word "but," it appears that Leah and Rachel are being contrasted. What differences does the text state or imply?

_____

_____

> ❧
>
> Perhaps Rachel is more outwardly beautiful, but Leah is more sensitive and kind.
> ALICE OGDEN BELLIS

8. A woman's beauty is an integral element in several Old Testament stories. Take a brief look at the following passages and make note of what you find there.

	Who is beautiful?	Why might that be dangerous?
Genesis 12:10-13	_____	_____
Genesis 26:6-7	_____	_____
2 Samuel 11:2-4	_____	_____

9. In your experiences, have you seen a situation where a woman's beauty led to trouble?

_____

Given what we've seen in Scripture and know to be true in our own lives, how might Rachel's beauty point to future problems for Jacob?

_____

_____

10. Physical beauty doesn't have to lead to trouble. We see in Esther 2:15-17 that Esther used her beauty—combined with courage—for godly purposes. How else might a woman's beauty be used of God for his glory?

_____

_____

_____

11. Take a personal inventory by comparing your outward beauty care with your inward beauty care. List below what you do daily or weekly to enhance your beauty in each area.

Physical beauty regimen	Spiritual beauty regimen
_____	_____
_____	_____
_____	_____
_____	_____

Are your regimens in the proper balance? If not, what adjustments could you make?

_____

_____

_____

Prayer

Heavenly Father, I want to become a beautiful woman in your sight. Help me look at myself and see what you see—my heart, my thoughts, my attitudes. And in those areas where I need a beauty makeover, guide me in your regimen for transforming my spirit. Thank you for being patient with me and for not giving up on me, even when I am the most unlovely…

WEEK FOUR

Day Five: The Price of Love

Read Genesis 29:18-20.

1. Whether it was love at first sight—that kiss by the well—or whether it took a month for him to know his feelings, Jacob's affection for Rachel is clearly stated. In our first week together we learned that Isaac loved Rebekah (Genesis 24:67). There are only a few scattered mentions in the Old Testament of such romantic feelings between men and women—Elkanah loved Hannah (1 Samuel 1:4-5), and Michal loved David (1 Samuel 18:20). But nearly all of the 733 appearances in the NIV of the words "love," "loves," "loving," or "loved" refer to God's loving us or to our being called to love one another. A great example of both can be found in 1 John 4:7-12. State at least three principles about love that you find in these verses.

a. _____

b. _____

c. _____

2. We say that we "love God," and you probably say "I love you" to certain people—a spouse, a parent, a child. Surely these emotions, and the practical ways they are expressed, are not identical. How would you describe your love for God and your love for a certain person who is dear to you? Circle any words that appear in both columns.

Love for God   Love for _____

_____   _____

_____   _____

_____   _____

_____   _____

How might your love for God enhance the earthly relationship you've listed here?

_____

_____

Does your love for God strain that relationship in any way?

_____

The following verses teach us how to love others in a way that's pleasing to God. Note a brief, helpful lesson from each one.

John 13:34-35_____

1 Peter 1:22-23_____

1 John 3:18 _____

1 John 4:20-21 _____

3. Now look back over Genesis 29:1-18, beginning right after Jacob's personal encounter with God.

Is there any mention of God in these eighteen verses? _____

Does Jacob thank God, as Abraham's servant did, for guiding him? _____

Does Jacob offer praises to him for beautiful Rachel? _____

After reviewing those verses, what conclusion(s) might you draw about Jacob and his relationship with God at this point in the story?

_____

_____

4. Laban, you'll remember, asked Jacob what his wages should be. Now Jacob states how long he is willing to work, that is, _____, and his expected compensation, namely, _____. What detail does Jacob include, lest there be any question which daughter he means?

_____

5. Laban's response is curious. How would you interpret Laban's answer to Jacob's offer?

_____

_____

And what does Laban *not* say that you might have expected?

_____

_____

6. Jacob is a man of his word here; we learn that he fulfills his part of the bargain. Perhaps you've held the same job for seven years; imagine working all those years *without getting paid!* Clyde Francisco wrote, "No man who loved that unselfishly could be an essentially self-centered person." Do you agree…or disagree? Have we seen Jacob behave unselfishly before? If not, how might you explain his behavior here?

_____

_____

_____

7. Especially when compared to today's marital standards, Jacob's commitment to wait and work for Rachel is remarkable. While we may not be asked to sacrifice seven years of hard labor for someone we love, we are asked to make daily sacrifices in the name of love. According to the following verses, in what specific and practical ways are we to show love to those around us?

Leviticus 19:18_____

Proverbs 10:12_____

Proverbs 17:9 _____

Custom regards the father of the bride as entitled to some compensation for the trouble had in her training, and for the loss of service experienced by her departure from home. If this compensation cannot be rendered in money, jewels, or cattle, it may be given in labor.

JAMES M. FREEMAN

WEEK FOUR

Matthew 5:44_____

Romans 12:9-18 _____

1 Peter 3:8 _____

Select one of these practical ways to show love and commit to expressing it to someone today.

After Your Group Discussion...

Restate in your own words the most important principles you learned this week.

How will you respond to these truths?

Prayer

Loving Father, you have shown overwhelming love to me, especially by sending your Son to die for my sins. And you continue to show your love for me in providing for my needs, in continually forgiving me, in protecting me from harm. May the love that you pour into my life flow out to others. Help me release my impatience, my frustration, my expectations of others and replace it with your love...

Video Notes

Insights:

A Deceiver Deceived

God Disciplines the Ones He Loves

GENESIS 29:21–29

A Deceiver Deceived

God Disciplines the Ones He Loves

Read Genesis 29:21-29.

Major events:

■ After seven years of labor, Jacob is more than ready to be married.

■ On the wedding night Laban secretly presents Leah—not Rachel—to eager Jacob.

■ The next morning Jacob discovers his father-in-law's deceit and protests loudly.

■ Laban blames local custom and strikes a second deal for Rachel's hand.

This week's verse to remember:
"My child, don't ignore it when the LORD disciplines you, and don't be discouraged when he corrects you. For the LORD corrects those he loves, just as a father corrects a child in whom he delights." (Proverbs 3:12, NLT)

 hen Isaac and Rebekah sent their younger son, Jacob, off to Paddan Aram to marry one of Laban's daughters, they surely did not foresee a turnabout like *this* one…nor did Jacob! If this story is new to you, Laban's deceptive move no doubt caught you by surprise as well. Even those of us who knew what was coming still shake our heads with more questions than answers as we read this cruel twist in the story.

Our lesson this week will inch along through only nine verses. As we grapple with the myriad issues at hand—ethical, moral, legal, sexual, emotional, and spiritual —we must remind ourselves that we're studying the story of *one* family in a specific time and place, a family greatly influenced by their primitive culture and their developing faith in the one true God within a polytheistic society (one that worshiped many pagan gods).

Having said all that, we *can* learn from this unseemly situation and can apply these lessons to our lives. Paul assures us that "all Scripture is God-breathed and is useful for teaching, rebuking, correcting and training in righteousness, so that the man of God may be thoroughly equipped for every good work" (2 Timothy 3:16-17). Much as we might be tempted to put aside some stories in the Bible and say,

"No thanks. That one doesn't appeal or apply to me," the truth is, every story in some way points to our fallible human nature and our desperate need for a Savior.

The key is not to get so caught up in studying the lives of people in the Bible that we forget to examine our own lives, our own failings, our own motives, our own need for repentance. Jesus cautioned the Jews who were persecuting him, "You diligently study the Scriptures because you think that by them you possess eternal life. These are the Scriptures that testify about me, yet you refuse to come to me to have life" (John 5:39-40). As you study this week, come to the Scriptures to learn, and come to the Savior to discover what unique lessons he has for *you* that will draw you closer to him.

Day One: A Big Switch

Read Genesis 29:21-23.

1. After the seven long years come to an end, Jacob tells Laban to uphold his end of their bargain. Based on last week's study, what had Jacob promised to do?

_____

_____

Had he fulfilled his promise?

_____

Precisely what does Jacob tell Laban to do to fulfill his part?

_____

_____

In your translation, does the name "Rachel" appear in the verse? In truth it does *not* appear in the Hebrew, which is literally rendered, "please grant my woman." Why is this omission significant?

_____

_____

2. According to verse 22, how does Laban respond to Jacob's demand?

_____

_____

Who is on the guest list?

_____

What is provided for them?

_____

> It was customary among the Hebrews…to eat together when entering into a covenant.
>
> JAMES M. FREEMAN

3. The Hebrew word describing this "feast" is derived from the root meaning "drink." Consequently, it would seem they were not only eating food but drinking wine. Similarly, Jesus' first miracle took place at a wedding where wine was served (read John 2:1-3). Drinking wine was not shameful, but being drunk on wine was another matter entirely. Note in each of the passages below what is the outcome of drinking too much wine:

Genesis 9:20-25 _____

Genesis 19:30-36 _____

Proverbs 23:20-21 _____

What does Paul have to say about being inebriated, as found in Ephesians 5:18?

_____

_____

4. In *The Storyteller's Companion to the Bible,* Michael Williams wrote, "The culmination of the feast is always the procession of the bride as she is taken to the tent of the anxious groom." According to Genesis 29:23, at what time of day does this occur?

_____

Why might that be crucial to the story?

_____

_____

What travesty occurs?

_____

_____

Who appears to be responsible?

_____

Does Jacob seem aware of the switch?

_____

5. Now I'm going to turn the tables and ask *you* to jot down any unanswered questions this deceptive scene brings to mind:

a. _____

_____

b. _____

_____

c. _____

_____

6. Given what we know of Laban's nature from previous scenes, can you answer the most compelling question: Why did Laban give *Leah* to Jacob rather than *Rachel,* the woman Jacob loved (and for whom he had labored)? Think of as many possible explanations as you can.

_____

_____

_____

7. Now read back through the following verses leading up to this week's lesson, and note the various clues that foreshadow this wedding night fiasco. I found at least *one* clue in every single verse. See if you can do the same. (Not to worry if some leave you clueless!)

Genesis 29:12 _____

Genesis 29:13 _____

Genesis 29:14 _____

Genesis 29:15 _____

Genesis 29:16 _____

Genesis 29:17 _____

Genesis 29:18 _____

Genesis 29:19 _____

Genesis 29:20 _____

Genesis 29:21 _____

Genesis 29:22 _____

Genesis 29:23 _____

8. One of the ironies of this scene is that Jacob has behaved honorably (for a change *and* for seven years!), yet he is now on the receiving end of deception. Have you ever been in a situation where you were deceived and mistreated even though you had acted honorably and in good faith? Have you...

❏ honored your marriage vows only to have your husband break them?

❏ trusted a friend with a confidence only to have that friend share it with others?

❏ granted a child a privilege only to have that child abuse it?

❏ entered a business deal only to have your partner cheat you?

❏ paid someone to do a job only to have that person not do the work properly?

❏ _____

How did you feel about yourself?

_____

_____

How did you feel about the other person?

_____

_____

How did you feel about God?

_____

_____

What actions did you take?

_____

_____

What wisdom could you gain from Jacob's experience?

_____

_____

Prayer

Merciful Father, when I am mistreated and don't "deserve" it, my first reaction is definitely not to ask you to bless those who have offended me. In fact, I find it difficult ever to ask with sincerity that you bless them. Please help me relinquish any need for pay-back so that my heart stays clean, because I know I need your grace and mercy just as much as anyone else on earth…

Day Two: Vixen or Victim?

Read Genesis 29:23.

1. At last, after a day-long wedding celebration, Jacob is alone in his tent with his bride. But as Genesis 29:23 tells us, it is not his beloved Rachel who shares his bed; it is her older sister, Leah, thanks to Laban who "gave" or "brought" Leah to Jacob. Laban was nothing if not self-serving. In what ways did Laban stand to benefit from this bridal bait-and-switch?

_____

_____

> *This week's verse to remember:*
> "My child, don't ignore it when the LORD disciplines you, and don't be discouraged when he corrects you. For the LORD corrects those he loves, just as a father corrects a child in whom he delights." (Proverbs 3:12, NLT)

2. This deceptive scene echoes one earlier in our study, that of Jacob's pretending to be Esau. Reread Genesis 27:15-16. Then using your imagination and common sense, list below some practical ways Laban might have disguised Leah in order to fool Jacob.

_____

_____

_____

3. Compare the consequences of Laban's deception of Jacob to Jacob's deception of Isaac, considering, among other things, who was affected in each case, how relationships were changed, and how the future was affected. Refer to earlier passages you have read for your answers.

Jacob's deception of Isaac   Laban's deception of Jacob

_____   _____

_____   _____

_____   _____

_____   _____

4. We know that even if he wasn't eager to deceive his father, Jacob at least cooperated with his mother, Rebekah, in the plan. But in this scene, we don't hear from Leah, so we cannot be certain *why* she participated with her father in the scheme. Below are several possibilities. Number them in order from *most likely* (1) to *least likely* (5), and then add a few words of explanation for your top two choices.

_____ Desperate for a husband _____

_____ In love with Jacob _____

_____ Anxious for children _____

_____ Forced by her father _____

_____ Jealous of her sister _____

If you've come up with another possible reason, list it below and number it as well:

_____ _____ _____

> Until we ourselves are injured we do not see how mean and evil it is to injure someone else.
> **FRANCES VANDER VELDE**

5. Regardless of why Leah participated in the deception, what do the following verses say about our responsibility for our actions?

   a. Ezekiel 18:20 _____

   b. Matthew 12:36-37 _____

   c. Romans 14:11-13 _____

6. How easy it is not to accept responsibility for our behavior. Put a check mark by any of the following thinking patterns you're tempted to engage in.

   ❏   I can't help it; this is just the way I am.

   ❏   I'm just like my mother (or father).

   ❏   My husband (or "my family") won't let me...

   ❏   I've been this way all my life; it's too late to change now.

   ❏   We all have shortcomings; mine aren't worse than anyone else's.

   ❏   I'm not perfect, but God's grace is sufficient.

What is the danger in thinking this way?

_____

_____

In what specific area do you need to take more responsibility for your actions or thoughts or habits?

_____

_____

What specific steps can you take to become more responsible in this area?

_____

_____

Prayer

Gracious Father, I sometimes rationalize away my responsibilities—responsibility for my thoughts, my words, my behavior, my relationship with you. I presume on your grace—and the kindness of others—to overlook my irresponsible behavior. I praise you for your grace and mercy, and I ask that the Holy Spirit guide me in taking control of my thoughts, words, and actions so they come more in line with your will...

Day Three: Just Deserts?

Read Genesis 29:23.

1. At least with old, blind Isaac, we understood how he might have been deceived. But based on what we've studied so far this week, how do you explain young Jacob's not recognizing he had the wrong bride on his wedding night? List below any contributing factors that might account for Jacob's being so easily deceived.

_____

_____

_____

> *This week's verse to remember:*
> "My child, don't ignore it when the LORD disciplines you, and don't be discouraged when he corrects you. For the LORD corrects those he loves, just as a father corrects a child in whom he delights." (Proverbs 3:12, NLT)

2. In his book *When Brothers Dwell Together,* Frederick Greenspahn comments, "Laban's actions have long been recognized as just retribution for Jacob's earlier deceit." Do you agree that Jacob got what he deserved? Why or why not?

_____

_____

What do the following verses teach us about getting what we deserve?

Job 34:10-11 _____

_____

Jeremiah 17:10 _____

_____

3. If we truly got what we deserve for our sins, we would *all* be in trouble. Note below what each of the following verses says about these questions: What do all of us deserve? What have we been given? How do we receive this gift?

Romans 3:21-24 _____

_____

Romans 6:22-23 _____

_____

Ephesians 2:1-9 _____

_____

> This was Laban's sin; he wronged both Jacob and Rachel, whose affections, doubtless, were engaged to each other, and, if (as some say) Leah was herein no better than an adulteress, it was no small wrong to her too.
> MATTHEW HENRY

WEEK FIVE

4. What encouragement does Psalm 103:8-14 provide for those who fear the Lord?

_____

_____

What three images, or pictures, does the psalmist use in verses 11-13 to help us understand the extent of the Lord's love, forgiveness, and compassion?

_____

_____

_____

Which image is most comforting to you, and why? Consider writing that verse on a note card and putting it in a spot where you will see it daily.

_____

_____

5. Read Psalm 140:4-5, David's cry to God for protection from those who had set traps to ensnare him. It seems a trap was set for Jacob. Have you ever felt as if you walked into a trap of some kind or were set up to fail? Describe (a) the situation, (b) how you felt when you discovered what had happened, and (c) what you learned from the experience.

a. _____

_____

b. _____

_____

c. _____

_____

6. When people are suffering from a painful or seemingly unfair situation, Christians are quick to quote Romans 8:28 as a word of encouragement. Take a moment to jot down that verse here:

_____

_____

One Bible translation, the Contemporary English Version, words this verse a bit differently than most other translations: "We know that God is always at work for the good of everyone who loves him. They are the ones God has chosen for his purpose." Consider both wordings—and look at other translations, if possible—then restate this principle in your own words.

_____

_____

When this verse is misunderstood or misused, it can give people a wrong impression of God, causing anger at God rather than bringing comfort. Have you seen an instance when this happened? If so, describe it.

_____

_____

_____

How could a correct understanding of this verse help us address difficult times?

_____

_____

♥ 7. Another verse that Christians often quote in such circumstances is 1 Corinthians 10:13. Write out that verse below.

_____

_____

Do you find, as I have, that this verse is often misused? How do people often misstate its promise?

_____

_____

What point *is* Paul making in this verse?

_____

_____

8. For a thorough and practical discussion of what we can do when trouble comes, read Ephesians 6:12-18. What insight does each verse provide?

verse 12 _____

verse 13 _____

verse 14 _____

verse 15 _____

verse 16 _____

verse 17 _____

verse 18 _____

Prayer

All-wise Father, I realize that being your child does not insulate me from sad and unfair and difficult circumstances. When I am engulfed in these trials, help me not to blame you or to turn my back on you but to turn toward you to redeem the circumstances. Help my faith grow deeper through these times so that others may be drawn to you as the source of all goodness, all comfort, and all hope…

WEEK FIVE

Day Four: A Rude Awakening

Read Genesis 29:24-25.

1. In the middle of this dramatic scene of Jacob's mistaking Leah for his bride, we have verse 24, which seems an intrusive detail at this point. In fact, the Revised Standard Version and the New Revised Standard Version put this verse in parentheses. What fact do we learn?

_____

_____

This week's verse to remember:
"My child, don't ignore it when the LORD disciplines you, and don't be discouraged when he corrects you. For the LORD corrects those he loves, just as a father corrects a child in whom he delights." (Proverbs 3:12, NLT)

2. Even this detail offers us an insight into the culture and into Laban. It was a wedding custom for the father of the bride to provide her with a personal slave girl. Sharon Pace Jeansonne says, "Laban presumes that Leah will be fertile and gives Zilpah to Leah as a servant—one who could be used as a nursemaid." Yet how does Laban's gift to Leah compare with his gift to Rebekah when she was leaving to marry Isaac (see Genesis 24:59, 61)? What might that tell us about Laban?

_____

_____

3. The title of the Cat Stevens song "Morning Has Broken" (originally a hymn dating from 1931) comes to mind when reading verse 25. Lives were broken and hearts were broken that fateful morning. Most translations include an exclamation point. Does yours? What might that communicate about Jacob's discovery that morning?

_____

_____

To whom does Jacob first turn for an explanation?

_____

What might *that* indicate?

_____

_____

4. In verse 25, Jacob asks three questions in a row without even giving Laban time to respond. Jot down these three brief questions here, and then answer them as Laban *might* have, based on his character and motives.

Jacob: "_____"

Laban: "_____"

Jacob: "_____"

Laban: "_____"

Jacob: "_____"

Laban: "_____"

5. Note that Jacob does not even mention Leah. Why might that be the case?

_____

_____

What do *you* feel toward Leah at this point in the story? Disgust? Pity? Apathy? Take a moment to put your thoughts about Leah into words

_____

_____

_____

6. As with the earlier deception scene in which Jacob was the deceiver and his father was the deceived, we find ourselves asking, "Where is God in all this?" Earlier at Bethel, Jacob had clearly said, "The LORD will be my God" (Genesis 28:21). What evidence do you see of a godly Jacob in this week's verses?

_____

_____

7. When you find yourself in difficult circumstances, which of the following describes how you often *feel?* You may find yourself checking more than one; in any case, see if you can explain why you chose the one(s) you did.

- ❏ God is too busy or too far away to notice what's happening to me.

- ❏ God is interested in what's happening to me, but he doesn't get directly involved.

- ❏ God is disciplining me for my sins.

- ❏ God is orchestrating the events for my good.

- ❏ God is with me, sustaining me, but he isn't the author of these events.

_____

_____

8. How might the following verses help provide a biblical response to these perceptions of God?

Psalm 145:18-19_____

_____

Ephesians 2:13-14_____

_____

Romans 8:31-39_____

_____

Hebrews 12:5-11_____

_____

> Jacob's reaction made it utterly clear that there was no place for Leah in his heart.
>
> GIEN KARSSEN

Prayer

Patient Father, help me to see your hand more clearly in my life. In the midst of blessings—so many of which I take for granted—I want to praise you more for your faithfulness and generosity. In the midst of trials, I want to feel your comforting presence and to know that you are with me and that you will lead me. I want to trust more fully that you never abandon me, that you never quit loving me, that you always hear my prayers and respond…

WEEK FIVE

Day Five: A Second Wife

Read Genesis 29:26-29.

1. Laban speaks at last, but, goodness…that wasn't what I expected him to say! Study his few words carefully, and then answer the following:

Does Laban express any regret?

_____

This week's verse to remember:

"My child, don't ignore it when the LORD disciplines you, and don't be discouraged when he corrects you. For the LORD corrects those he loves, just as a father corrects a child in whom he delights." (Proverbs 3:12, NLT)

Has he mentioned this custom earlier?

_____

Although it was customary, was it a biblical command?

_____

Is either of his daughters named here?

_____

Does his statement leave room for negotiation?

_____

Based on the above answers, how would you describe Laban's response to Jacob that morning?

_____

_____

The excuse was frivolous.…If there had been such a custom, and he had resolved to observe it, he should have told Jacob so.

MATTHEW HENRY

2. We've yet to hear a peep from the two sisters. When we last heard of Rachel, she was preparing to wed Jacob. When we last heard of Leah, she was in her sister's marriage bed. Does it seem to you that Jacob and Laban are taking the women's opinions, feelings, or needs into account? Why might that be the case?

_____

_____

3. The following passages make it clear that what happened on Jacob's wedding night should have been avoided at all costs. Jot down the central message of each verse.

1 Thessalonians 4:3-5_____

_____

2 Timothy 2:22_____

_____

Hebrews 13:4_____

_____

4. In her book *The Women of Genesis,* author Sharon Pace Jeansonne wrote, "Where Laban appears selfish, Jacob appears resigned." Indeed, when we read verse 28, it seems that Jacob agreed to Laban's terms without protest. What reasons might you offer for Jacob being so resigned?

_____

_____

5. Just as Isaac irreversibly blessed the younger son, we have another situation that couldn't be revoked. According to *Nelson's New Illustrated Bible Commentary,* "a public feast in recognition of the union made the marriage between Jacob and Leah official, even though Leah was the wrong woman." Under the circumstances, what could Jacob do to bring any good out of the situation?

_____

_____

6. Read Leviticus 18:18. Uh-oh…sure sounds like what we have going on here! Clyde Francisco, in *The Broadman Bible Commentary,* wrote, "The prohibition probably resulted from the trouble experienced in this family." Without question, Jacob and company are a prime example of how *not* to create a harmonious home life. How does God view such heartless behavior? Proverbs 6:16-19 lists seven things God hates. Note these seven things below and give an example of each—if there is one—from our study of these families.

a. _____

b. _____

c. _____

d. _____

e. _____

f. _____

g. _____

7. Sum up the week's study by stating the various consequences of Laban's switching his daughters:

a. Ethical _____

b. Moral _____

c. Legal _____

d. Sexual _____

e. Emotional _____

f. Spiritual_____

When we sin, we generally don't see all the consequences that ripple out from it. Consider for a moment one sin that is hard for you to overcome, and list below the possible consequences—for you and for others—of your continuing to tolerate that sin.

_____

_____

_____

After Your Group Discussion…

Restate in your own words the most important principles you learned this week.

How will you respond to these truths?

Video Notes

Insights:

A Heart for God

God's Love Is Powerful Enough to Change Our Hearts

GENESIS 29:30-35

A Heart for God

God's Love Is Powerful Enough to Change Our Hearts

Read Genesis 29:30-35.

Major events:

■ Jacob remains married to both women but loves Rachel rather than Leah.

■ When God sees that Leah is unloved, he opens her womb and closes Rachel's.

■ As Leah bears and names four sons, we see her drawing closer to God.

■ Leah discovers an important truth for all of us: God is worthy of our praise.

This week's verse to remember:
"Whom have I in heaven but you? I desire you
more than anything on earth. My health may fail,
and my spirit may grow weak, but God remains
the strength of my heart; he is mine forever."
(Psalm 73:25-26, NLT)

Jacob got what he wanted…or did he? Two miserable wives instead of one happy one. And another seven years of labor without pay. He also got a household that was torn asunder with jealousy and strife. Leah and Rachel apparently dwelled in separate tents (Genesis 31:33), but their days and nights spent with Jacob forever tied their sibling relationship into a hard, bitter knot.

Although lovely Rachel seems the innocent party, it's the plight of unloved Leah that tugs at my heart. Imagine waking to find yourself married to someone who did not choose you and does not love you. Who, instead, loves your beautiful, younger sister. Who, in fact, loves her enough to work fourteen *years* for the honor of calling her his wife yet wouldn't willingly work a single *day* for your hand in marriage. *Groan.* Does anyone love Leah? Apparently not her father. Definitely not Jacob. Probably not Rachel.

Only God. But is God's love enough to sustain her—and us? This week in Genesis 29:30-35 we will find our answers.

Day One: Room for Two?

Read Genesis 29:30.

1. One husband, two wives, and two maidservants who later bore Jacob children also—a most unusual means of building a family! *The Interpreter's Dictionary of the Bible* offers several reasons for polygamy: "love and lust, the desire for children, and diplomacy on the part of the nation's rulers. Undoubtedly the need and the desire for sons was the most prominent factor." Those are man's ideas; God's idea was one husband for one wife. Note what the following verses tell us on that subject.

    Genesis 2:24 _____

    _____

    Matthew 19:4-9 _____

    _____

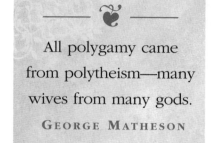

All polygamy came from polytheism—many wives from many gods.

GEORGE MATHESON

2. This verse makes it very clear where Jacob's affections rest. The King James Version states, "He loved also Rachel more than Leah," and the New English Bible says, "He loved her rather than Leah." Big difference there! How does your translation compare Jacob's feelings for Rachel to his feelings for Leah? Does your version include "also" or "more than" or "rather than"…or something else altogether?

    _____

    What indications do we have at this point in the story regarding Jacob's true feelings for Leah, positive or negative?

    _____

3. Verse 30 concludes with this simple statement: "He worked for Laban another seven years." What would have been *different* about those seven years compared to the first seven? Think through all the dimensions—practical, emotional, spiritual—that might have been part of Jacob's experience throughout that *second* term of unpaid labor.

    _____

    _____

    _____

    _____

4. Although Laban may have intended those seven additional years to benefit him alone, God can use such times in our lives to test and refine our faith. What do the following verses teach us about the value of trials?

    James 1:2-4 _____

    _____

    James 1:12 _____

    _____

    1 Peter 1:6-7 _____

    _____

1 Peter 4:12-13 _____

_____

5. And what Jacob may have seen only as Laban's greed and deceit, God may have seen as an opportunity to discipline the chosen Jacob (something that many of us have longed to see!). What do the following passages have to say about the value of discipline and especially the value of God's discipline?

Job 5:17_____

Proverbs 3:11-12_____

Proverbs 10:17_____

Proverbs 12:1-2 _____

Proverbs 15:32 _____
What warnings do these verses give about those who reject discipline?

_____

_____

And what positive outcome is suggested if we accept God's discipline?

_____

_____

6. According to the dictionary, discipline can in part be defined as "the rigor or training effect of experience, adversity, etc." Describe a time when you felt that God was disciplining you through an experience of adversity.

What was the discipline?

_____

_____

What changes did it bring about?

_____

_____

How might your life have been different if God had not disciplined you?

_____

_____

How might other lives have been affected if you had not been disciplined?

_____

_____

Can you now say, as Paul did, that the discipline was to your benefit and God's glory?

_____

_____

Prayer

Gracious Father, you know I don't like to be disciplined. My pride is wounded, and often something I have "idolized" is wrested out of my hands. Even though I don't like it, I understand that your discipline shows you haven't given up on me and that you are trying to form me more into the image of your Son. Help me to accept your discipline with humility and understanding so that you will be glorified…

Day Two: Precious in God's Sight

Read Genesis 29:31.

1. Jacob is not the only one whom God was watching over. Write out the first phrase found in verse 31:

_____

_____

_____.

> *This week's verse to remember:*
> "Whom have I in heaven but you? I desire you more than anything on earth. My health may fail, and my spirit may grow weak, but God remains the strength of my heart; he is mine forever." (Psalm 73:25-26, NLT)

It's easy to get so caught up in the description of Leah's loveless state that we miss the important opening words, "When the LORD saw…" Restate and personalize each of the following verses to encourage *you* to remember that God sees you, even when you (like Leah) fear no one is paying attention to you at all.

2 Chronicles 16:9a_____

_____

Job 34:21 _____

_____

Psalm 33:13-15 _____

_____

2. With those promises fresh in your mind, why not ask the Lord to "keep his eye on you" concerning a particular situation you are dealing with right now. Write it below as a prayer request and note the date. Later you can rejoice when you see your prayer has been answered. No need to share this with your small group if you're not comfortable doing so; this is between you and the One who sees.

Today's Date: _____   Date God Answered: _____

Dear Lord, please keep your eye on me as I…

_____

_____

_____

3. These very words—"When the Lord saw"—appear in the NIV translation only once in the New Testament, as part of a story involving the Lord Jesus and another woman in distress. Read Luke 7:11-17 and then note what you've learned from this passage.

What do we know about the woman in this story?

_____

_____

How does Jesus initially respond to her—physically, emotionally, then verbally?

_____

_____

What actions does Jesus take to remedy the dire situation?

_____

_____

To whom do the people give credit?

_____

How does this story build *your* faith in a Lord who "sees" our sorrow and takes action?

_____

_____

_____

♥ **4.** According to *Nelson's New Illustrated Bible Commentary*, "As near as we can tell, many cultures in the ancient world viewed women as little more than property. Furthermore, the men who recorded the literature of those times tended to overlook the presence and significance of their female counterparts. By contrast, the Bible not only includes women but also tells about their leadership, contributions, and feelings, and not just their sins and failures." In addition to Leah and the widow just mentioned, we find many examples in the Bible of God's seeing the plight of women—and responding. Let's look at three of them. How does God intervene in each of these women's lives?

	The woman	The problem	God's intervention
1 Samuel 1:1-20	_____	_____	_____
Mark 5:24-34	_____	_____	_____
John 4:3-29	_____	_____	_____

5. While the NIV translates the Hebrew as "Leah was not loved," others render it "Leah was hated" (RSV) and "Leah was despised" (AMP). Ouch! Take a moment to compare various translations of that phrase with others in your small group. To be "unloved" (NASB) suggests a passive, unemotional detachment; to be "hated" (KJV) sounds more aggressive and intentional.

Which of these phrases best describes Jacob's treatment of Leah?

_____

Why do you say that?

_____

_____

How might he have demonstrated these feelings toward her on a day-to-day basis?

_____

_____

6. As for Leah, we can imagine her calling out to God in her prayers, beseeching his favor, just as David often did many centuries later. Read the following verses from Psalms and note what comfort or wisdom you find in each. Choose the verse or verses that best apply to your situation mentioned in question 2, and consider making it a part of your store of memory verses.

Psalm 10:14_____

Psalm 25:19-21_____

Psalm 86:17_____

Psalm 109:25-27_____

7. The Lord not only *sees* that Leah is unloved, he *saves* her from despair. According to verse 31, what does God do for Leah?

_____

By contrast, what is Rachel's situation?

_____

Rachel's condition was not unique among the matriarchs of the Old Testament or among the godly mothers of the New Testament, according to the following verses.

	Woman's name	Her affliction	God's response
Genesis 11:30; 17:19	_____	_____	_____
Genesis 25:21	_____	_____	_____
Luke 1:7, 24-25	_____	_____	_____

8. Based on all these examples of what God has done for women in the Bible, how would you describe his ability and willingness to help you in your present circumstances?

_____

_____

_____

Prayer

Merciful Father, I am overwhelmed by the thought that you see my every move and hear my every cry. I bring to you my burdens, and I take shelter in your arms. And for every blessing you put in my life and every time you rescue me, I praise you and give you all the glory. Thank you that I am not less important to you just because I am a woman…

Day Three: Blessings for the Humble

Read Genesis 29:32.

1. Leah's womb is not only opened; it is filled. Unto Leah a child is born. Note your answers to the following questions based on this verse.

   Is it a boy or girl? _____

   Why does that matter?_____

   Who names this child? _____

   What is that name?_____

   Whom does Leah credit for her son?_____

   What outcome does Leah hope for? _____

This week's verse to remember:

"Whom have I in heaven but you? I desire you more than anything on earth. My health may fail, and my spirit may grow weak, but God remains the strength of my heart; he is mine forever." (Psalm 73:25-26, NLT)

2. According to the Law of Moses, which reflects many long-standing principles, this child from Leah is to be favored over any child from Rachel. Let's look at Deuteronomy 21:15-17 and find out why.

   What situation does the Law address here that suits the Leah-Rachel fiasco to a *T*?

   _____

   _____

   Which son is to receive the greater honor in the father's will?

   _____

   In what specific way is the father to honor this son?

   _____

   _____

   Why do you think this law was put into place?

   _____

   _____

3. "Reuben" literally means "Look, a son!" What do the following verses from Psalms tell us about the value of children to a father?

   Psalm 45:16-17 _____

   Psalm 127:3-5 _____

   Psalm 128:3-4 _____

   Do we find any evidence in our story that Jacob responded to the birth of this first son or to the woman who bore him?

   _____

Barrenness was a shame and a reproach in Israel; it was interpreted as divine punishment or at least a sign of divine displeasure.

PHYLLIS A. BIRD

4. It is clear that Jacob does *not* favor Leah; it is equally clear that God *does*. Examine closely 1 Corinthians 1:27-29 and see if the truth we find there fits our unloved Leah.

How has Leah been "foolish"?

_____

_____

In what way is Leah viewed as "weak"?

_____

_____

How might the word "lowly" suit Leah?

_____

_____

Who "despises" Leah?

_____

What "things" might Leah "not" possess?

_____

_____

To what end does God use all of the above?

_____

_____

5. Of the many words that might describe Leah, *humble* is surely one of the best. Using your dictionary, give two or three definitions for *humble* that apply to Leah.

_____

_____

And in what way might each of the following verses describe Leah?

Isaiah 66:2_____

Ephesians 4:1-3_____

James 4:10_____

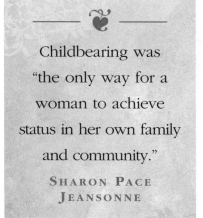

Childbearing was "the only way for a woman to achieve status in her own family and community."

SHARON PACE JEANSONNE

6. Humility is not our favorite virtue to pursue. As a friend said, "I'd be willing to be humble if everybody else would go first." What do the following verses teach us about God's view of humility?

Psalm 25:9-10 _____

Proverbs 22:4 _____

1 Peter 5:6-7 _____

7. How would you rate your humility level? Put an "X" to show where you would place yourself on the scale below.

Pride   Humility

1   2   3   4   5

In what specific ways could you work on moving away from pride and toward humility?

_____

_____

_____

Prayer

Heavenly Father, just like Leah, I don't always receive the answers to my prayers that I want. But I pray that you will help me see the answers you send and that I will humbly receive them as what is best for me. Help me see the ways in which my pride hinders me from learning what you would teach me. Help me be able to say, as Mary did, "I am the Lord's servant, and I am willing to accept whatever he wants" (Luke 1:38, NLT)…

Day Four: The One Who Always Hears

Read Genesis 29:33-34.

1. One child would have been sufficient for Leah to have considered herself blessed. Sarah in the Old Testament and Elizabeth in the New Testament each gave birth to just one son. But fertile Leah gives birth again.

   Was this second child a son or daughter? _____

   To whom does Leah give credit? _____

   With the first child, she said God *saw* her misery. What does Leah say this time?

   _____

   Again, who named the babe? _____

   And what is the child's name? _____

2. It is comforting to know that our God watches over us and even more encouraging to realize he *hears* and *listens*. Restate in your own words the assurance you find in the following verses from Psalms.

   Psalm 10:17-18 _____

   _____

   Psalm 22:23-24 _____

   _____

   Psalm 34:17-18 _____

   _____

3. The name "Simeon" means "listening." Not only was God listening to Leah, even as he is listening now to us, but God also calls us to listen to *him*. Spend a few moments in the New Testament and note what Jesus asks us to do.

   Luke 6:46-49_____

   Luke 9:35_____

   John 10:27-28 _____

4. In these verses we also learn that a third son is born to Leah and Jacob. At the previous birth, Leah mentions God but not Jacob. What do we see at *this* birth?

   _____

   What does Leah hope will happen this time?

   _____

   And why is she convinced it will?

   _____

> *This week's verse to remember:*
>
> "Whom have I in heaven but you? I desire you more than anything on earth. My health may fail, and my spirit may grow weak, but God remains the strength of my heart; he is mine forever."
> (Psalm 73:25-26, NLT)

> The names Leah gave her children testified to the miraculous faith God had planted in her heart.
>
> HERBERT LOCKYER

Who named this third baby?

_____

And what is the child's name, which in Hebrew means "to cleave"?

_____

5. The sons of Levi were very important to the nation of Israel. Read Deuteronomy 10:8 and 21:5. What were the duties of the Levites?

_____

_____

Perhaps the most famous of the Levites is introduced in Exodus 2:1-10. What's the name of this baby, born to a Levite couple?

_____

According to Hebrews 11:24-26, what legacy of faith did this famous Levite leave?

_____

_____

6. God has watched, God has listened, God has blessed Leah's womb three times, the number of holiness. Does Jacob seem to be paying attention?

_____

What explanation would you offer?

_____

_____

_____

7. Have you ever been in a situation that sounds similar to Leah's—thinking you can win or earn someone's appreciation or love but seeing no results? Might that person be a man, a husband, a parent, an in-law, a sibling, a child? Based on what you have learned from Leah's life thus far, what words of wisdom would you offer to a person stuck in this situation?

_____

_____

_____

Prayer

Heavenly Father, what a comfort it is to know that you listen to my prayers. Now I want to be more attuned to you. To hear your wisdom and guidance through your Word, through godly people, through your Spirit. I want to be so at peace with you that any lack of a person's love loses its power to control or hurt me...

Day Five: Praise the Lord

Read Genesis 29:35.

1. When Leah gives birth to her fourth child, something extraordinary happens to her spiritually.

   What does Leah say about Jacob? _____

   What does she say about God? _____

   _____

   _____

   How would you describe her attitude? _____

   Who names this child? _____

   And what name is he given?_____

> *This week's verse to remember:*
> "Whom have I in heaven but you? I desire you more than anything on earth. My health may fail, and my spirit may grow weak, but God remains the strength of my heart; he is mine forever." (Psalm 73:25-26, NLT)

2. "Judah" means "praise," a jubilant expression of Leah's heart toward God. In the NIV translation, this is the first time in Scripture we see the exact phrase "Praise the Lord"…but it is not the last. (In fact, the word "praise" and its variant forms appear 420 times in the NIV!) There are innumerable reasons to praise God. Note below just a few of them as found in the following verses.

   Psalm 68:19_____

   Psalm 86:5-10_____

   Psalm 93:1-2_____

   Jeremiah 10:6_____

   2 Corinthians 1:3-4 _____

   Revelation 4:11_____

3. Knowing all the heartache that has come before this moment, describe what *you* see happening in Leah's life, emotionally and spiritually, with the birth of this fourth child and why this might be the case.

   _____

   _____

4. Have you had a similar epiphany in your spiritual journey, an instance when you discovered some life-changing truth? Leah came to a point of desperation before she came to a place of praise. Is that how it was for you? Take a moment to put your experience into words.

   _____

   _____

   Did you, like Leah, "praise the Lord" at the time it happened?

_____

How would you praise God now for the changes that discovery has brought to your life?

_____

_____

_____

_____

"Three people never started life together against greater odds, but God was in it with them." In fact, "God is the main Character in the drama."

EUGENIA PRICE

5. When Judah is grown, his father, Jacob, speaks a prophetic word over this son. Read Genesis 49:8-10 and note all that is to come in Judah's life.

_____

_____

What elements of Judah's blessing do you find in Isaac's blessing of Jacob (Genesis 27:28-29)?

_____

_____

6. In truth, it is not only Judah himself who will rule nor simply the tribe that bears his name. Centuries later a ruler will come from the lineage of Judah who will reign for all time. Note what the following verses teach us about this Lion of Judah.

Matthew 1:1-2_____

Matthew 2:6 _____

Hebrews 7:14 _____

7. In her book *Caught in a Higher Love,* author Carolyn Baker writes: "On the one hand Leah's story is one of heartbreak. On the other it is a story of triumph." The heartbreak is obvious. How is Leah's story one of triumph?

_____

_____

_____

8. Although the story of Leah, Rachel, and Jacob is far from over, I've chosen to end our study here with good purpose: The focus rests on God and on the coming of his Son, Jesus. Just as Leah realized that the Lord was her only hope, her true source of joy, and worthy of her praise, so must we come to the same conclusion if we are to be truly at peace with ourselves and with God. Though David wrote Psalm 62:5, the words sound like something Leah might have whispered while she cradled the baby Judah in her arms. Write out Psalm 62:5 here:

_____

_____

Now put these same thoughts in your own words, personalizing them by applying them to your own life and your own desire to trust in the promises of God and experience his blessings. Treat it as the Amplified Bible would—expanding the words and phrases to make the verse more specific and applicable to you.

_____

_____

_____

9. I said at the beginning of this study that I had a three-point mission: (1) for you to know how much God loves you; (2) for you to realize that you can trust his promises—as long as you don't hold him to your timing; and (3) for you to experience his blessings—as long as you are willing to look at a new definition of "blessing." As we close this series, let's reflect on these three goals.

How has your awareness of how much God loves you grown?

_____

_____

_____

What verse or biblical example helped reinforce your awareness of God's love for you?

_____

_____

In what ways has your trust in his promises increased?

_____

_____

Which of his promises has made the greatest impact on you?

_____

_____

What blessings have you become more aware of in your life?

_____

_____

How do you want to respond to God in light of what you've learned?

_____

_____

_____

Prayer

Loving Father, thank you for providing your written Word so I can read and study your heart-changing message throughout my life. Open my eyes to see who you are and what you have done for me. Sharpen my hearing to perceive the leading of your Spirit. Soften my heart to respond to your will for my life. I pray that I will draw closer to you every day and will grow into the likeness of your Son…

Closing thoughts from Liz...

Dear one, this time with you—on video and on paper—has been an absolute delight! As I prepared the seven messages and crafted the many questions you've answered, I prayed for you, knowing we had much ground to cover together as we explored the timeless truths of God's Word. Bless you for being willing to make the journey!

Now I'll continue to pray that the lessons you've learned here will take root and blossom in your life…that your trust in him will grow deeper and your awareness of his many blessings will increase. Truly, my friend, you are loved by God!

Liz Curtis Higgs

P.S. Isn't it wonderful that Christian sisters never need to say a last good-bye? Instead, I'll leave you with a long-distance hug and these encouraging words from 2 Thessalonians 2:16-17:

May our Lord Jesus Christ himself and God our Father,
who loved us and by his grace gave us eternal encouragement and good hope,
encourage your hearts and strengthen you in every good deed and word.

After Your Group Discussion…

Restate in your own words the most important principles you learned this last week of the study.

How will you respond to these truths?

Video Notes

Insights:

Fifteen Recommended Study Resources for

Loved by God

A Bible Study with Liz Curtis Higgs

Alter, Robert. *Genesis: Translation and Commentary*. New York: W.W. Norton & Company, 1996.

Baker, Carolyn Nabors. *Caught in a Higher Love*. Nashville: Broadman & Holman Publishers, 1998.

Elliott, Ralph H. *The Message of Genesis*. St. Louis: Abbot Books, 1962.

Francisco, Clyde. *Genesis: The Broadman Bible Commentary*. Vol. 1. Nashville: Broadman Press, 1969.

Freeman, James M. *Manners and Customs of the Bible*. New Kensington, Pa.: Whitaker House, 1996.

Hartley, John E. *New International Biblical Commentary: Genesis*. Peabody, Mass.: Hendrickson Publishers, 2000.

Henry, Matthew. *Matthew Henry's Commentary on the Whole Bible*. Vol. 1. 1706. Reprint, Peabody, Mass: Hendrickson Publishers, 1991.

Jeansonne, Sharon Pace. *The Women of Genesis*. Minneapolis: Fortress Press, 1990.

Kam, Rose Salberg. *Their Stories, Our Stories*. New York: Continuum Publishing Company, 1995.

Kidner, Derek. *Genesis: An Introduction and Commentary*. Downers Grove, Ill.: Tyndale Press, 1967.

Owens, Virginia Stem. *Daughters of Eve*. Colorado Springs: NavPress, 1995.

Raver, Miki. *Listen to Her Voice: Women of the Hebrew Bible*. San Francisco: Chronicle Books, 1998.

von Rad, Gerhard. *Genesis: A Commentary*. Philadelphia: Westminster Press, 1972.

Wiersbe, Warren W. *Be Authentic*. Colorado Springs: Chariot Victor Publishing, 1997.

Williams, Michael E., ed. *The Storyteller's Companion to the Bible*. Vol. 4, *Old Testament Women*. Nashville: Abingdon Press, 1993.

Notes

Welcome to the Family!

1. "God often outdoes…," Matthew Henry, *Matthew Henry's Commentary on the Whole Bible,* vol. 1 (1706; reprint, Peabody, Mass: Hendrickson Publishers, 1991), 124.

2. "Isaac wasn't praying selfishly…," Warren W. Wiersbe, *Be Authentic* (Colorado Springs: Chariot Victor Publishing, 1997), 12.

Week One: Sibling Rivalry

1. "They personified two ways…," Gerhard von Rad, *Genesis: A Commentary* (Philadelphia: Westminster Press, 1972), 265-66.

2. "applied to certain advantages…," H. L. Willmington, *Willmington's Guide to the Bible* (Wheaton, Ill.: Tyndale House, 1981), commentary on Genesis 25:27-34.

3. "He was defrauded…," Ralph H. Elliott, *The Message of Genesis* (St. Louis, Mo.: Abbot Books, 1962), 162.

4. "Blessing is the transmission…," von Rad, *Genesis,* 277.

5. "She operates behind the scenes…," Christiana de Groot, *The IVP Women's Bible Commentary (Genesis)* (Downers Grove, Ill.: InterVarsity Press, 2002), 17.

6. "The deceiver…," Meredith G. Kline, *Genesis,* of *The New Bible Commentary,* rev. ed. (Grand Rapids: Wm. B. Eerdsman Publishing, 1970), 102.

7. "An abundant measure…," James G. Murphy, *Barnes' Notes: Genesis* (1873; reprint, Grand Rapids: Baker Books, 1998), 382.

Week Two: Running from God

1. "It is almost as impossible…," Clyde Francisco, *The Broadman Bible Commentary: Genesis,* vol. 1 (Nashville: Broadman Press, 1969), 206.

2. "The tree was shaken…," Francisco, *The Broadman Bible Commentary: Genesis,* 207.

3. "Esau's tears were not…," Wiersbe, *Be Authentic,* 30.

4. "The paternal benediction…," Murphy, *Barnes' Notes: Genesis,* 383.

5. "The history of Edom…," Murphy, *Barnes' Notes: Genesis,* 383.

6. "Her tactics are questionable…," de Groot, *The IVP Women's Bible Commentary: Genesis,* 18.

7. "The Old Testament term…," Derek Kidner, *Genesis: An Introduction and Commentary* (Downers Grove, Ill.: Tyndale Press, 1967), 158.

8. "God left [Rebekah]…," Henry, *Matthew Henry's Commentary on the Whole Bible,* 131.

9. "Esau's response to this news…," Wiersbe, *Be Authentic,* 31.

Week Three: A Dream Come True

1. "There could not have been …," Francisco, *The Broadman Bible Commentary,* 210.

2. "This is the greatest promise…," John E. Hartley, *New International Biblical Commentary: Genesis* (Peabody, Mass.: Hendrickson Publishers, 2000), 256.

3. "When God appears…," Trent C. Butler, ed., *Holman Bible Dictionary* (Nashville: Holman Bible Publishers, 1991), see "religious fear: fear of God."

4. "In pagan belief a site…," Hartley, *New International Biblical Commentary: Genesis,* 255-56.

5. "The biblical concept of naming…," Butler, *Holman Bible Dictionary,* see "naming."

6. "By making such a contribution…," Hartley, *New International Biblical Commentary: Genesis,* 258.

Week Four: Blinded by Love

1. "He tries to rid the scene…," Rose Salberg Kam, *Their Stories, Our Stories* (New York: Continuum Publishing, 1995), 62.

2. "In rolling the stone…," Francisco, *The Broadman Bible Commentary,* 212.

3. "Tradition has it…," Barbara L. Thaw Ronson, *The Women of the Torah* (Jerusalem: Jason Aronson, Inc., 1999), 120.

4. "Perhaps Rachel is…," Alice Ogden Bellis, *Helpmates, Harlots, and Heroes* (Louisville, Ky.: Westminster/John Knox Press, 1994), 85.

5. "Custom regards the father…," James M. Freeman, *Manners and Customs of the Bible* (New Kensington, Pa.: Whitaker House, 1996), 37.

6. "No man who loved…," Francisco, *The Broadman Bible Commentary,* 213.

Week Five: A Deceiver Deceived

1. "It was customary…," Freeman, *Manners and Customs of the Bible,* 34.

2. "The culmination of the feast…," Michael E. Williams, ed., *The Storyteller's Companion to the Bible* (Nashville, Abingdon Press, 1991), 146.

3. "Until we ourselves are injured…," Frances Vander Velde, *Women of the Bible* (Grand Rapids: Kregel Publications, 1985), 61.

4. "Laban's actions have long…," Frederick E, Greenspahn, *When Brothers Dwell Together* (Oxford: Oxford University Press, 1994), 128.

5. "This was Laban's sin…," Henry, *Matthew Henry's Commentary on the Whole Bible,* 141.

6. "Laban presumes that…," Sharon Pace Jeansonne, *The Women of Genesis* (Minneapolis: Fortress Press, 1990), 73.

7. "Jacob's reaction…," Gien Karssen, *Her Name Is Woman,* book 2 (Colorado Springs: NavPress, 1977), 49.

8. "The excuse was frivolous…," Henry, *Matthew Henry's Commentary on the Whole Bible,* 141.

9. "Where Laban appears selfish…," Jeansonne, *The Women of Genesis,* 73-74.

10. "a public feast…," Earl D. Radmacher, gen. ed., *Nelson's New Illustrated Bible Commentary* (Nashville: T. Nelson Publishers, 1999), commentary on Genesis 29:23.

11. "This prohibition probably…," Francisco, *The Broadman Bible Commentary,* 214.

Week 6: A Heart for God

1. "love and lust…," George Arthur Buttrick, ed., *The Interpreter's Dictionary of the Bible,* vol. 3 (New York: Abingdon Press, 1962), 280.

2. "All polygamy…," George Matheson, *The Representative Women of the Bible* (London: Hodder and Stoughton, 1908), 120.

3. "As near as we can tell…," Radmacher, *Nelson's New Illustrated Bible Commentary,* commentary at Genesis 29:30, 31, entitled "Women in the Ancient World."

4. "God cared for these women…," Julia Staton, *What the Bible Says About Women* (Joplin, Mo.: College Press Publishing, 1980), 54-55.

5. "Barrenness was a shame…," Phyllis A. Bird, *Missing Persons and Mistaken Identities* (Minneapolis: Augsburg Fortress Press, 1997), 35.

6. "the only way for a woman…," Jeansonne, *The Women of Genesis,* 75.

7. "The names Leah gave…," Herbert Lockyer, *All the Women of the Bible* (Grand Rapids: Zondervan, 1967), 82.

8. "Three people never started…," "God is the main Character…," Eugenia Price, *God Speaks to Women Today* (Grand Rapids: Zondervan Publishing, 1964), 69, 64.

9. "On the one hand…," Carolyn Nabors Baker, *Caught in a Higher Love* (Nashville: Broadman & Holman Publishers, 1998), 70.

FOR ORGANS, PIANOS & ELECTRONIC KEYBOARDS

E-Z PLAY TODAY

182

Amazing Grace

100 Inspirational Favorites

HAL•LEONARD
CORPORATION

7777 W. BLUEMOUND RD. P.O. BOX 13819 MILWAUKEE, WI 53213

ISBN 0-7935-0147-4

ABIDE WITH ME
(Fast Falls The Eventide)

Registration 1

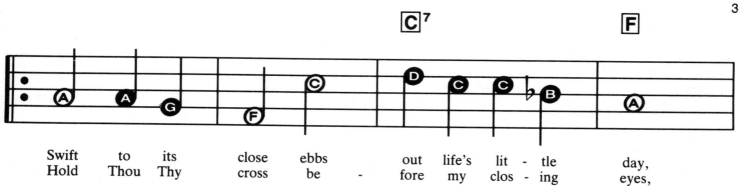

Swift to its close ebbs out life's lit - tle day,
Hold Thou Thy cross be - fore my clos - ing eyes,

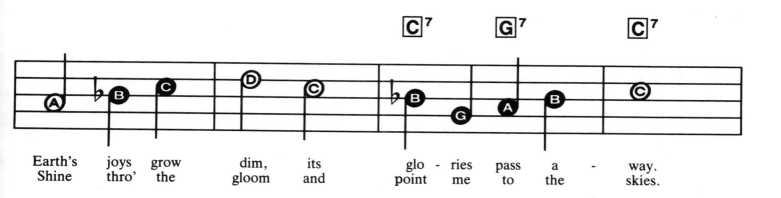

Earth's joys grow dim, its glo - ries pass a - way.
Shine thro' the gloom and point me to the skies.

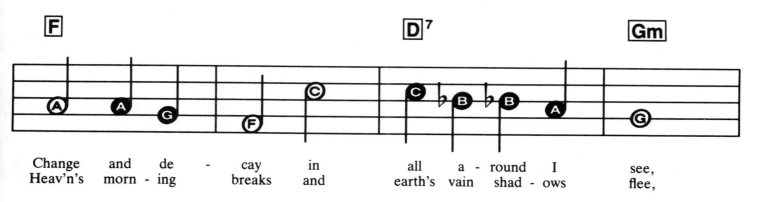

Change and de - cay in all a - round I see,
Heav'n's morn - ing breaks and earth's vain shad - ows flee,

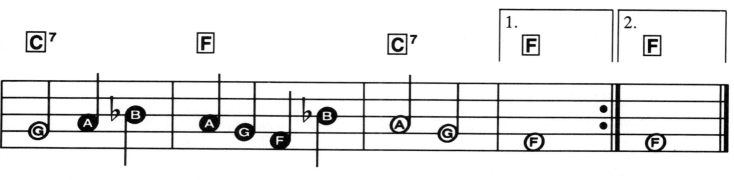

O Thou, who chang - est not, a - bide with me.
In life, in death, O Lord, a - bide with me.

ALL HAIL THE POWER
OF JESUS' NAME

Registration 2
Rhythm: March

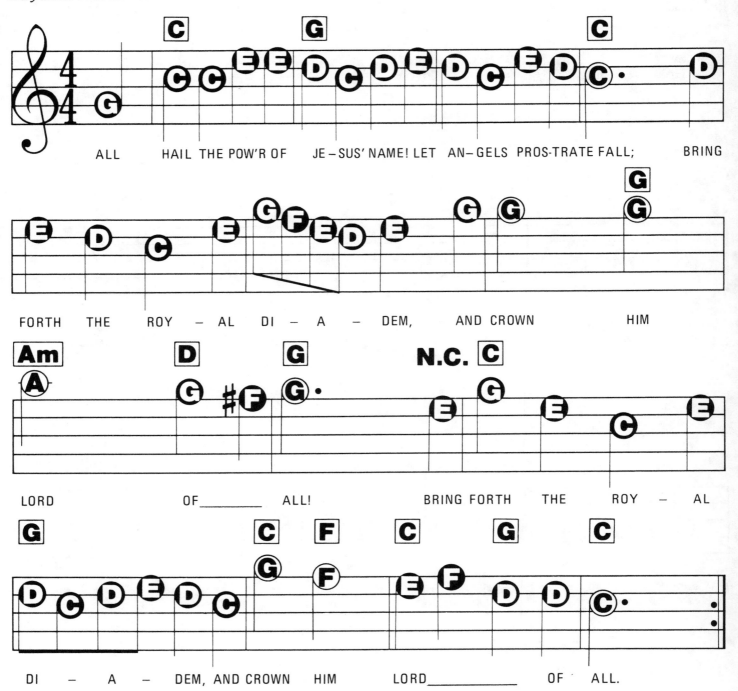

ALL HAIL THE POW'R OF JE—SUS' NAME! LET AN—GELS PROS-TRATE FALL;   BRING

FORTH THE ROY — AL DI — A — DEM,   AND CROWN   HIM

LORD   OF_____ ALL!   BRING FORTH   THE   ROY — AL

DI — A — DEM, AND CROWN HIM   LORD_____ OF ALL.

2.) LET EV'RY KINDRED, EV'RY TRIBE ON THIS TERRESTIAL BALL,
TO HIM ALL MAJESTY ASCRIBE AND CROWN HIM LORD OF ALL.
TO HIM ALL MAJESTY ASCRIBE AND CROWN HIM LORD OF ALL.

3.) OH, THAT WITH YONDER SACRED THRONG WE AT HIS FEET MAY FALL.
WE'LL JOIN THE EVERLASTING SONG AND CROWN HIM LORD OF ALL.
WE'LL JOIN THE EVERLASTING SONG AND CROWN HIM LORD OF ALL.

AMAZING GRACE

5

Registration 9
Rhythm: Waltz

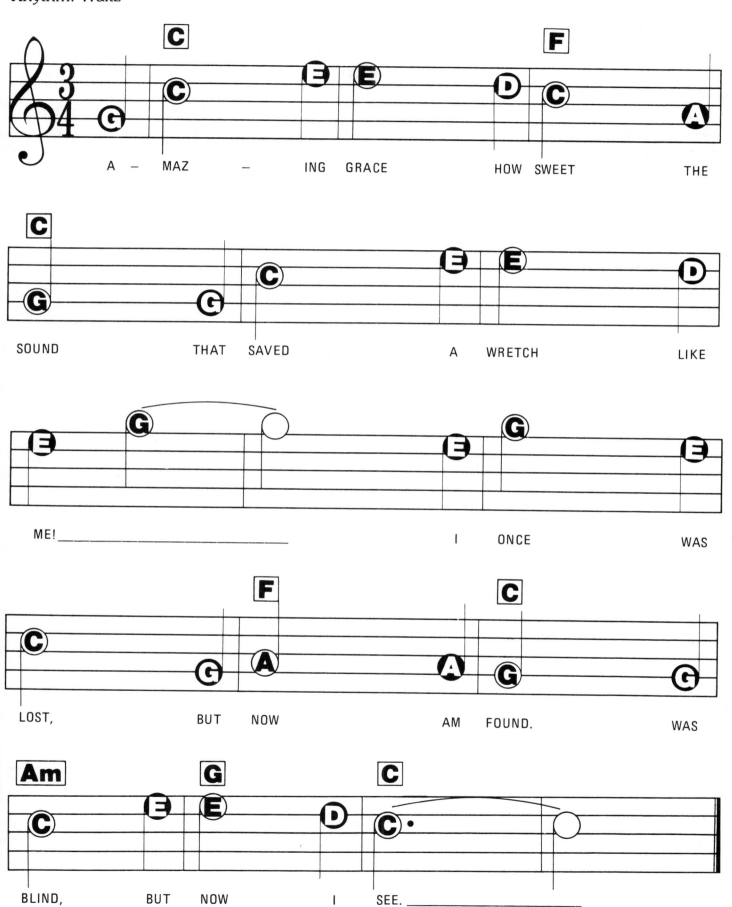

AVE MARIA

Registration 3
Rhythm: Waltz

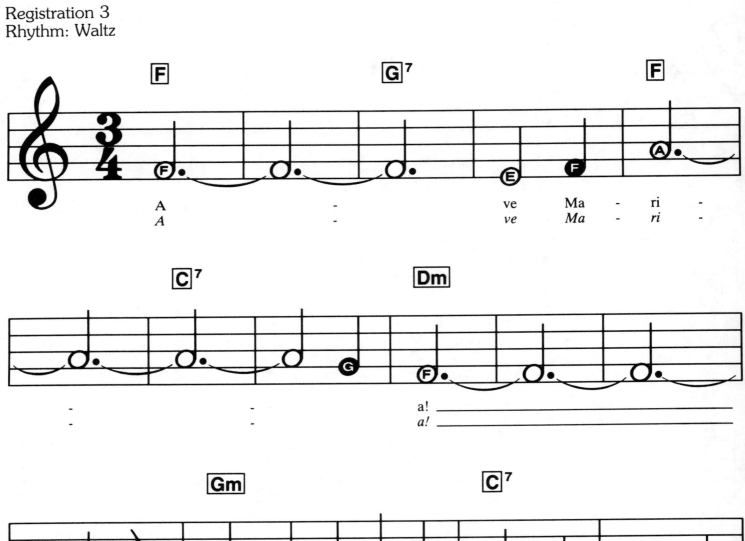

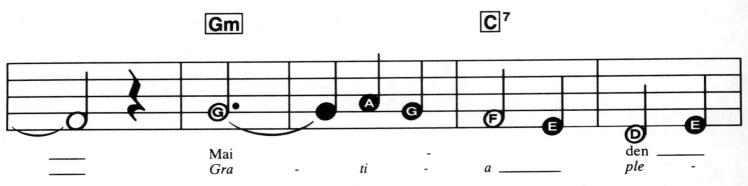

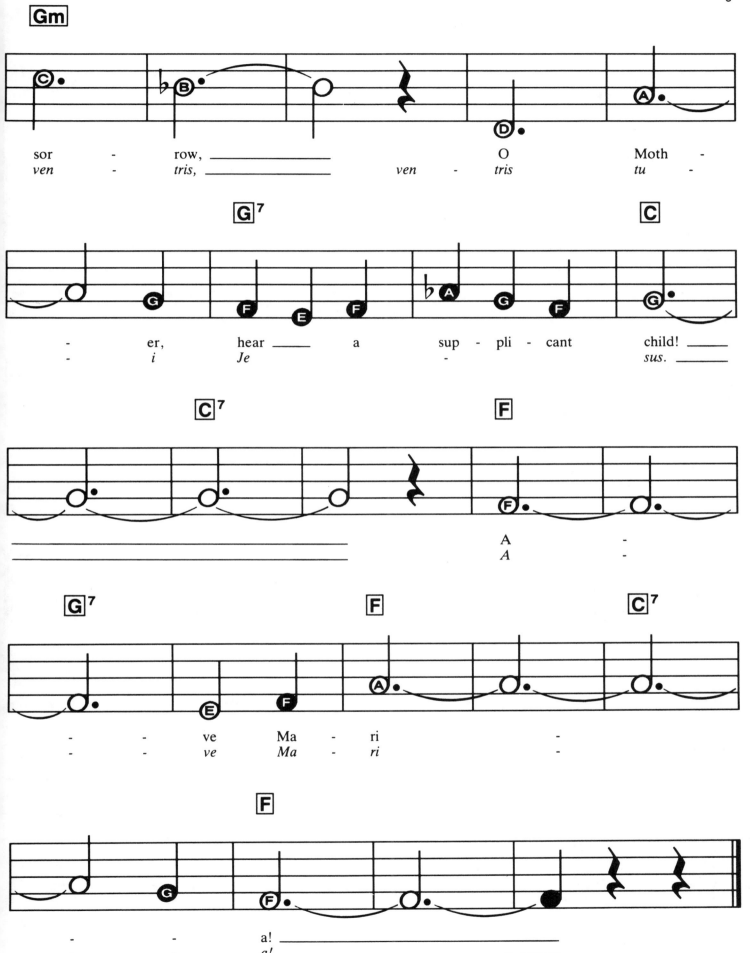

ALL THINGS BRIGHT AND BEAUTIFUL

Registration 4

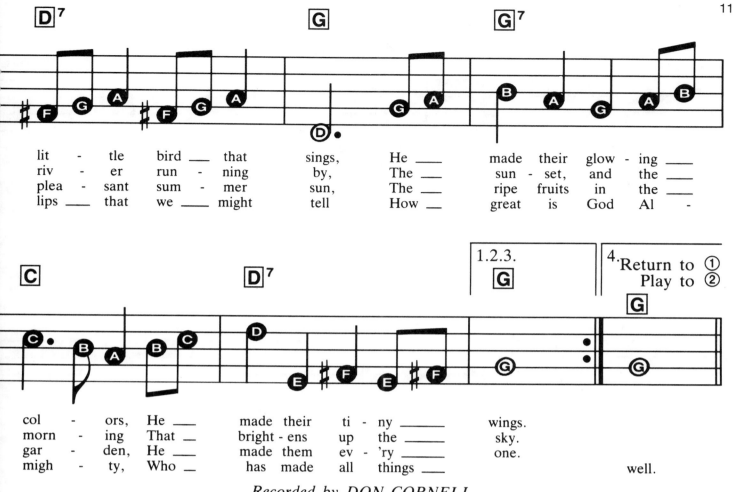

lit - tle bird ___ that sings, He ___ made their glow - ing ___
riv - er run - ning by, The ___ sun - set, and the ___
plea - sant sum - mer sun, The ___ ripe fruits in the ___
lips ___ that we ___ might tell How ___ great is God Al -

col - ors, He ___ made their ti - ny ___ wings.
morn - ing That ___ bright - ens up the ___ sky.
gar - den, He ___ made them ev - 'ry ___ one.
migh - ty, Who ___ has made all things ___ well.

Recorded by DON CORNELL

THE BIBLE TELLS ME SO

Registration 7
Rhythm: Swing

Words and Music by
By DALE EVANS

Have faith, hope and char - i - ty,

That's the way to live suc - cess - ful - ly. How do I know? The

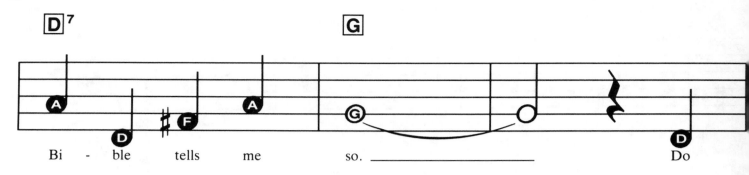

Bi - ble tells me so. _____ Do

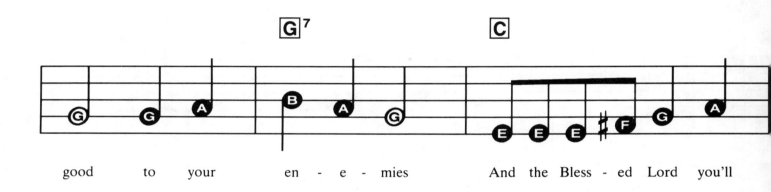

good to your en - e - mies And the Bless - ed Lord you'll

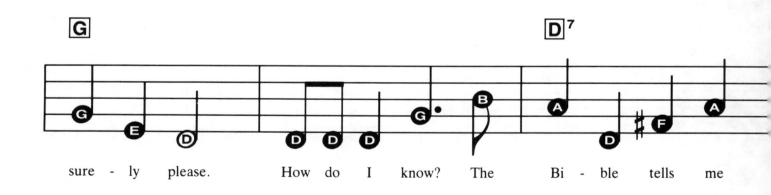

sure - ly please. How do I know? The Bi - ble tells me

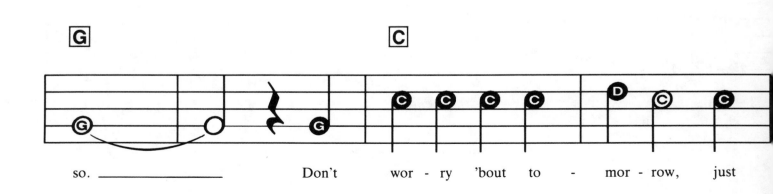

so. _____ Don't wor - ry 'bout to - mor - row, just

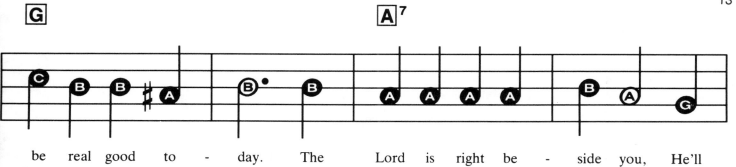

be real good to - day. The Lord is right be - side you, He'll

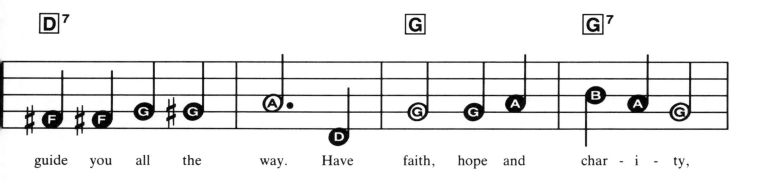

guide you all the way. Have faith, hope and char - i - ty,

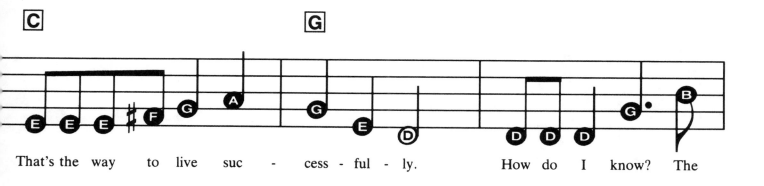

That's the way to live suc - cess - ful - ly. How do I know? The

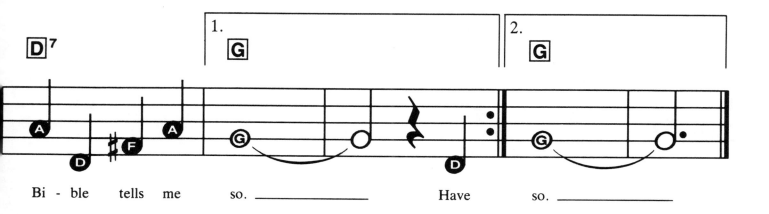

Bi - ble tells me so. _____ Have so. _____

BE STILL, MY SOUL

Registration 10

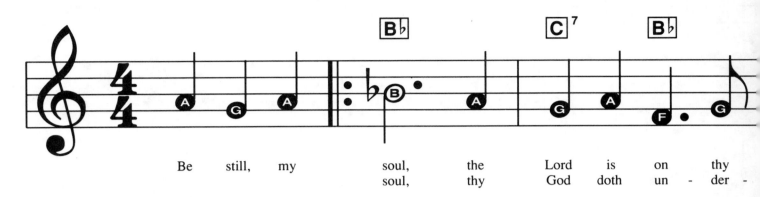

Be still, my soul, the Lord is on thy
soul, thy God doth un - der -

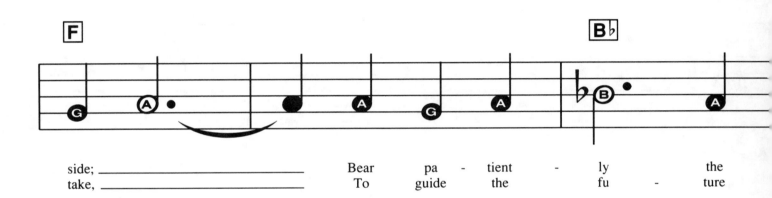

side; _____ Bear pa - tient - ly the
take, _____ To guide the fu - ture

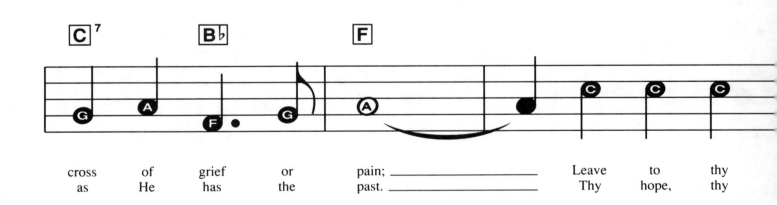

cross of grief or pain; _____ Leave to thy
as He has the past. _____ Thy hope, thy

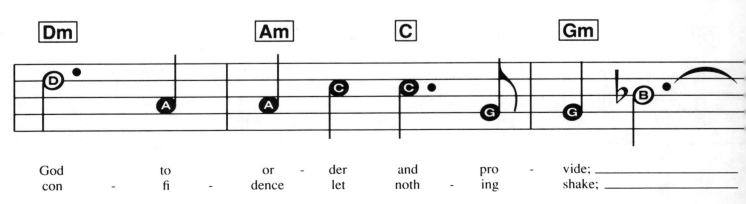

God to or - der and pro - vide; _____
con - fi - dence let noth - ing shake; _____

15

BEAUTIFUL ISLE OF SOMEWHERE

Registration 4
Rhythm: Waltz

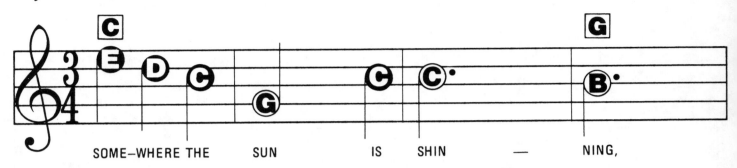

SOME—WHERE THE SUN IS SHIN — NING,

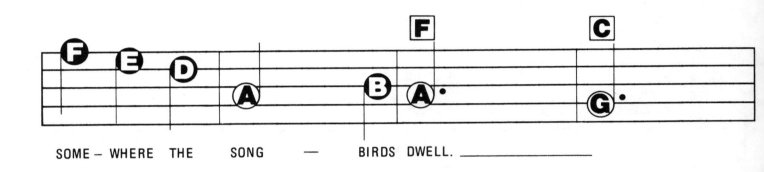

SOME — WHERE THE SONG — BIRDS DWELL. _____

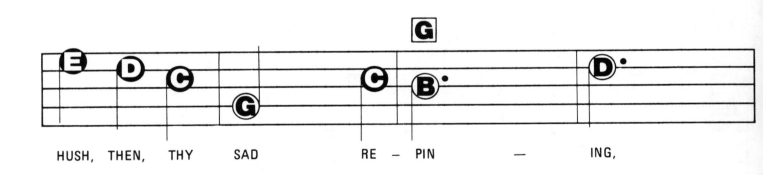

HUSH, THEN, THY SAD RE - PIN — ING,

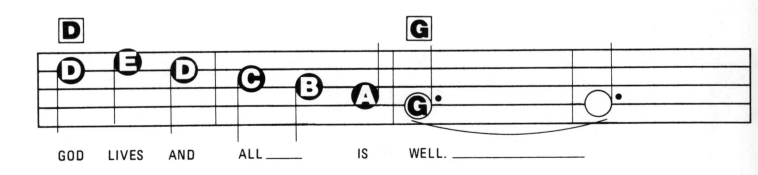

GOD LIVES AND ALL ____ IS WELL. _____

17

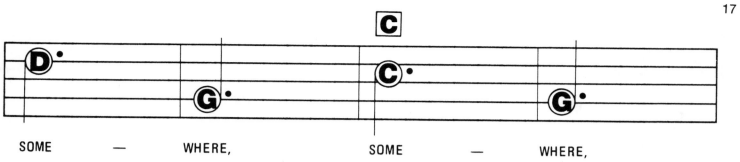

SOME — WHERE, SOME — WHERE,

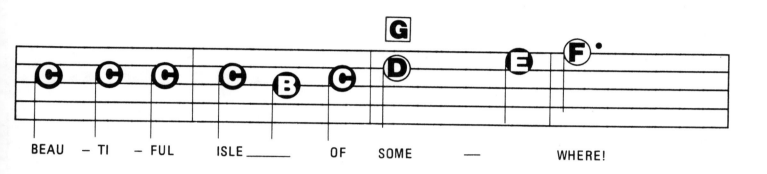

BEAU — TI — FUL ISLE____ OF SOME — WHERE!

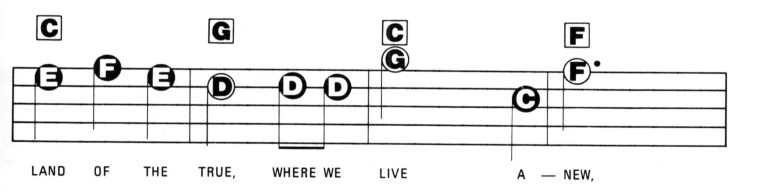

LAND OF THE TRUE, WHERE WE LIVE A — NEW,

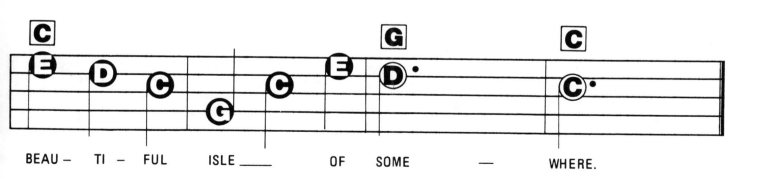

BEAU — TI — FUL ISLE____ OF SOME — WHERE.

ALLELUIA! SING TO JESUS

Registration 6
Rhythm: Waltz

BEAUTIFUL SAVIOR

Registration 9

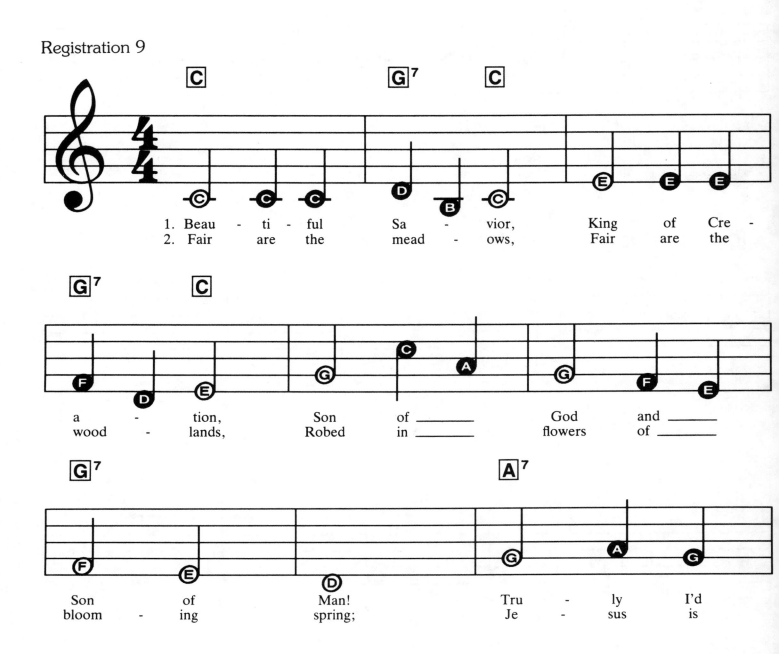

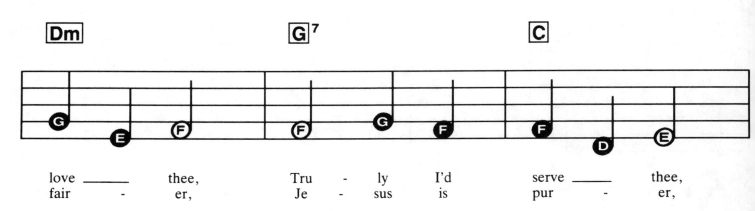

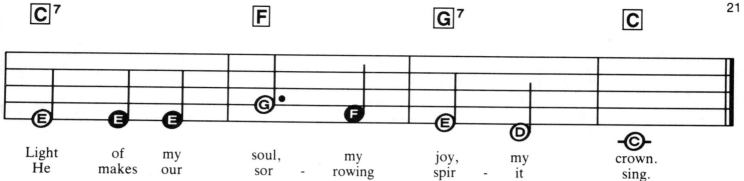

Light of my soul, my joy, my crown.
He makes our sor - rowing spir - it sing.

3. Fair is the sunshine
Fair is the moonlight,
Bright the sparkling stars on high;
Jesus shines brighter,
Jesus shines purer,
Than all the angels in the sky.

4. Beautiful Savior,
Lord of the nations,
Son of God and Son of Man!
Glory and honor,
Praise, adoration,
Now and for evermore be thine!

BLESSING AND HONOR

Registration 10

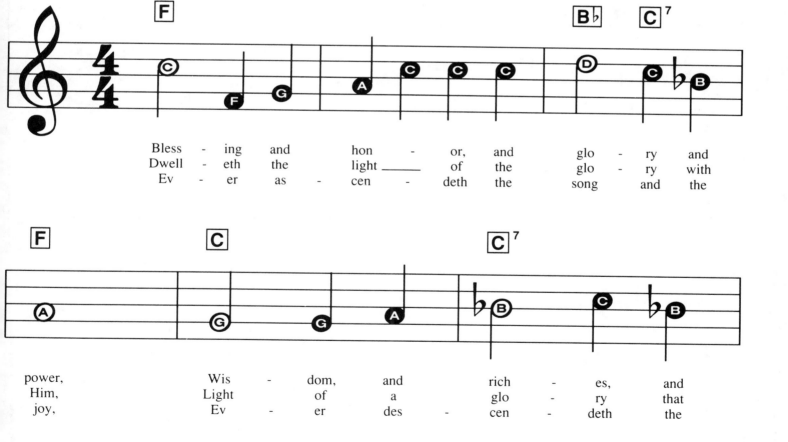

Bless - ing and hon - or, and glo - ry and
Dwell - eth and the light ____ of the glo - ry with
Ev - er as - cen - deth the song and the

power, Wis - dom, and rich - es, and
Him, Light of a glo - ry that
joy, Ev - er des - cen - deth the

BLEST BE THE TIE THAT BINDS

Registration 2
Rhythm: Waltz

3. We share our mutual woes
   Our mutual burdens bear,
   And often for each other flows
   The sympathizing tear.

4. When we asunder part
   It gives us inward pain.
   But we shall still be joined in heart
   And hope to meet again.

BRINGING IN THE SHEAVES

Registration 4

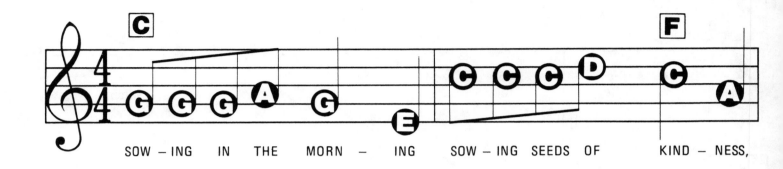

SOW – ING IN THE MORN – ING SOW – ING SEEDS OF KIND – NESS,

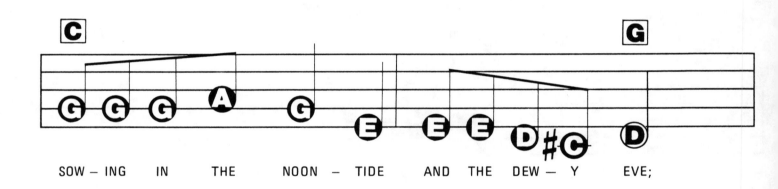

SOW – ING IN THE NOON – TIDE AND THE DEW – Y EVE;

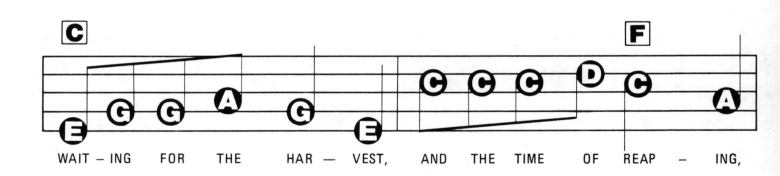

WAIT – ING FOR THE HAR — VEST, AND THE TIME OF REAP – ING,

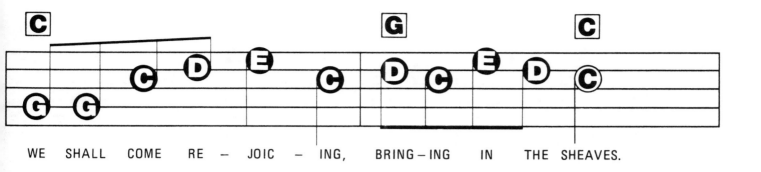

WE SHALL COME RE — JOIC — ING, BRING — ING IN THE SHEAVES.

Chorus

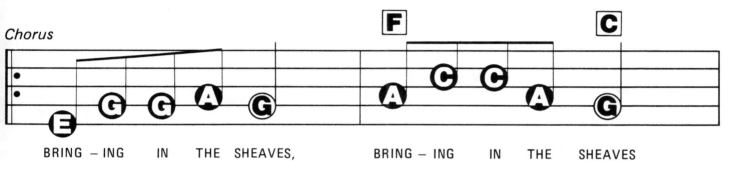

BRING — ING IN THE SHEAVES, BRING — ING IN THE SHEAVES

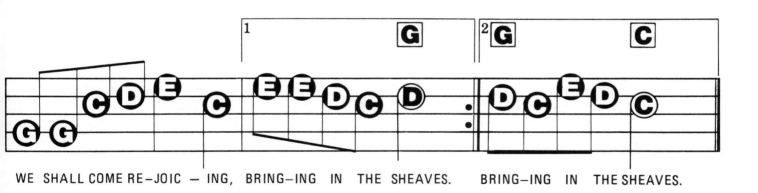

WE SHALL COME RE—JOIC — ING, BRING—ING IN THE SHEAVES. BRING—ING IN THE SHEAVES.

2.) SOWING IN THE SUNSHINE, SOWING IN THE SHADOWS,
   FEARING NEITHER CLOUDS NOR WINTER'S CHILLING BREEZE;
   BY AND BY THE HARVEST, AND THE LABOR ENDED,
   WE SHALL COME REJOICING,
   BRINGING IN THE SHEAVES.
   Chorus

3.) GOING FORTH WITH WEEPING, SOWING FOR THE MASTER,
   THO' THE LOSS SUSTAINED OUR SPIRIT OFTEN GRIEVES;
   WHEN OUR WEEPING'S OVER, HE WILL BID US WELCOME,
   WE SHALL COME REJOICING,
   BRINGING IN THE SHEAVES.
   Chorus

BRING THEM IN

Registration 1
Rhythm: Swing

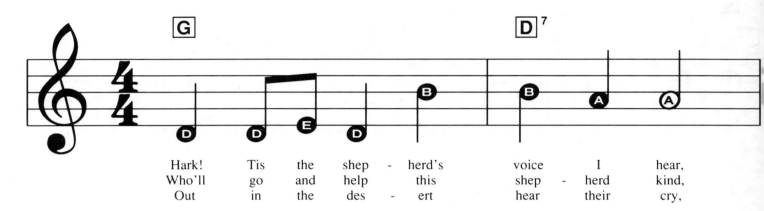

Hark!	Tis	the	shep	herd's	voice	I	hear,
Who'll	go	and	help	this	shep	herd	kind,
Out	in	the	des	ert	hear	their	cry,

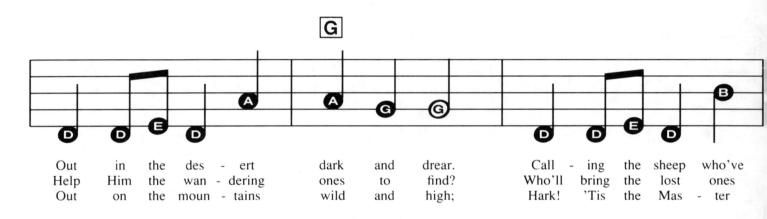

Out	in	the	des	ert	dark	and	drear.	
Help	Him	the	wan - dering		ones	to	find?	
Out	on	the	moun - tains		wild	and	high;	

Call - ing	the	sheep	who've
Who'll	bring	the	lost ones
Hark!	'Tis	the	Mas - ter

gone	a -	stray
to	the	fold
speaks	to	thee,

Far	from	the	shep - herd's
Where	they'll	be	shel - tered
"Go,	find	my	sheep wher - e'er

fold	a -	way.
from	the	cold.
they		be."

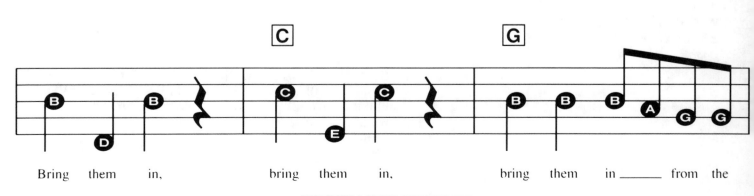

Bring	them	in,	bring	them	in,

bring	them	in _____	from the

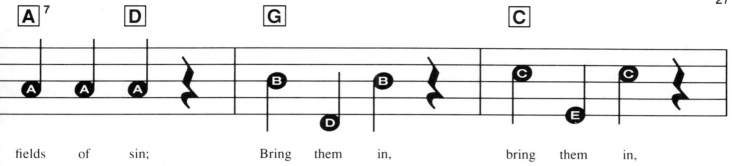

fields of sin;   Bring them in,   bring them in,

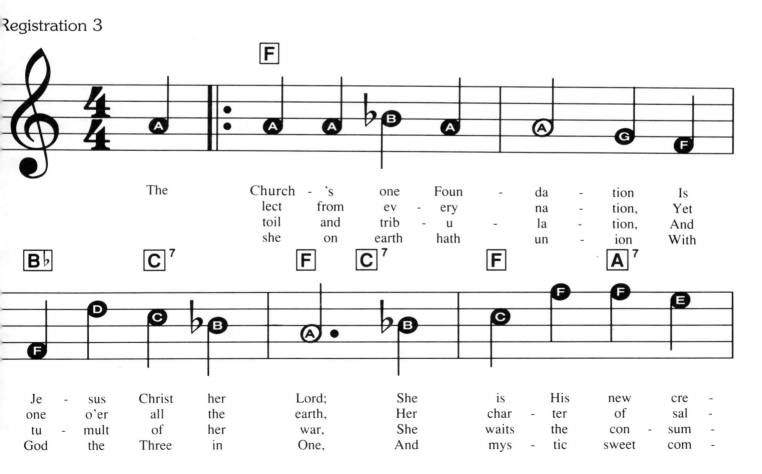

bring the wand - ering ones to   Je - sus.   Je - sus.

THE CHURCH'S ONE FOUNDATION

Registration 3

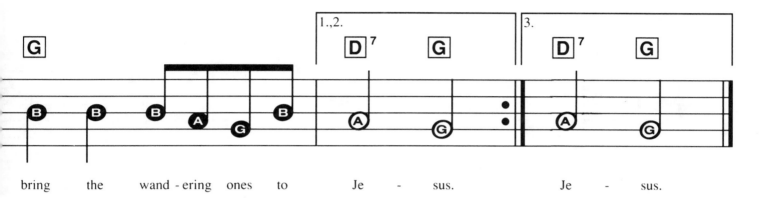

The   Church - 's   one   Foun - da - tion   Is
lect   from   ev - ery   na - tion,   Yet
toil   and   trib - u - la - tion,   And
she   on   earth   hath   un - ion   With

Je - sus   Christ   her   Lord;   She   is   His   new   cre -
one   o'er   all   her   earth,   Her   char - ter   of   sal -
tu - mult   of   her   war,   She   waits   the   con - sum -
God   the   Three   in   One,   And   mys - tic   sweet   com -

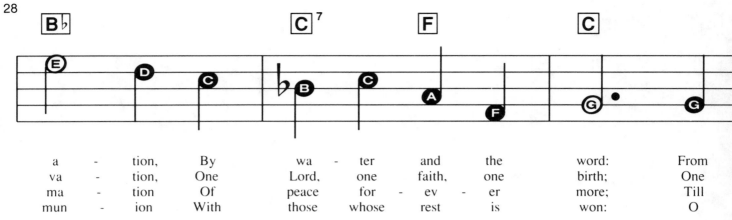

a	-	tion,	By	wa	ter	and	the	word:	From
va	-	tion,	One	Lord,	one	faith,	one	birth;	One
ma	-	tion	Of	peace	for - ev - er			more;	Till
mun	-	ion	With	those	whose	rest	is	won:	O

heaven	He	came	and	sought	her	To	be	His	ho - ly
ho - ly	name	she	bless -	es,	Par -	takes	one	ho - ly
with	the	vi - sion	glo -	rious	Her	long - ing	eyes	are
hap - py	ones	and	ho -	ly!	Lord,	give	us	grace	that

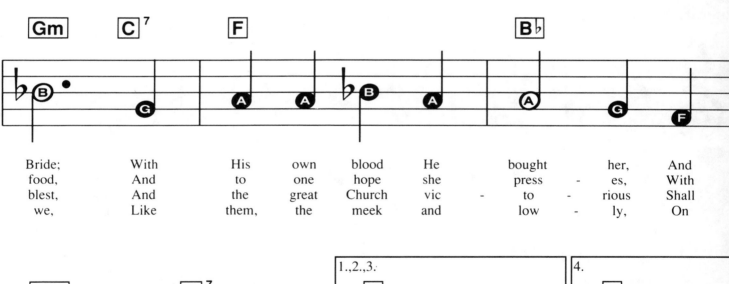

Bride;	With	His	own	blood	He	bought	her,	And
food,	And	to	one	hope	she	press -	es,	With
blest,	And	the	great	Church	vic -	to -	rious	Shall
we,	Like	them,	the	meek	and	low -	ly,	On

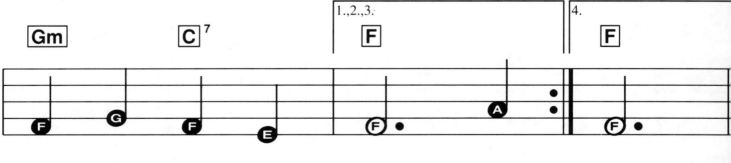

for	her	life	He	died.	E -
ev - ery	grace	He	en -	dued.	'Mid
be	the	Church	at	rest.	Yet
high	may	dwell	with		Thee.

CHRIST AROSE

Registration 9

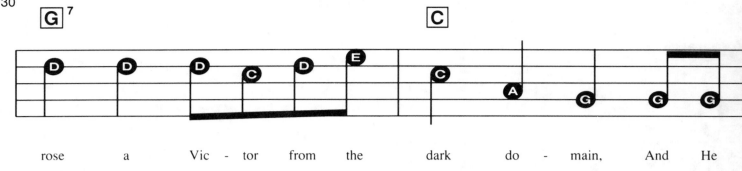

rose a Vic - tor from the dark do - main, And He

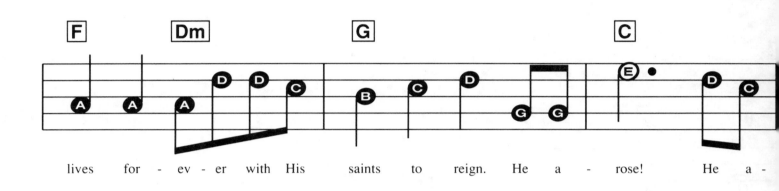

lives for - ev - er with His saints to reign. He a - rose! He a -

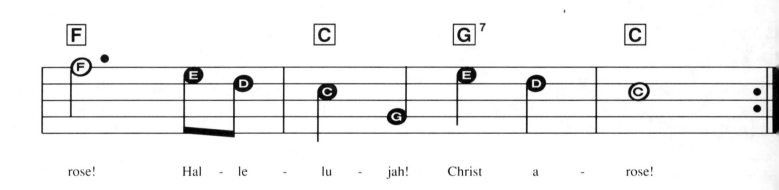

rose! Hal - le - lu - jah! Christ a - rose!

CROWN HIM WITH MANY CROWNS

Registration 6

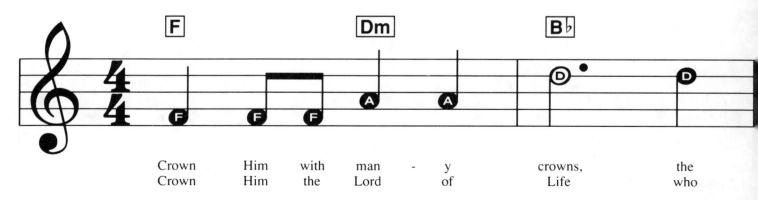

Crown Him with man - y crowns, the
Crown Him the Lord of Life who

BLESSED ASSURANCE

Registration 1
Rhythm: Waltz

COME THOU ALMIGHTY KING

Registration 10
Rhythm: Waltz

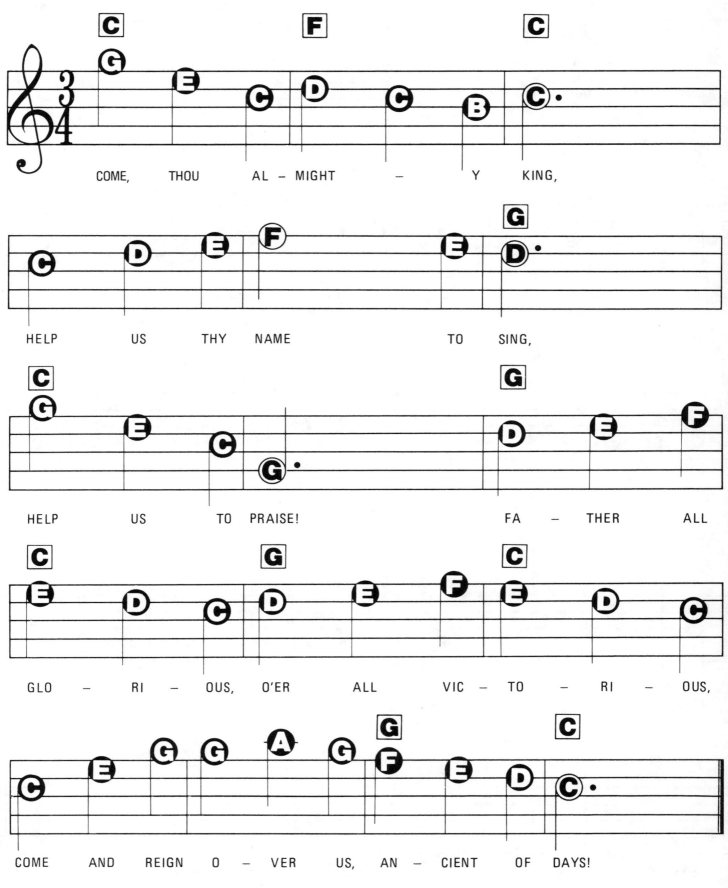

COME UNTO ME, YE WEARY

EV'RY TIME I FEEL THE SPIRIT

Registration 7
Rhythm: Rock or 8 Beat

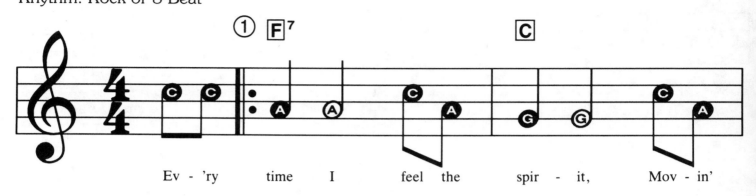

Ev - 'ry time I feel the spir - it, Mov - in'

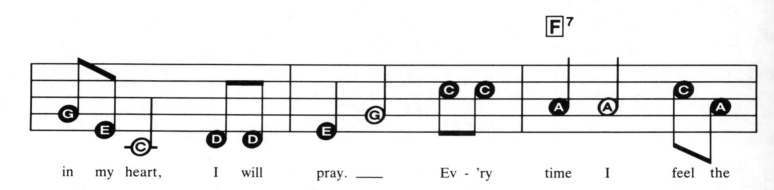

in my heart, I will pray. ___ Ev - 'ry time I feel the

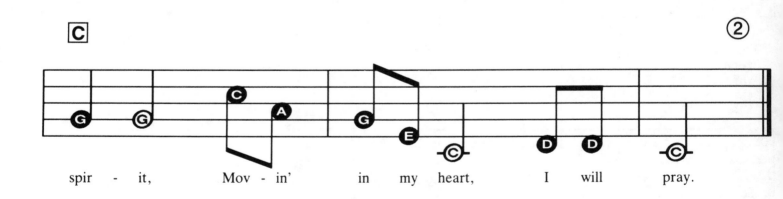

spir - it, Mov - in' in my heart, I will pray.

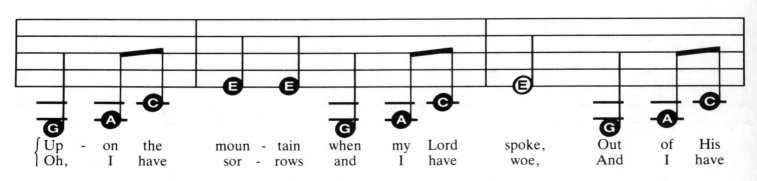

Up - on the moun - tain when my Lord spoke, Out of His
Oh, I have sor - rows and I have woe, And I have

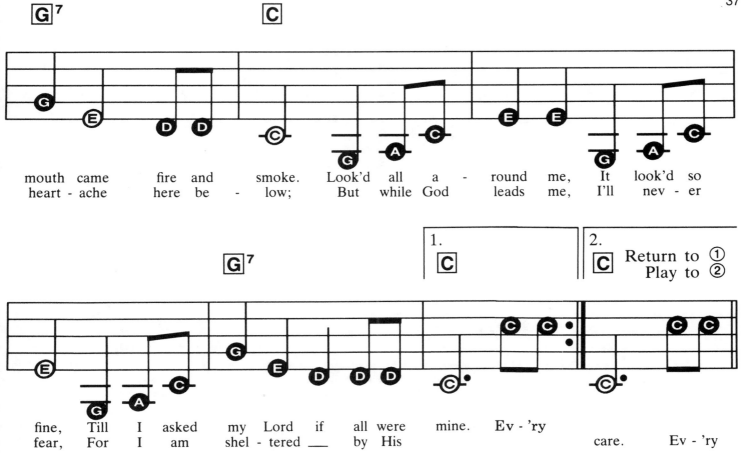

G⁷　　　　C

mouth came　　fire and　　smoke.　Look'd all a - round me,　It　look'd so
heart - ache　　here be - low;　　But while God　leads me,　I'll　nev - er

G⁷

1.
C

2.
C　Return to ①
　　Play to ②

fine,　Till　I　asked　my Lord if　all were　mine.　Ev - 'ry
fear,　For　I　am　shel - tered ___ by His　care.　Ev - 'ry

COME, HOLY GHOST

Registration 4
Rhythm: Waltz

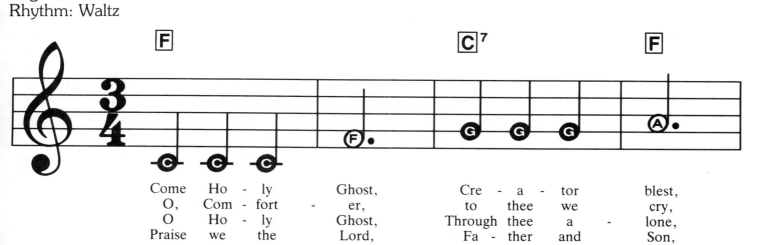

F　　　　　　　C⁷　　　　F

Come Ho - ly　Ghost,　　Cre - a - tor　blest,
O, Com - fort - er,　　　to thee we　cry,
O Ho - ly　Ghost,　　Through thee a - lone,
Praise we the　Lord,　　Fa - ther and　Son,

38

DOMINIQUE

Registration 9
Rhythm: Swing

English Lyrics by
Noel Regney
Music by
Soeur Sourire, O.P.

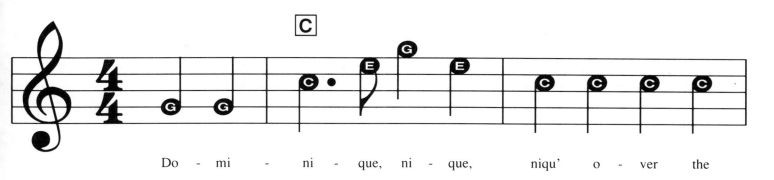

Do - mi - ni - que, ni - que, niqu' o - ver the

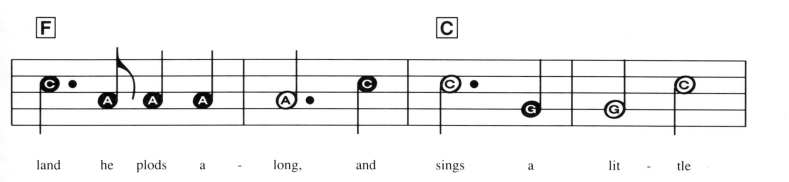

land he plods a - long, and sings a lit - tle

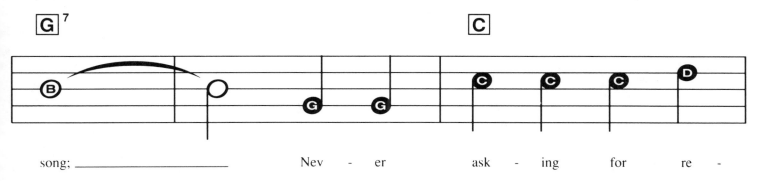

song; _____ Nev - er ask - ing for re -

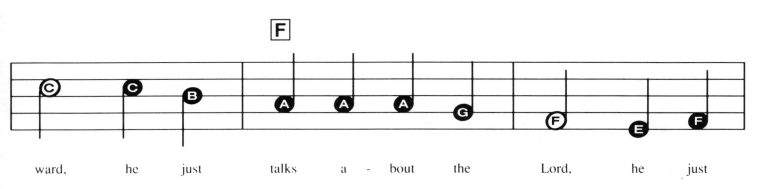

ward, he just talks a - bout the Lord, he just

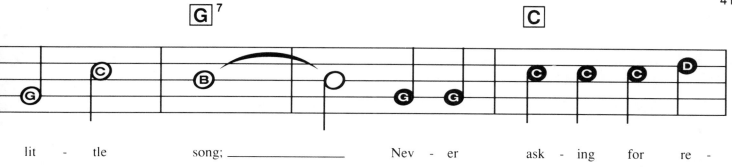

lit - tle   song; _____   Nev - er   ask - ing   for   re -

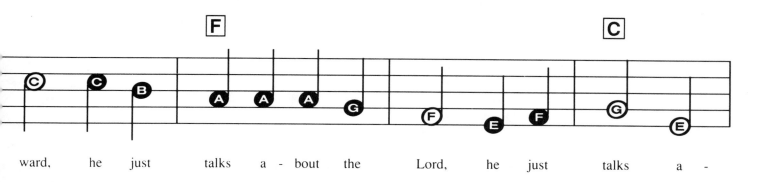

ward,   he   just   talks   a - bout   the   Lord,   he   just   talks   a -

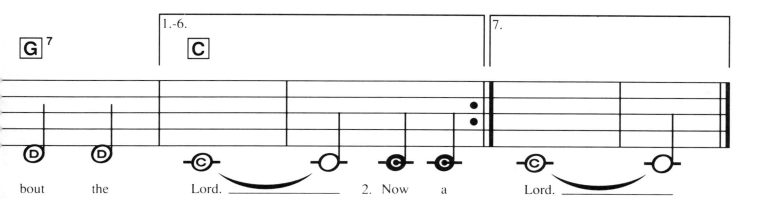

bout   the   Lord. _____   2. Now   a   Lord. _____

Additional Lyrics

2. Now a heretic, one day,
   Among the thorns forced him to crawl.
   Dominique with just one prayer,
   Made him hear the good Lord's call.
   To Chorus

3. Without horse or fancy wagon,
   He crossed Europe up and down.
   Poverty was his companion,
   As he walked from town to town.
   To Chorus

4. To bring back the straying liars
   And the lost sheep to his fold,
   He brought forth the preaching friars,
   Heaven's soldiers, brave and bold.
   To Chorus

5. One day, in the budding order,
   There was nothing left to eat.
   Suddenly two angels walked in
   With a loaf of bread and meat.
   To Chorus

6. Dominique once, in his slumber,
   Saw the Virgin's coat unfurled
   Over friars without number,
   Preaching all around the world.
   To Chorus

7. Grant us now, oh Dominique,
   The grace of love and simple mirth,
   That we all may help to quicken
   Godly life and truth on earth.
   To Chorus

CLEANSE ME

Registration 9
Rhythm: Waltz

Search me, O God, _____ and
O Ho - ly Ghost, _____ re -

know my heart to - day; _____
vi - val my comes from Thee; _____

Try me, O Sav - ior,
Send a re - vi - val,

know my thoughts, I pray. _____
start the work in me. _____

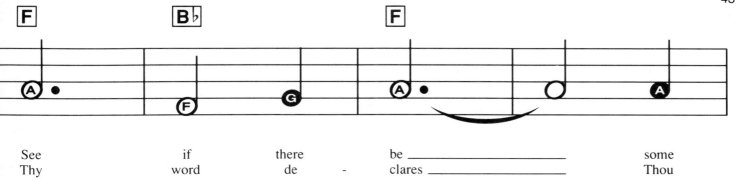

See if there be _____ some
Thy word de - clares _____ Thou

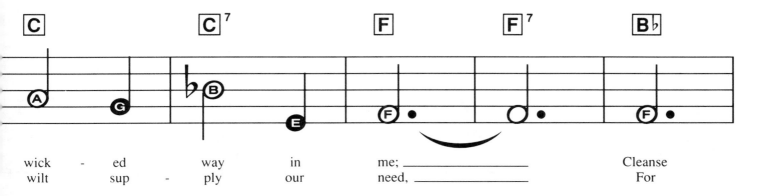

wick - ed way in me; _____ Cleanse
wilt sup - ply our need, _____ For

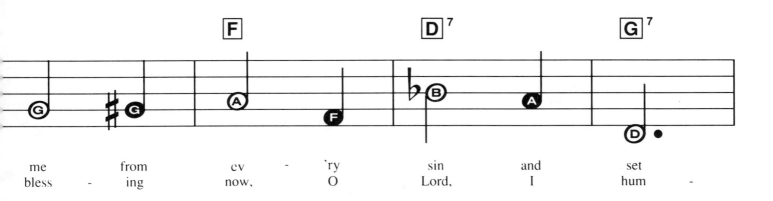

me from ev - 'ry sin and set
bless - ing now, O Lord, I hum -

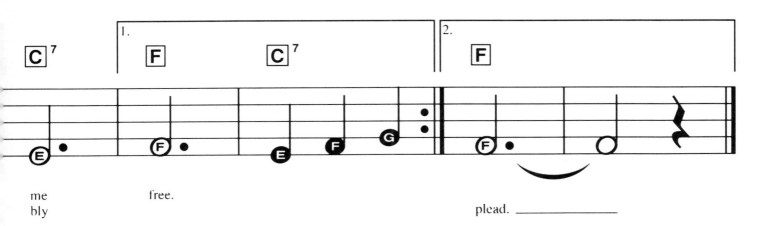

me free.
bly

plead. _____

DOXOLOGY

Registration 6

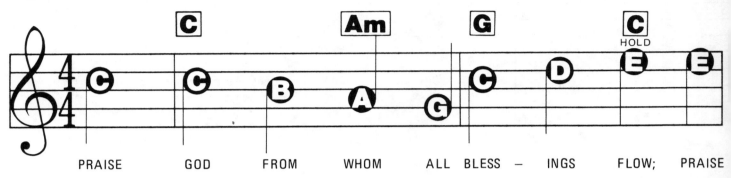

PRAISE GOD FROM WHOM ALL BLESS — INGS FLOW; PRAISE

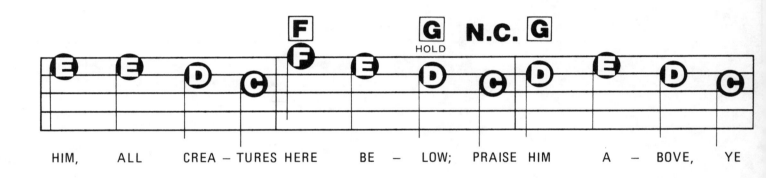

HIM, ALL CREA — TURES HERE BE — LOW; PRAISE HIM A — BOVE, YE

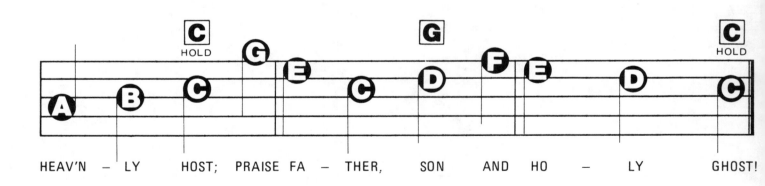

HEAV'N — LY HOST; PRAISE FA — THER, SON AND HO — LY GHOST!

FOR THE BEAUTY OF THE EARTH

Registration 9

GO DOWN, MOSES

Registration 4
Rhythm: March

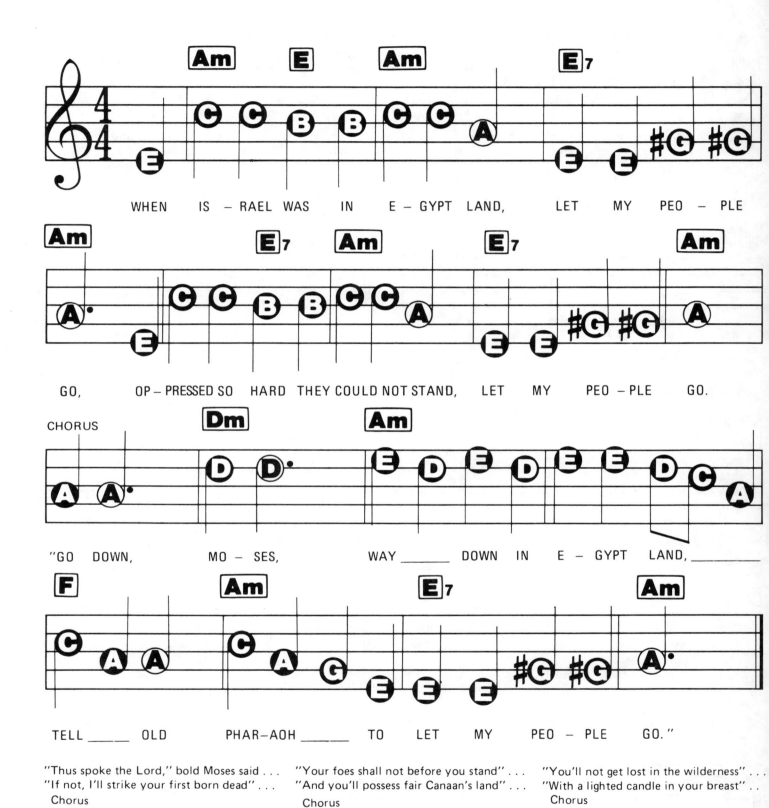

WHEN IS-RAEL WAS IN E-GYPT LAND, LET MY PEO-PLE

GO, OP-PRESSED SO HARD THEY COULD NOT STAND, LET MY PEO-PLE GO.

CHORUS

"GO DOWN, MO-SES, WAY _____ DOWN IN E-GYPT LAND, _____

TELL _____ OLD PHAR-AOH _____ TO LET MY PEO-PLE GO."

"Thus spoke the Lord," bold Moses said . . .   "Your foes shall not before you stand" . . .   "You'll not get lost in the wilderness" . . .
"If not, I'll strike your first born dead" . . .   "And you'll possess fair Canaan's land" . . .   "With a lighted candle in your breast" . .
Chorus   Chorus   Chorus

GOD OF OUR FATHERS
WHOSE ALMIGHTY HAND

47

Registration 9

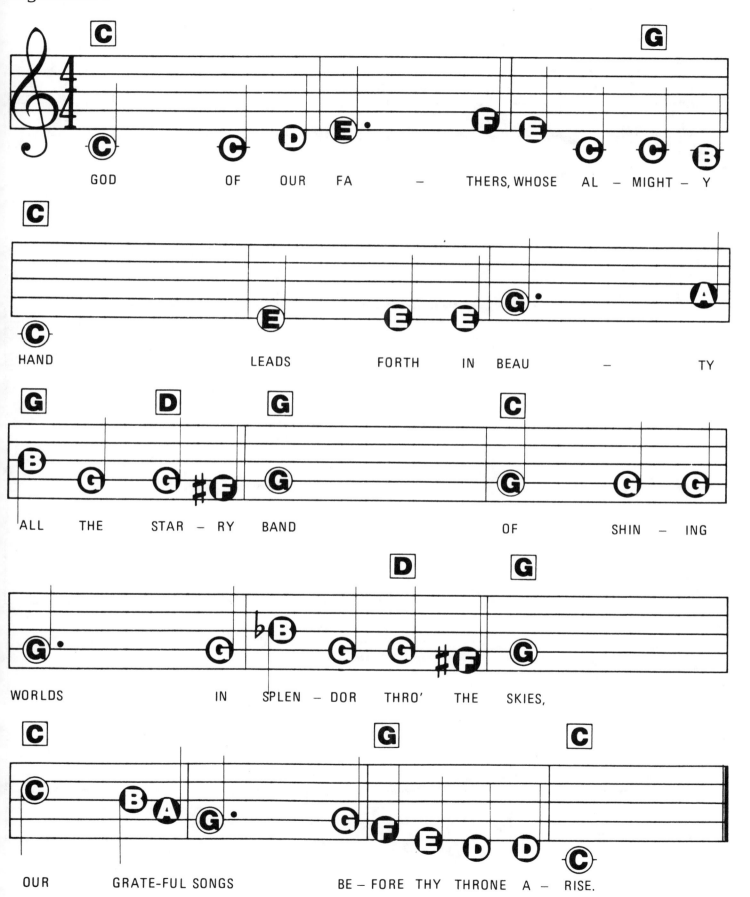

GOD BE WITH YOU TILL WE MEET AGAIN

Registration 2

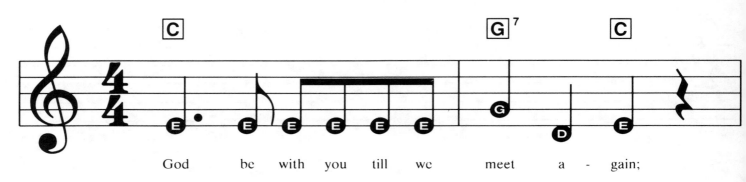

God be with you till we meet a - gain;

By	His	coun - sels	guide,	up - hold	you,
'Neath	His	wings pro - tect - ing	hide	you,
When	life's	per - ils	thick con - found	you,
Keep	love's	ban - ner	float - ing	o'er	you,

With	His	sheep se - cure - ly	fold	you;
Dai - ly	man - na	still pro - vide	you;
Put	His	arms un - fail - ing	round	you;
Smite	death's	threat -'ning	wave be - fore	you;

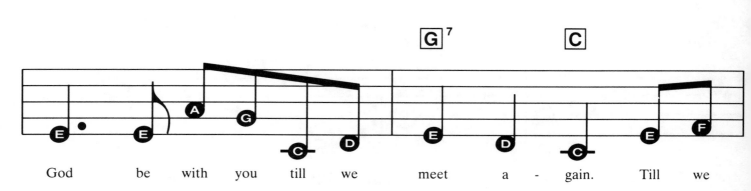

God be with you till we meet a - gain. Till we

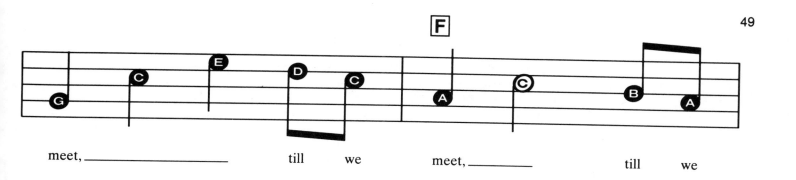

meet, _____ till we meet, _____ till we

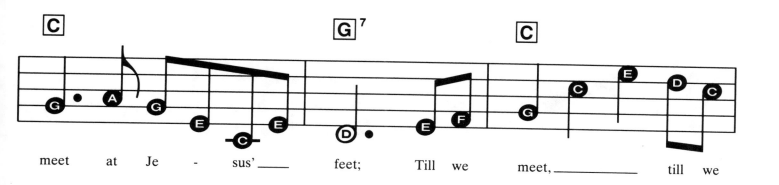

meet at Je - sus' _____ feet; Till we meet, _____ till we

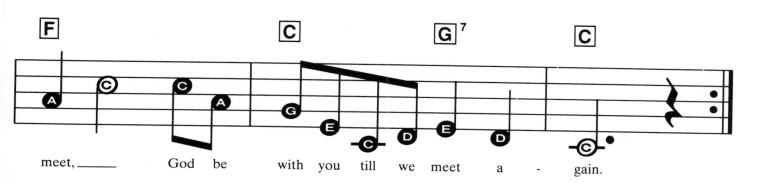

meet, _____ God be with you till we meet a - gain.

HE LEADETH ME, O BLESSED THOUGHT

Registration 8

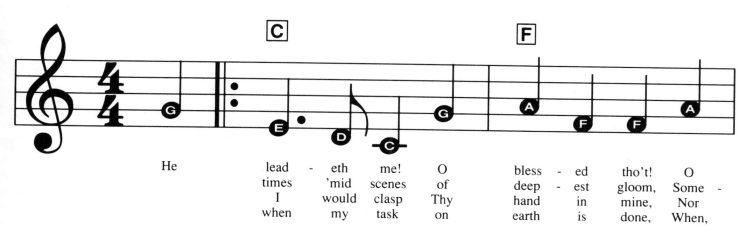

He lead - eth me! O bless - ed tho't! O
times 'mid scenes of deep - est gloom, Some -
I would clasp Thy hand in mine, Nor
when my task on earth is done, When,

HE'S GOT THE WHOLE WORLD IN HIS HANDS

Registration 7
Rhythm: Swing

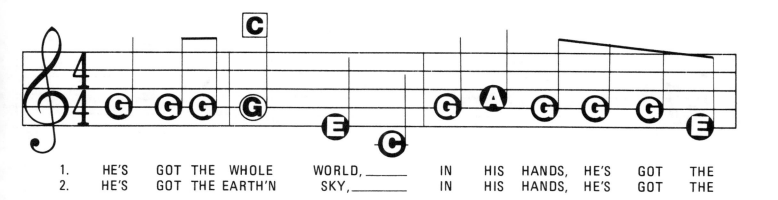

| | 1. | HE'S | GOT THE | WHOLE | WORLD, _____ | IN | HIS | HANDS, HE'S | GOT | THE |
| | 2. | HE'S | GOT THE | EARTH'N | SKY, _____ | IN | HIS | HANDS, HE'S | GOT | THE |

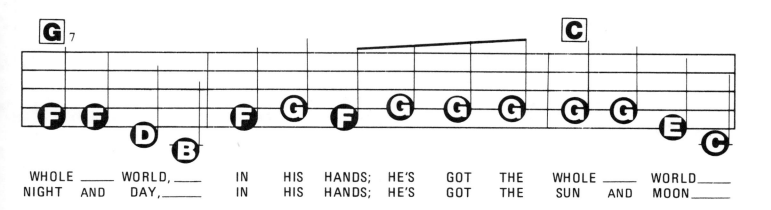

| WHOLE _____ | WORLD, ___ | IN | HIS | HANDS; HE'S | GOT | THE | WHOLE _____ | WORLD_____ |
| NIGHT AND | DAY,_____ | IN | HIS | HANDS; HE'S | GOT | THE | SUN AND | MOON_____ |

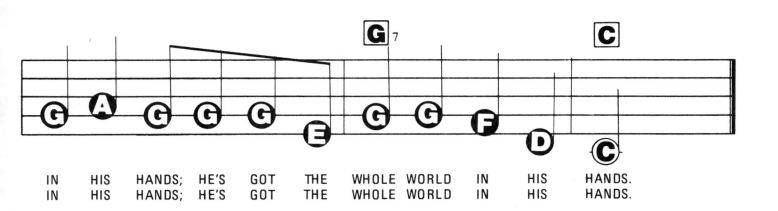

| IN | HIS | HANDS; HE'S | GOT | THE | WHOLE WORLD | IN | HIS | HANDS. |
| IN | HIS | HANDS; HE'S | GOT | THE | WHOLE WORLD | IN | HIS | HANDS. |

HOLY GOD, WE PRAISE THY NAME

Registration 1
Rhythm: Waltz

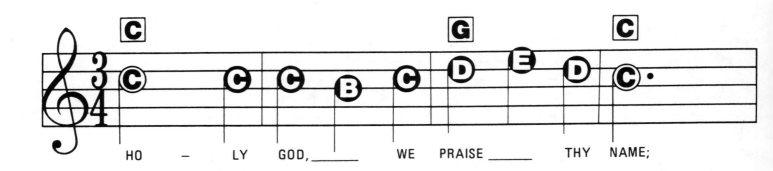

HO — LY GOD,_____ WE PRAISE _____ THY NAME;

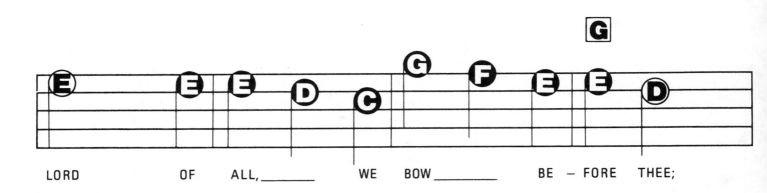

LORD OF ALL,_____ WE BOW _____ BE — FORE THEE;

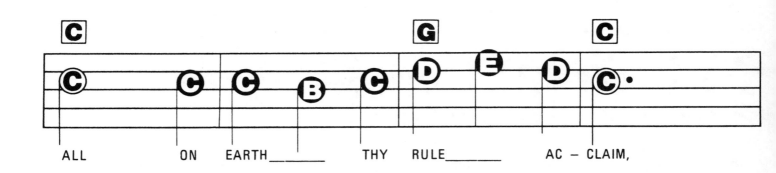

ALL ON EARTH_____ THY RULE_____ AC — CLAIM,

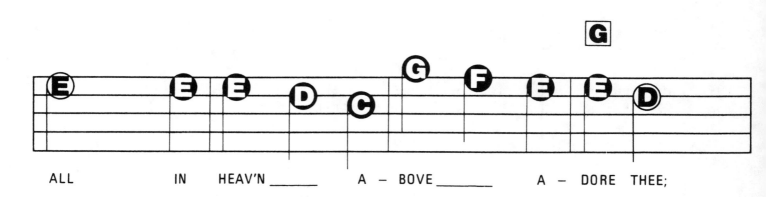

ALL IN HEAV'N_____ A — BOVE_____ A — DORE THEE;

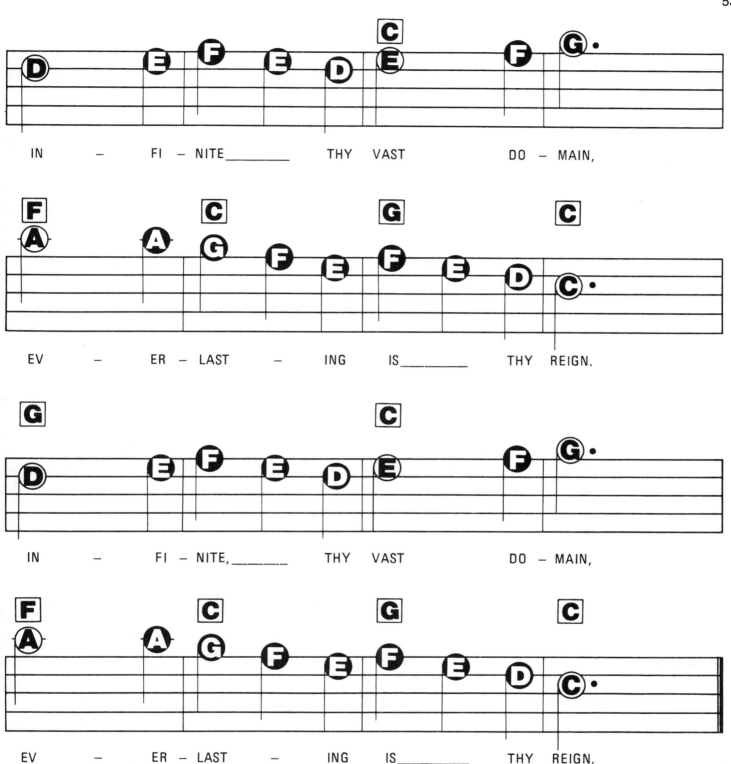

2.) HARK! THE LOUD CELESTIAL HYMN
ANGEL CHOIRS ABOVE ARE RAISING;
CHERUBIM AND SERAPHIM
IN UNCEASING CHORUS PRAISING;
FILL THE HEAV'NS WITH SWEET ACCORD;
HOLY, HOLY, HOLY, LORD!
FILL THE HEAV'NS WITH SWEET ACCORD;
HOLY, HOLY, HOLY, LORD!

3.) HOLY FATHER, HOLY SON,
HOLY SPIRIT, THREE WE NAME THEE;
WHILE IN ESSENCE ONLY ONE,
UNDIVIDED GOD WE CLAIM THEE;
AND ADORING, BEND THE KNEE,
WHILE WE OWN THE MYSTERY.
AND ADORING, BEND THE KNEE,
WHILE WE OWN THE MYSTERY.

HOLY, HOLY, HOLY

Registration 2

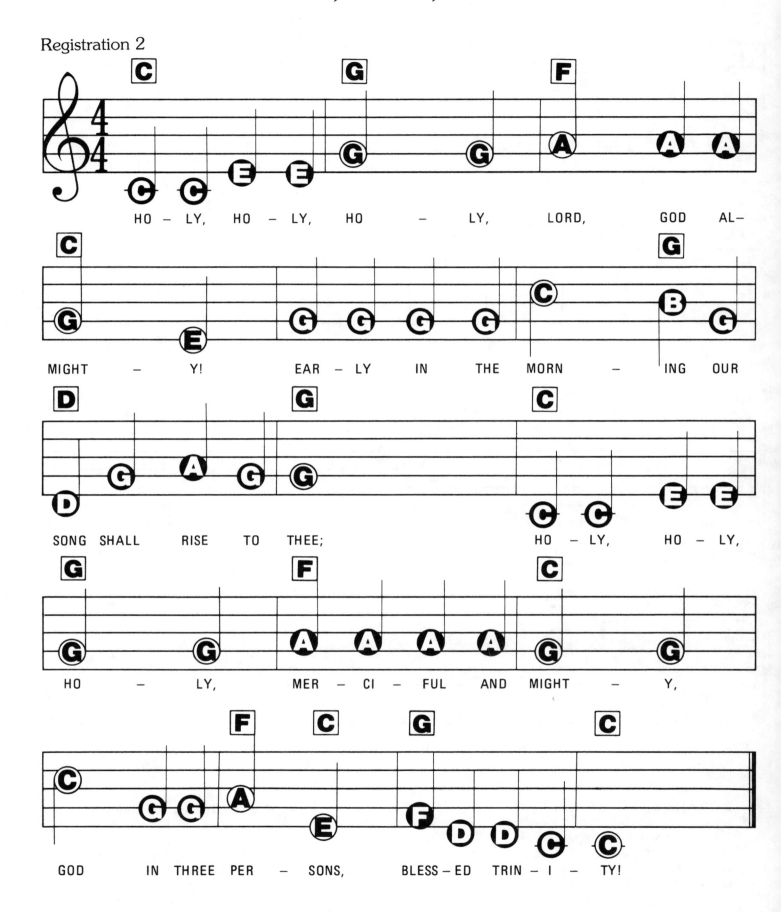

HOW SWEET THE NAME OF JESUS SOUNDS

Registration 3

FAITH OF OUR FATHERS

Registration 2
Rhythm: Waltz

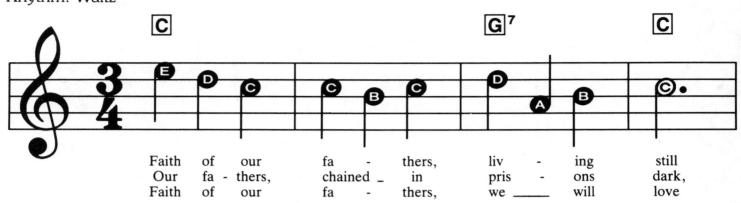

Faith of our fa - thers, liv - ing still
Our fa - thers, chained in pris - ons dark,
Faith of our fa - thers, we will love

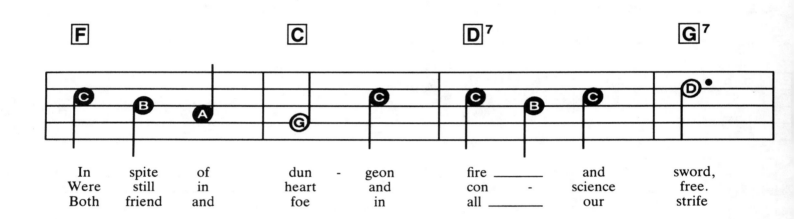

In spite of dun - geon fire and sword,
Were still in heart and con - science free.
Both friend and foe in all our strife

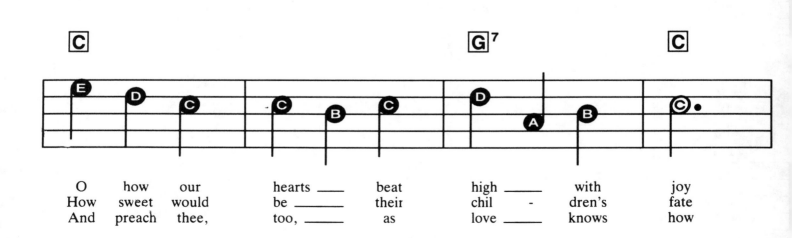

O how our hearts beat high with joy
How sweet would be their chil - dren's fate
And preach thee, too, as love knows how

I LOVE THY KINGDOM, LORD

58

Registration 1
Rhythm: March

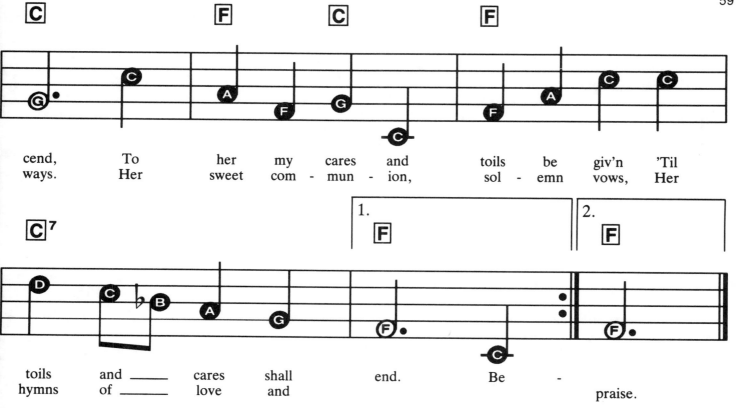

cend, To her my cares and toils be giv'n 'Til
ways. Her sweet com - mun - ion, sol - emn vows, Her

toils and _____ cares shall end. Be -
hymns of _____ love and praise.

I NEED THEE EV'RY HOUR

Registration 10
Rhythm: Waltz

1. I need Thee ev - 'ry hour, Most gra - cious _____
2. I need Thee ev - 'ry hour, Stay Thou _____ near _____

Lord; No ten - der voice like Thine Can peace _____ af -
by; Temp - ta - tions lose their power, When Thou _____ art _____

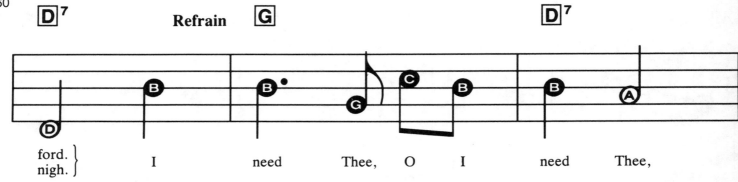

Refrain

ford.
nigh.
I need Thee, O I need Thee,

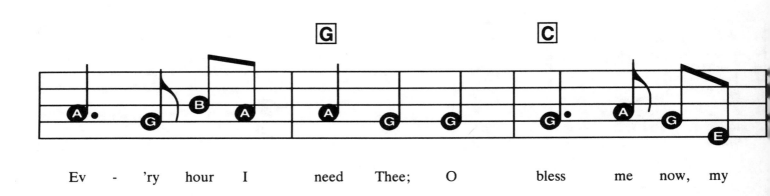

Ev - 'ry hour I need Thee; O bless me now, my

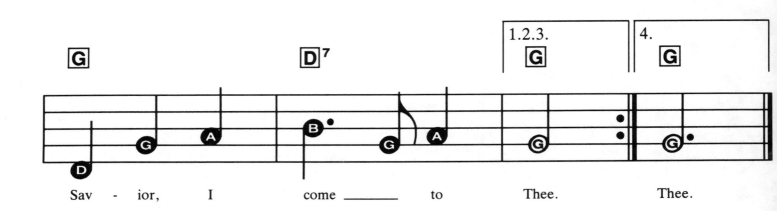

Sav - ior, I come to Thee. Thee.

3. I need Thee ev'ry hour,
   In joy or pain;
   Come quickly and abide,
   Or life is vain.
   Refrain

4. I need Thee ev'ry hour,
   Teach me Thy will;
   And Thy rich promises
   In me fulfill.
   Refrain

I SURRENDER ALL

Registration 9

All to Je - sus I sur - ren - der, All to Him I
All to Je - sus I sur - ren - der, Make me, Sav - ior,
All to Je - sus I sur - ren - der, Lord, I give my -

free - ly give; I will ev - er love and trust Him,
whol - ly Thine; Let me feel the Ho - ly Spir - it,
self to Thee; Fill me with Thy love and pow - er,

In His pres - ence dai - ly live. ⎫ I sur - ren - der
Tru - ly know that Thou art mine. ⎬
Let Thy bless - ing fall on me. ⎭

all, I sur - ren - der all;

All to Thee, my bless - ed Sav - ior, I sur - ren - der all.

IN THE SWEET BY AND BY

Registration 4

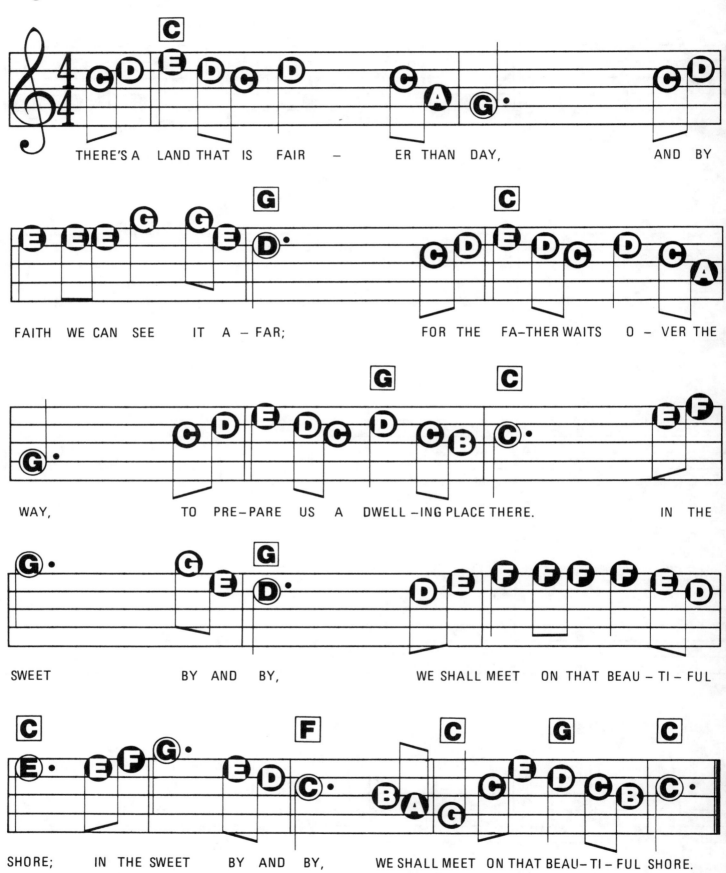

JESUS CALLS US

Registration 3
Rhythm: Waltz

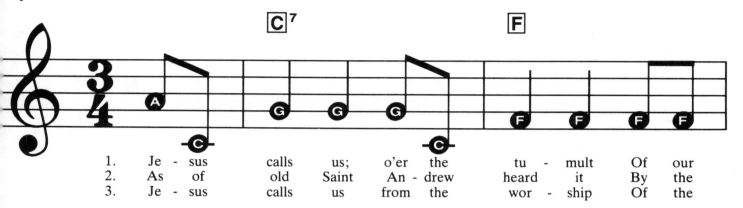

1. Je - sus calls us; o'er the tu - mult Of our
2. As of old Saint An - drew heard it By the
3. Je - sus calls us from the wor - ship Of the

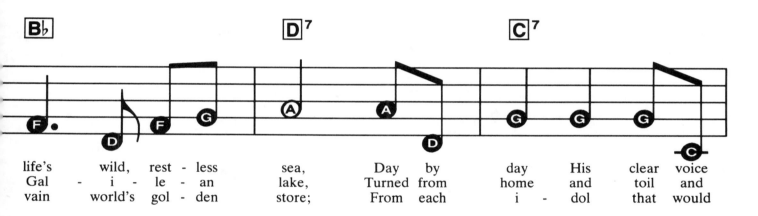

life's wild, rest - less sea, Day by day His clear voice
Gal - i - le - an lake, Turned from home and toil and
vain world's gol - den store; From each i - dol that would

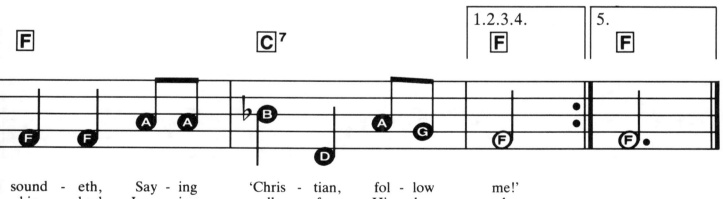

sound - eth, Say - ing, 'Chris - tian, fol - low me!'
kin - dred, Leav - ing all for His dear sake.
keep us, Say - ing, 'Chris - tian, love Me more.' all.

4. In our joys and in our sorrows,
Days of toil and hours of ease,
Still He calls, in cares and pleasures,
'Christian, love Me more than these.'

5. Jesus calls us! By Thy mercies,
Savior, make us hear Thy call,
Give our hearts to Thine obedience,
Serve and love Thee best of all.

JESUS CHRIST IS RISEN TODAY

Registration 9

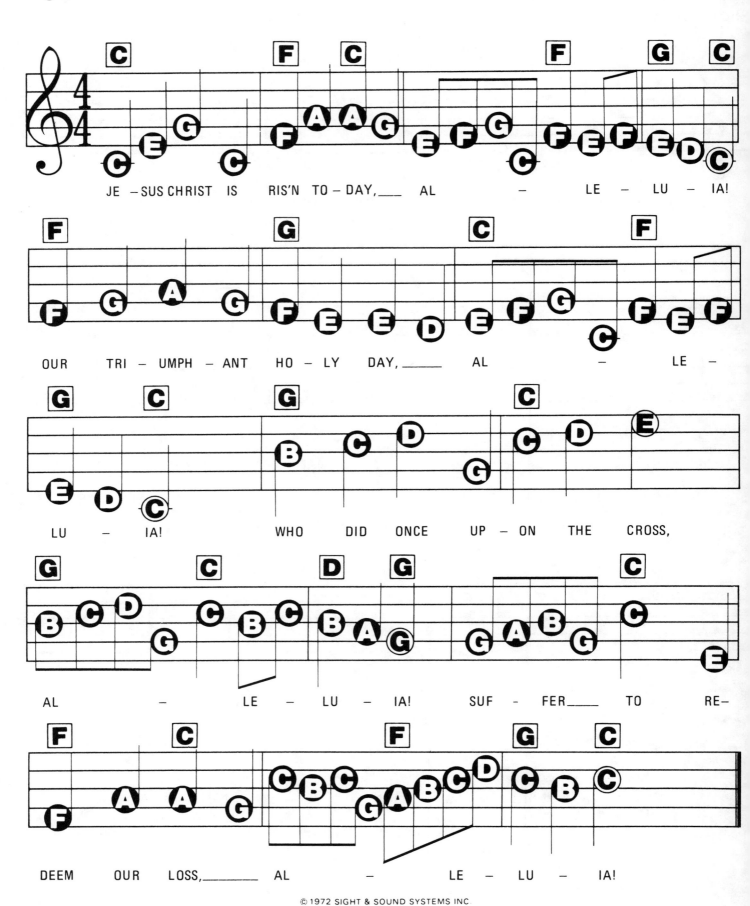

JESUS LOVES ME

Registration 2
Rhythm: Swing

I LOVE TO TELL THE STORY

Registration 6

I love to tell the sto - ry Of
love to tell the sto - ry; 'Tis

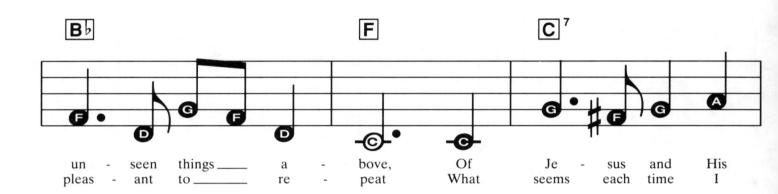

un - seen things _____ a - bove, Of Je - sus and His
pleas - ant to _____ re - peat What seems each time I

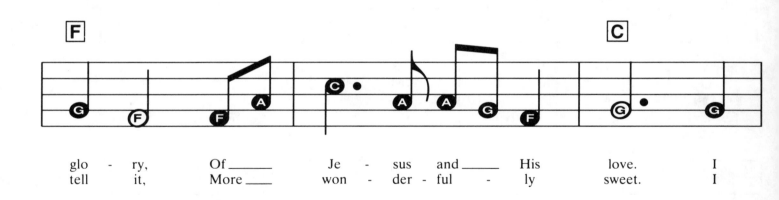

glo - ry, Of _____ Je - sus and _____ His love. I
tell it, More _____ won - der - ful - ly sweet. I

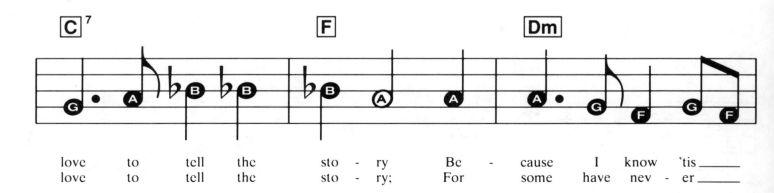

love to tell the sto - ry Be - cause I know 'tis _____
love to tell the sto - ry; For some have nev - er _____

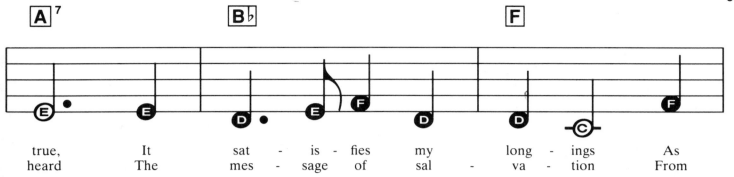

true, It sat - is - fies my long - ings As
heard The mes - sage of sal - va - tion From

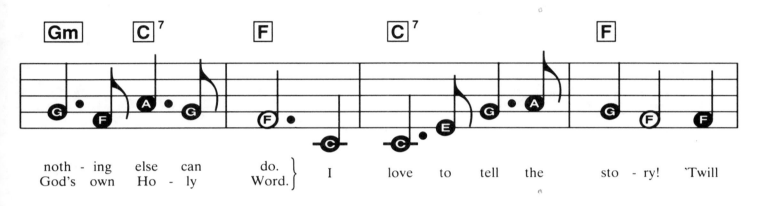

noth - ing else can do. I love to tell the sto - ry! 'Twill
God's own Ho - ly Word.

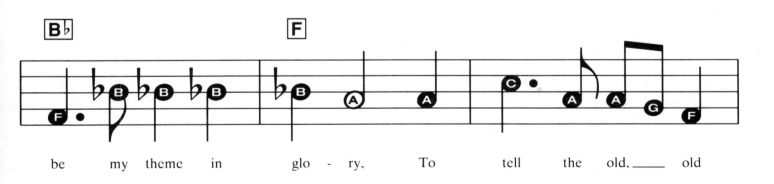

be my theme in glo - ry, To tell the old, ___ old

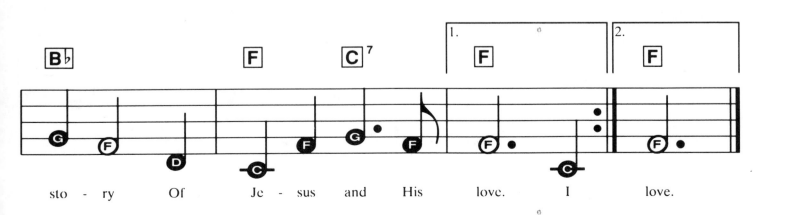

sto - ry Of Je - sus and His love. I love.

JOSHUA FIT THE BATTLE OF JERICHO

Registration 1
Rhythm: Swing

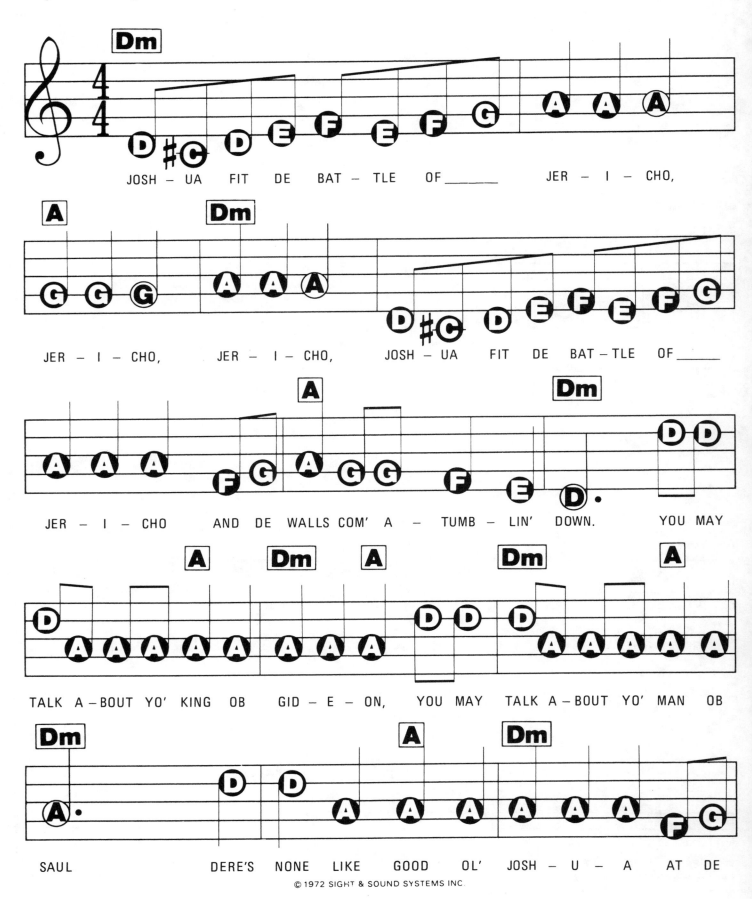

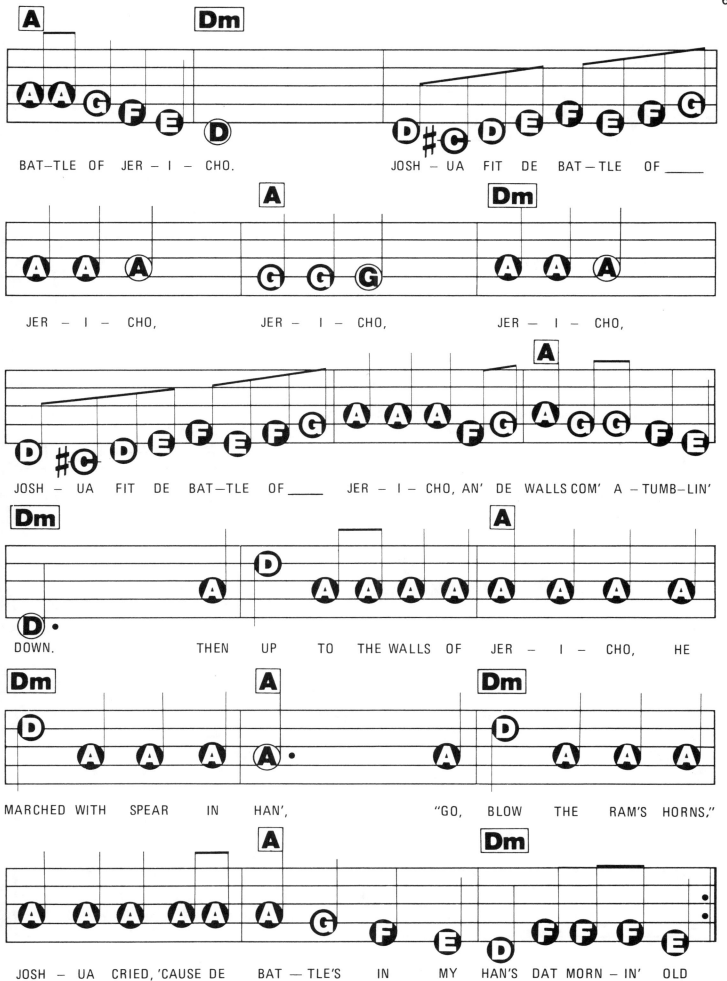

JUST A CLOSER WALK WITH THEE

JUST AS I AM

Registration 10
Rhythm: Waltz

KUMBAYA

Registration 8
Rhythm: Rock or 8 Beat

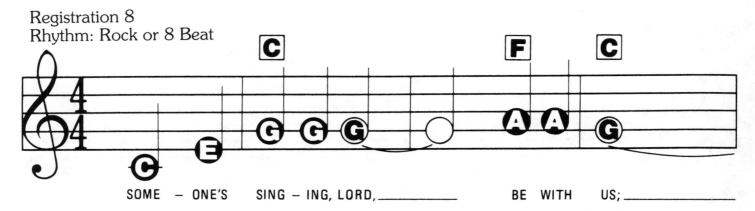

SOME – ONE'S   SING – ING, LORD,_____   BE   WITH   US;_____

_____ SOME–ONE'S   SING –ING, LORD,_____   BE   WITH   US;_____

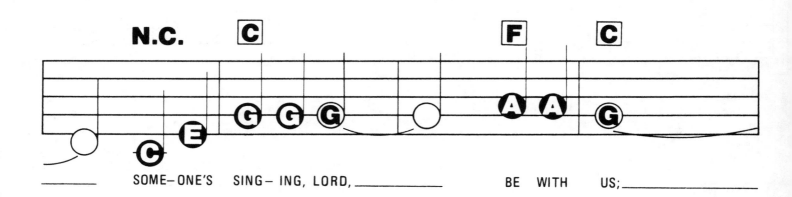

_____ SOME–ONE'S   SING – ING, LORD,_____   BE   WITH   US;_____

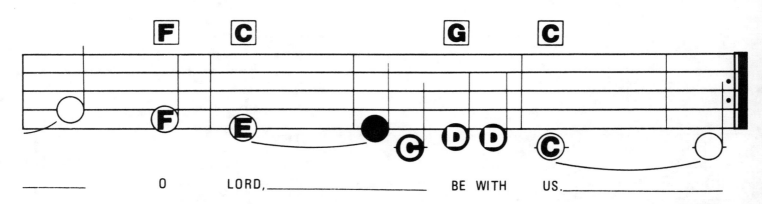

_____   O   LORD,_____   BE   WITH   US._____

2. SOMEONE'S PRAYING, ETC.
3. SOMEONE'S ASKING, ETC.
4. SOMEONE'S SEARCHING, ETC.
5. SOMEONE'S GIVING, ETC.
6. SOMEONE'S LOVING, ETC.

7. SOMEONE'S SUFF'RING, ETC.
8. SOMEONE'S HUNGRY, ETC.
9. SOMEONE'S DYING, ETC.
10. SOMEONE'S THANKING, ETC.
11. SOMEONE'S PRAISING, ETC.

I SING THE MIGHTY POW'R OF GOD

Registration 9

I sing the _____ might - y pow'r of God, That
sing the _____ good - ness of the Lord, That
not a _____ plant or flow'r be - low, But

made _____ the moun - tains rise; That spread the _____ flow - ing
filled _____ the earth with food; He formed the _____ crea - tures
makes _____ Thy glo - ries known. And clouds a - rise, and

seas a - broad, And built _____ the loft - y skies. I _____
with His word, And then _____ pro - nounced them good. Lord, _____
tem - pests blow, By or - der from Thy throne. While _____

sing the wis - dom that or - dained The _____ sun to rule the
how Thy won - ders are dis - played Wher - e'er I turn my
all that bor - rows life from _____ Thee Is _____ ev - er in Thy

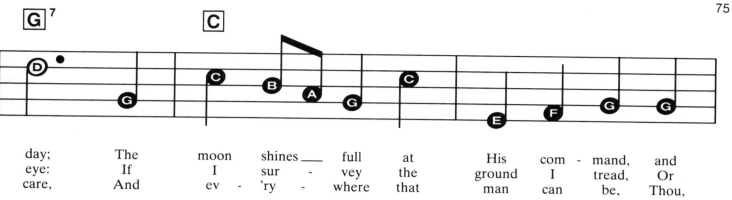

day; The moon shines___ full at His com - mand, and
eye: If I sur - vey at the ground I tread, Or
care, And ev - 'ry - where that man can be, Thou,

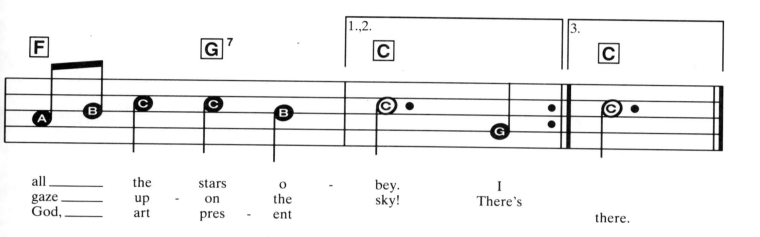

all_____ the stars o - bey. I
gaze_____ up - on the sky! There's
God,_____ art pres - ent

there.

LIFT EV'RY VOICE AND SING

Registration 8
Rhythm: Waltz

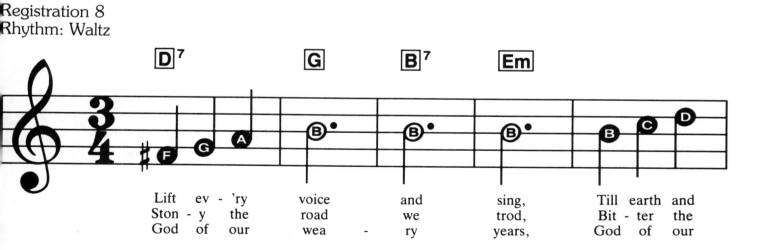

Lift ev - 'ry voice and sing, Till earth and
Ston - y the road we trod, Bit - ter the
God of our wea - ry years, God of our

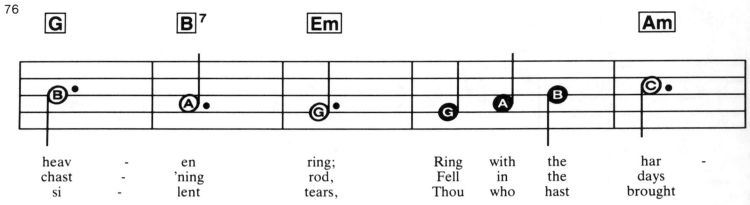

heav - en ring; Ring with the har -
chast - 'ning rod, Fell in the days
si - lent tears, Thou who hast brought

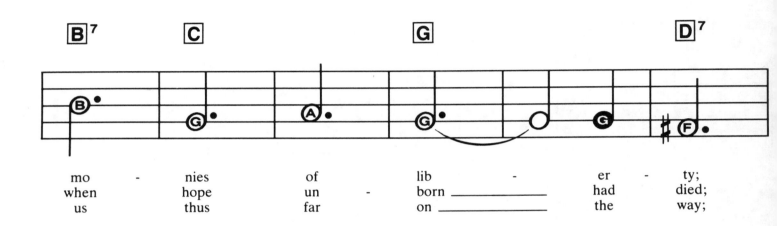

mo - nies of lib - er - ty;
when hope un - born _____ had died;
us thus far on _____ the way;

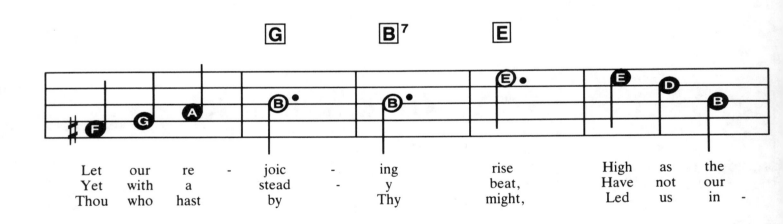

Let our re - joic - ing rise High as the
Yet with a stead - y beat, Have not our
Thou who hast by Thy might, Led us in -

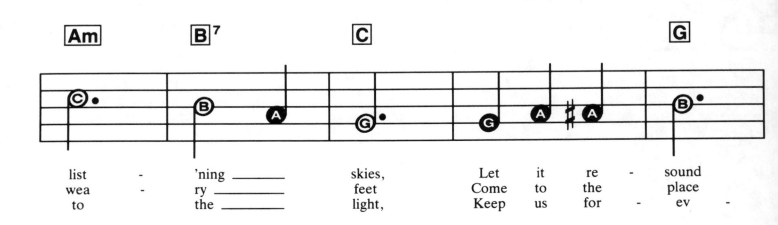

list - 'ning _____ skies, Let it re - sound
wea - ry _____ feet Come to the place
to the _____ light, Keep us for - ev -

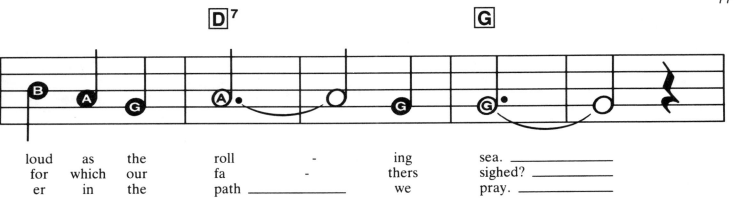

loud   as   the   roll   -   ing   sea. _____
for   which   our   fa   -   thers   sighed? _____
er   in   the   path _____   we   pray. _____

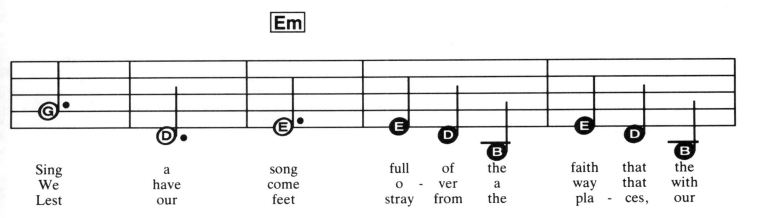

Sing   a   song   full   of   the   faith   that   the
We   have   come   o   -   ver   a   way   that   with
Lest   our   feet   stray   from   the   pla   -   ces,   our

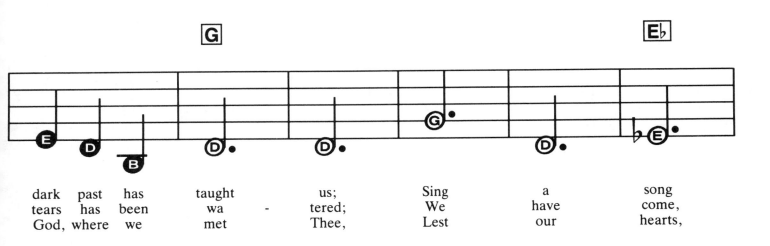

dark   past   has   taught   us;   Sing   a   song
tears   has   been   wa   -   tered;   We   have   come,
God,   where   we   met   Thee,   Lest   our   hearts,

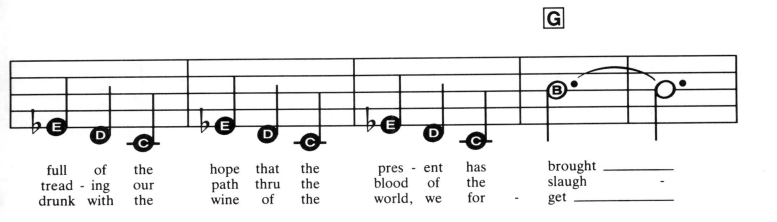

full   of   the   hope   that   the   pres   -   ent   has   brought _____
tread   -   ing   our   path   thru   the   blood   of   the   slaugh   -
drunk   with   the   wine   of   the   world,   we   for   -   get _____

THE LORD BLESS YOU AND KEEP YOU

Registration 10

JESUS LOVES THE LITTLE CHILDREN

Registration 2
Rhythm: Swing

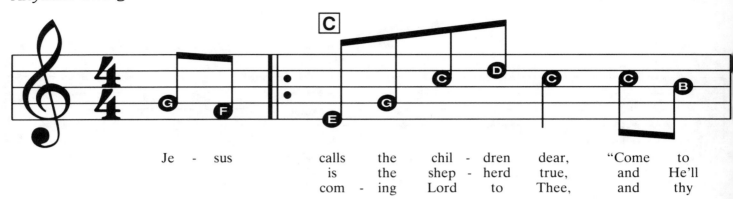

Je - sus
calls the chil - dren dear, "Come to
is the shep - herd true, and He'll
com - ing Lord to Thee, and thy

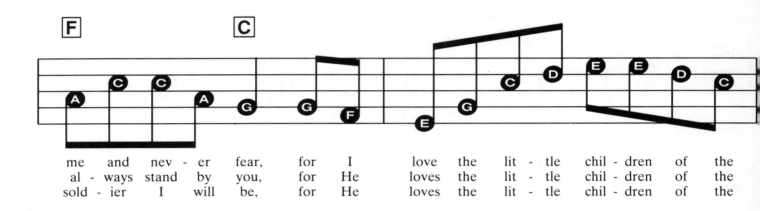

me and nev - er fear, for I love the lit - tle chil - dren of the
al - ways stand by you, for He loves the lit - tle chil - dren of the
sold - ier I will be, for He loves the lit - tle chil - dren of the

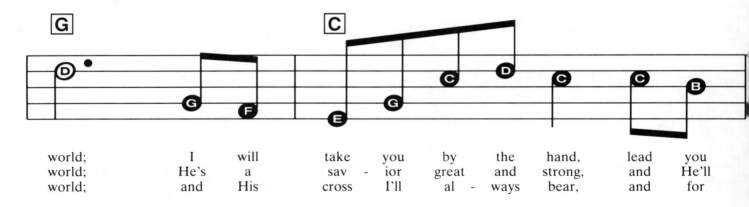

world; I will take you by the hand, lead you
world; He's a sav - ior great and strong, and He'll
world; and His cross I'll al - ways bear, and for

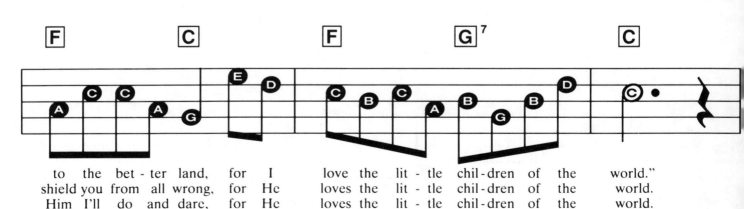

to the bet - ter land, for I love the lit - tle chil - dren of the world."
shield you from all wrong, for He loves the lit - tle chil - dren of the world.
Him I'll do and dare, for He loves the lit - tle chil - dren of the world.

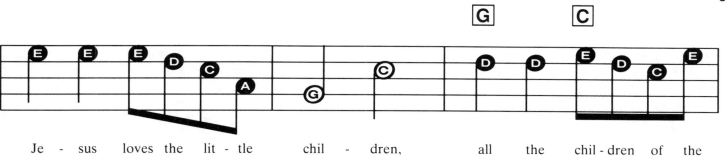

Je - sus loves the lit - tle chil - dren, all the chil - dren of the

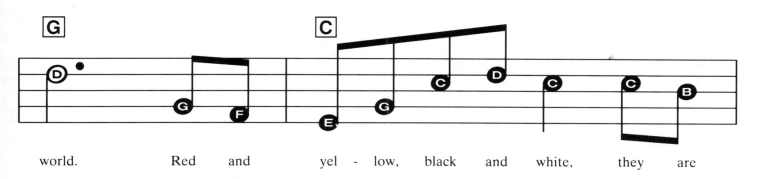

world.   Red   and   yel - low,   black   and   white,   they   are

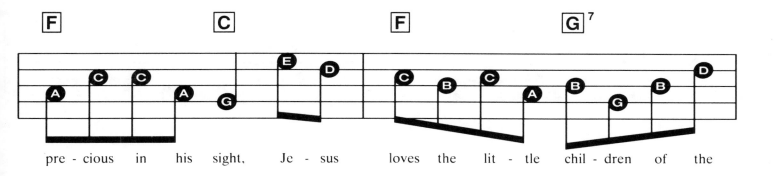

pre - cious   in   his   sight,   Je - sus   loves   the   lit - tle   chil - dren   of   the

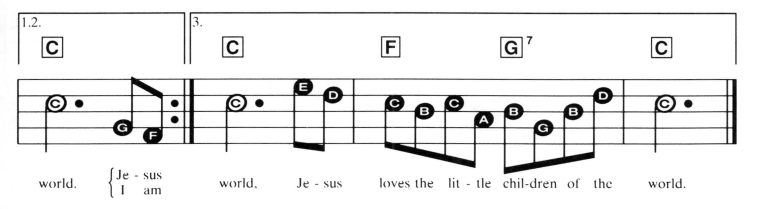

world. {Je - sus   world,   Je - sus   loves the lit - tle chil-dren of the   world.
         {I   am

LOVE DIVINE, ALL LOVES EXCELLING

Registration 1
Rhythm: Swing

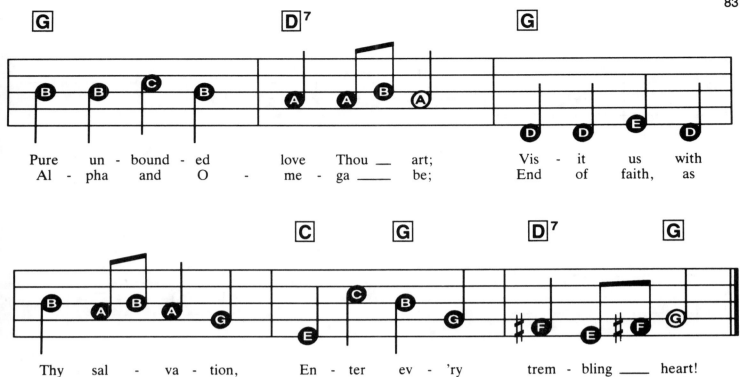

Pure un - bound - ed love Thou __ art; Vis - it us with
Al - pha and O - me - ga __ be; End of faith, as

Thy sal - va - tion, En - ter ev - 'ry trem - bling __ heart!
its be - gin - ning, Set our hearts at lib - er - ty!

3. Come, Almighty, to deliver,
   Let us all Thy life receive;
   Suddenly return and never,
   Nevermore Thy temples leave;
   Thee we would be always blessing,
   Serve Thee as Thy hosts above,
   Pray and praise Thee without ceasing,
   Glory in Thy **perfect** love!

4. Finish then Thy new creation,
   Pure and spotless may we be;
   Let us see our whole salvation,
   Perfectly secured in Thee;
   Changed from glory into glory,
   Till in heav'n we take our place,
   Till we cast our crowns before Thee,
   Lost in wonder, love, and praise!

O WORSHIP THE KING, ALL GLORIOUS ABOVE

Registration 4

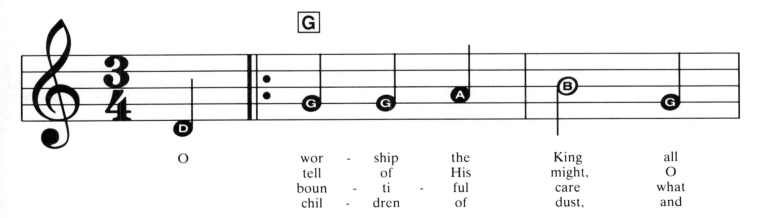

O wor - ship the King, all
tell of His might, O
boun - ti - ful care what
chil - dren of dust, and

LOVE LIFTED ME

Registration 10
Rhythm: Waltz

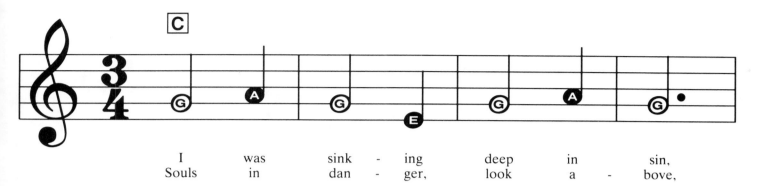

I   was   sink - ing   deep   in   sin,
Souls   in   dan - ger,   look   a - bove,

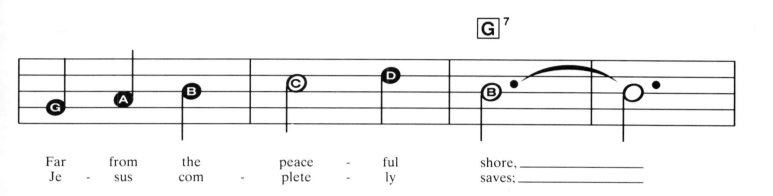

Far   from   the   peace - ful   shore,_____
Je - sus   com - plete - ly   saves;_____

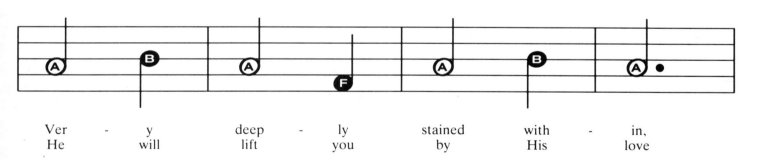

Ver - y   deep - ly   stained   with - in,
He   will   lift   you   by   His   love

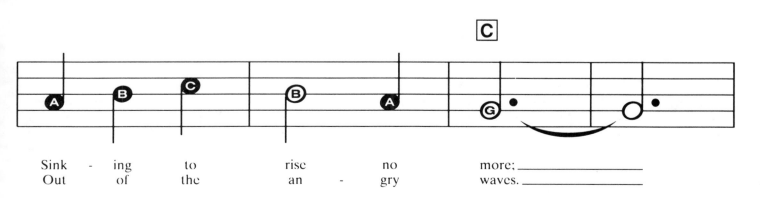

Sink - ing   to   rise   no   more;_____
Out   of   the   an - gry   waves._____

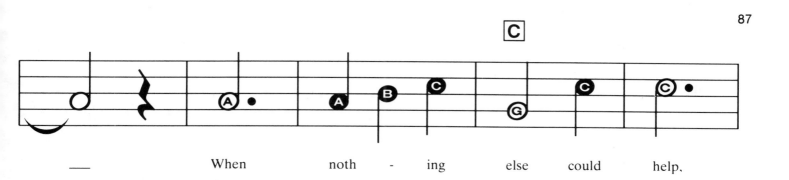

When noth - ing else could help,

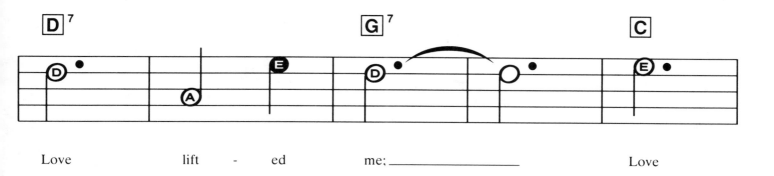

Love lift - ed me; _____ Love

lift - ed me, _____ Love lift - ed

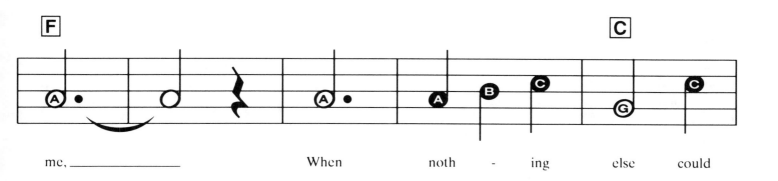

me, _____ When noth - ing else could

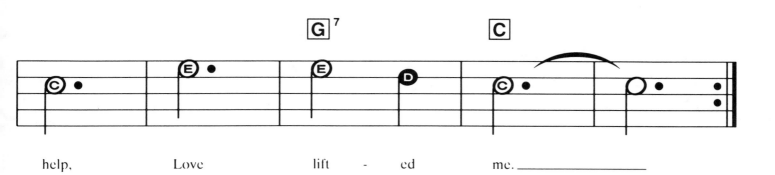

help, Love lift - ed me. _____

A MIGHTY FORTRESS IS OUR GOD

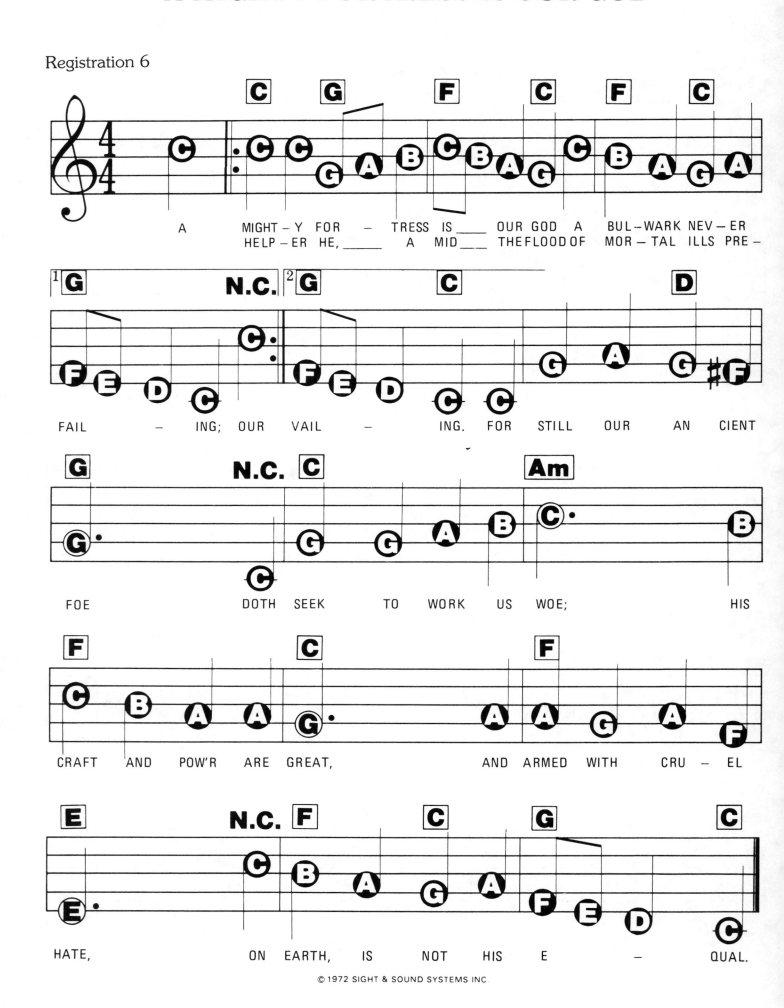

MY FAITH LOOKS UP TO THEE

Registration 9

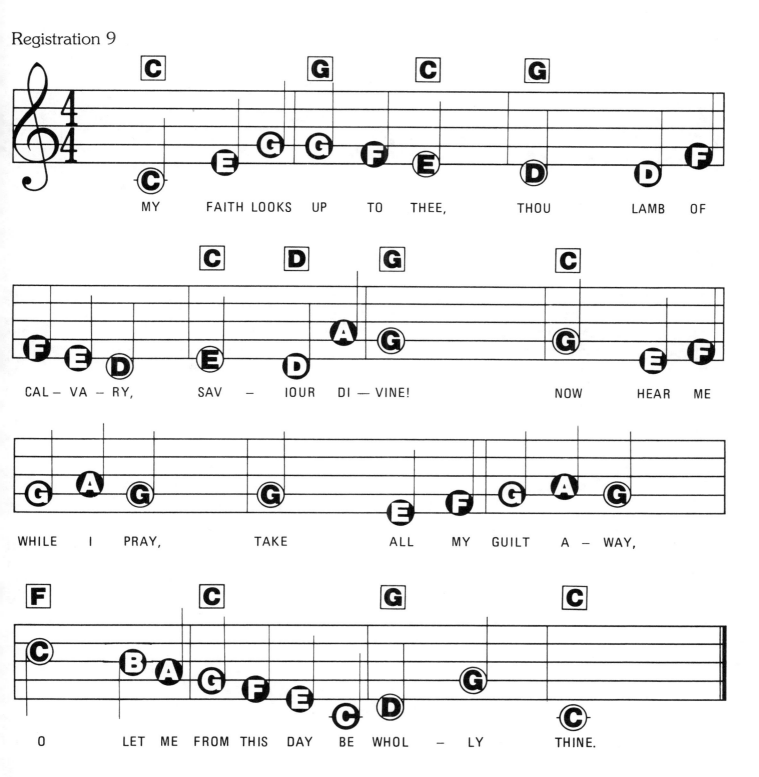

MY FAITH LOOKS UP TO THEE, THOU LAMB OF

CAL – VA – RY, SAV – IOUR DI — VINE! NOW HEAR ME

WHILE I PRAY, TAKE ALL MY GUILT A – WAY,

O LET ME FROM THIS DAY BE WHOL – LY THINE.

.) MAY THY RICH GRACE IMPART
STRENGTH TO MY FAINTING HEART,
MY ZEAL INSPIRE;
AS THOU HAST DIED FOR ME,
O MAY MY LOVE TO THEE
PURE, WARM AND CHANGELESS BE,
A LIVING FIRE!

3.) WHILE LIFE'S DARK MAZE I TREAD,
AND GRIEFS AROUND ME SPREAD,
BE THOU MY GUIDE;
BID DARKNESS TURN TO DAY,
WIPE SORROW'S TEARS AWAY,
NOR LET ME EVER STRAY
FROM THEE ASIDE.

4.) WHEN ENDS LIFE'S TRANSIENT DREAM,
WHEN DEATH'S COLD, SULLEN STREAM
SHALL O'ER ME ROLL;
BLEST SAVIOR, THEN, IN LOVE,
FEAR AND DISTRUST REMOVE;
O BEAR ME SAFE ABOVE,
A RANSOMED SOUL!

LITTLE BROWN CHURCH IN THE VALE

Registration 10

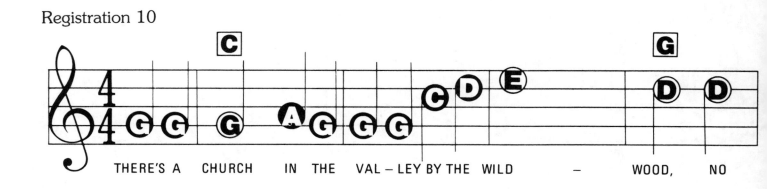

THERE'S A CHURCH IN THE VAL – LEY BY THE WILD – WOOD, NO

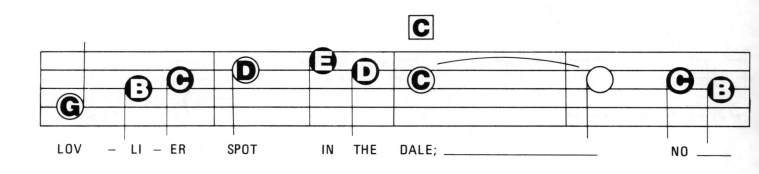

LOV – LI – ER SPOT IN THE DALE; _____ NO ____

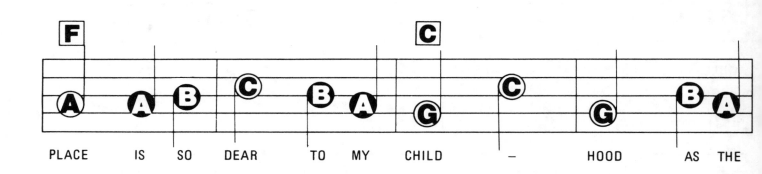

PLACE IS SO DEAR TO MY CHILD – HOOD AS THE

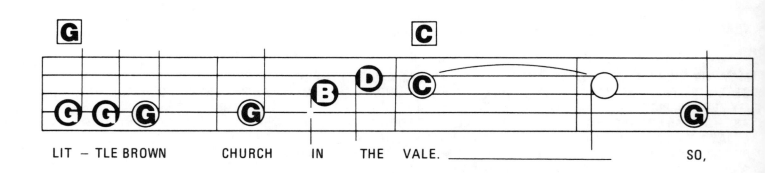

LIT – TLE BROWN CHURCH IN THE VALE. _____ SO,

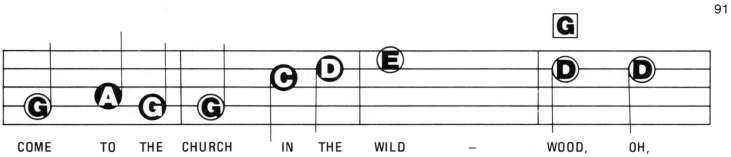

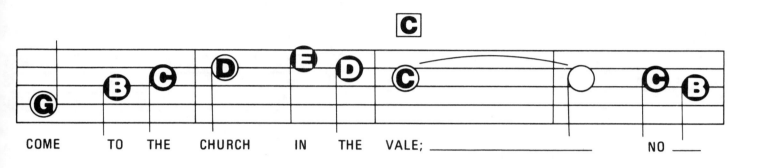

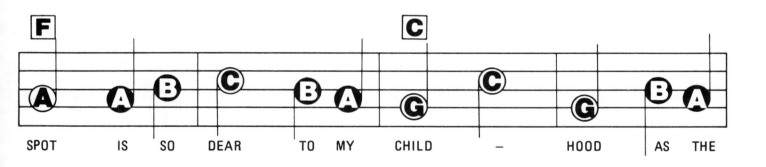

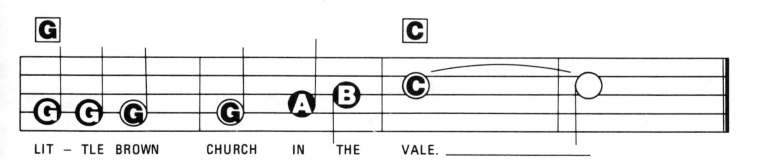

NOBODY KNOWS THE TROUBLE I'VE SEEN

Registration 2
Rhythm: Swing

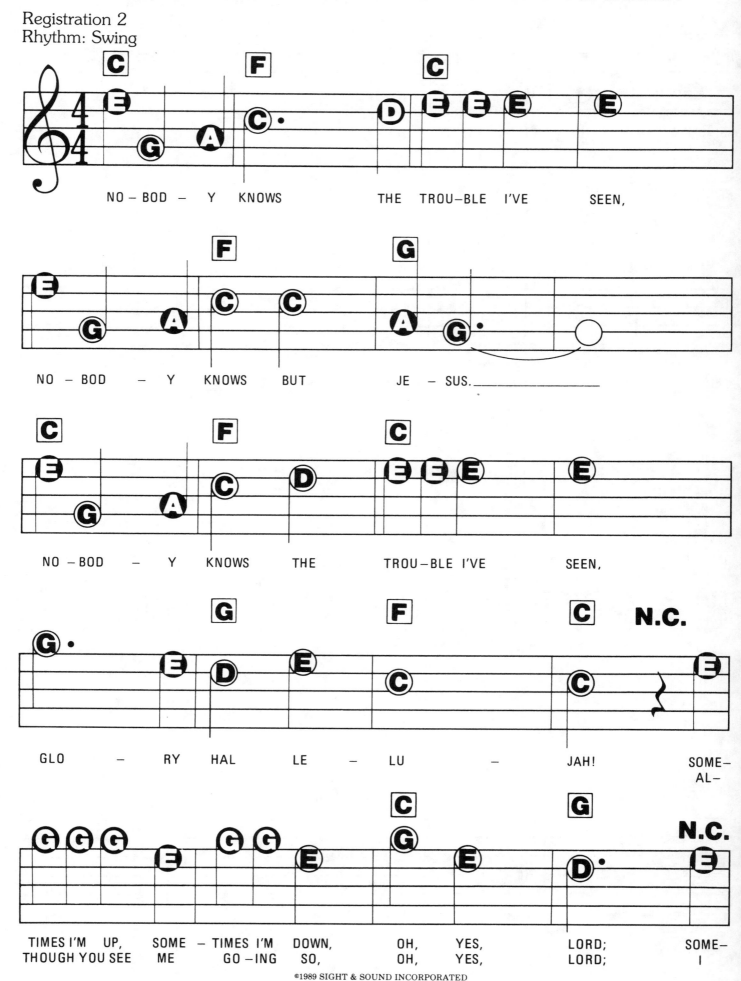

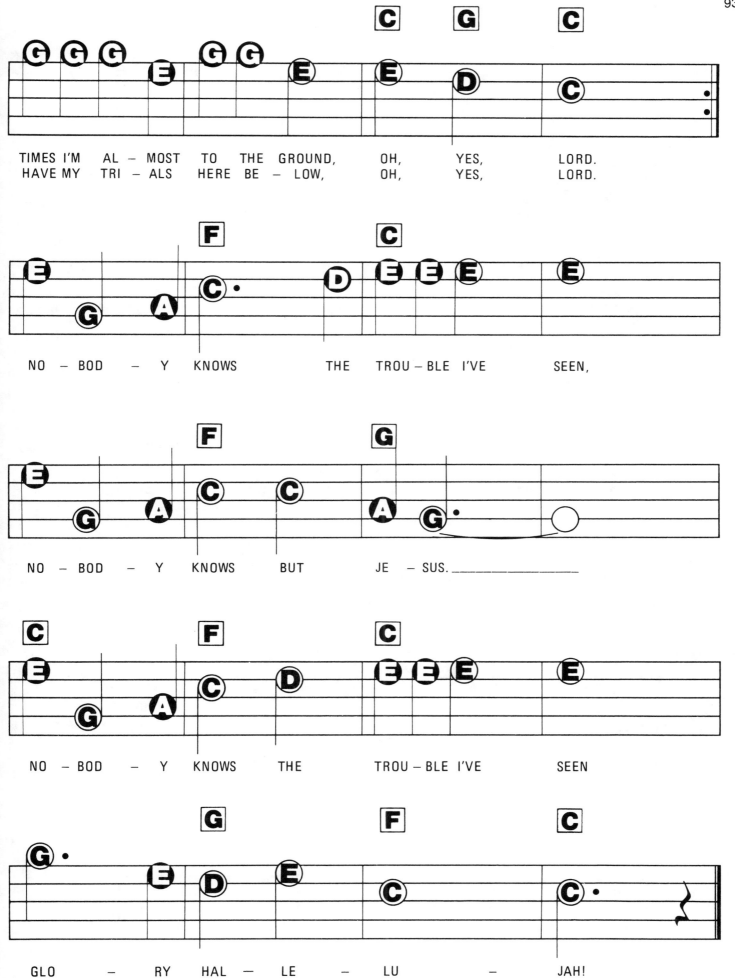

NOW THANK WE ALL OUR GOD

Registration 6

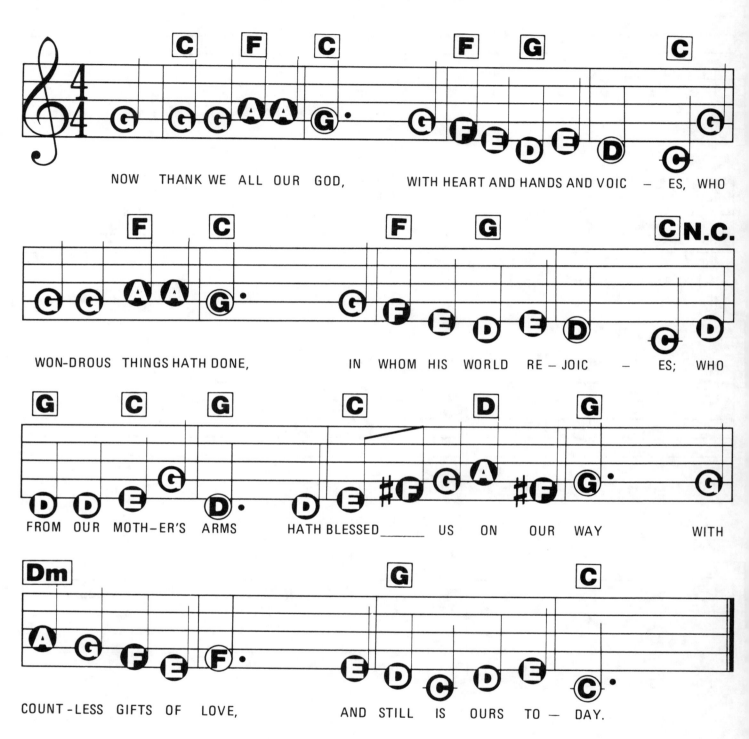

NOW THANK WE ALL OUR GOD, WITH HEART AND HANDS AND VOIC — ES, WHO

WON-DROUS THINGS HATH DONE, IN WHOM HIS WORLD RE — JOIC — ES; WHO

FROM OUR MOTH-ER'S ARMS HATH BLESSED_____ US ON OUR WAY WITH

COUNT-LESS GIFTS OF LOVE, AND STILL IS OURS TO — DAY.

2.) O MAY THIS BOUNTEOUS GOD,
THROUGH ALL OUR LIFE BE NEAR US!
WITH EVER JOYFUL HEARTS
AND BLESSED PEACE TO CHEER US;
AND KEEP US IN HIS GRACE,
AND GUIDE US WHEN PERPLEXED,
AND FREE US FROM ALL ILLS
IN THIS WORLD AND THE NEXT.

3.) ALL PRAISE AND THANKS TO GOD,
THE FATHER NOW BE GIVEN,
THE SON AND SPIRIT BLESSED
WHO REIGN IN HIGHEST HEAVEN;
ETERNAL, TRIUNE GOD,
WHOM EARTH AND HEAV'N ADORE;
FOR THUS IT WAS, IS NOW,
AND SHALL BE EVERMORE.

O GOD, OUR HELP IN AGES PAST

Registration 9

5. Time, like an ever-rolling stream,
   Bears all its sons **away**;
   They fly forgotten, as a dream
   Dies at the opening day.

6. O God, our help in ages past,
   Our hope for years to come,
   Be thou our guard while troubles last,
   And our eternal home.

NEARER, MY GOD, TO THEE

Registration 10
Rhythm: Waltz

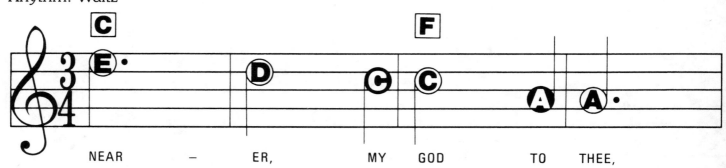

NEAR — ER, MY GOD TO THEE,

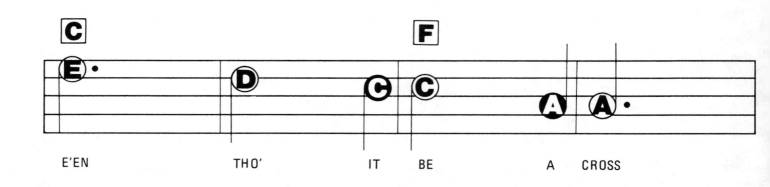

NEAR — ER TO THEE!_____

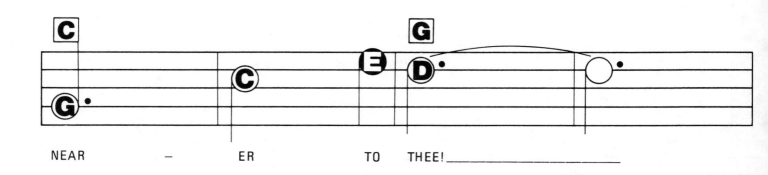

E'EN THO' IT BE A CROSS

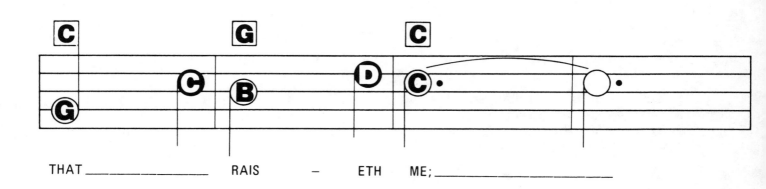

THAT_____ RAIS — ETH ME;_____

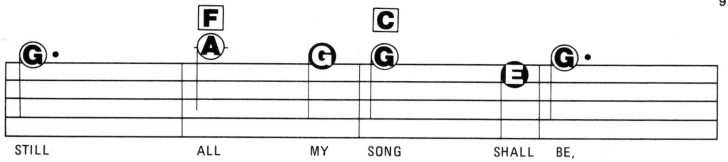

STILL   ALL   MY   SONG   SHALL   BE,

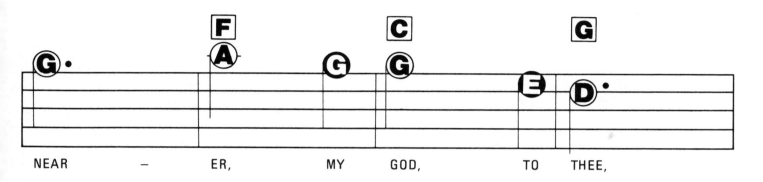

NEAR   —   ER,   MY   GOD,   TO   THEE,

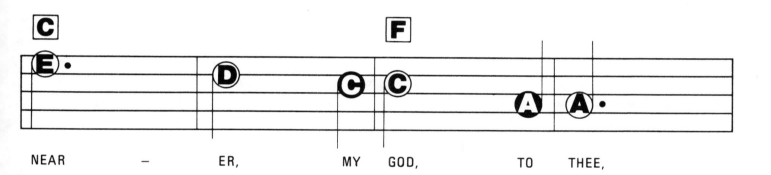

NEAR   —   ER,   MY   GOD,   TO   THEE,

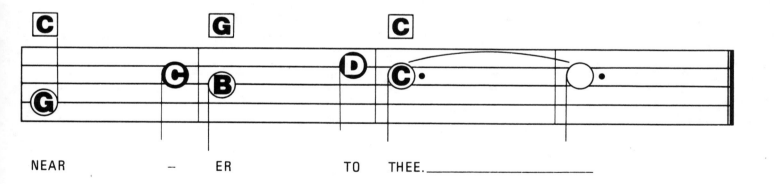

NEAR   —   ER   TO   THEE._____

2. THO' LIKE THE WANDERER,
   THE SUN GONE DOWN,
   DARKNESS BE OVER ME,
   MY REST A STONE,
   YET IN MY DREAMS I'D BE,
   NEARER, MY GOD, TO THEE,
   NEARER, MY GOD, TO THEE,
   NEARER TO THEE.

3. THERE LET THE WAY APPEAR
   STEPS UNTO HEAV'N;
   ALL THAT THOU SENDEST ME
   IN MERCY GIV'N;
   ANGELS TO BECKON ME,
   NEARER, MY GOD, TO THEE,
   NEARER, MY GOD, TO THEE,
   NEARER TO THEE.

4. OR IF ON JOYFUL WING
   CLEAVING THE SKY,
   SUN, MOON, AND STARS FORGOT,
   UPWARD I FLY,
   STILL ALL MY SONG SHALL BE,
   NEARER, MY GOD, TO THEE,
   NEARER, MY GOD, TO THEE,
   NEARER TO THEE.

O MASTER, LET ME WALK WITH THEE

Registration 1
Rhythm: Waltz

FAIREST LORD JESUS

Registration 4

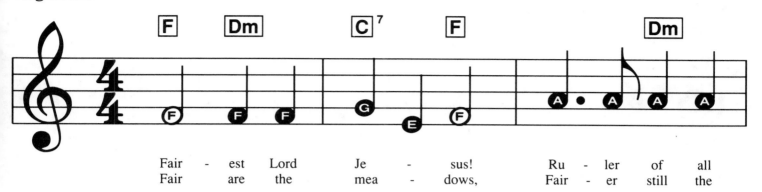

Fair - est Lord Je - sus! Ru - ler of all
Fair are the mea - dows, Fair - er still the

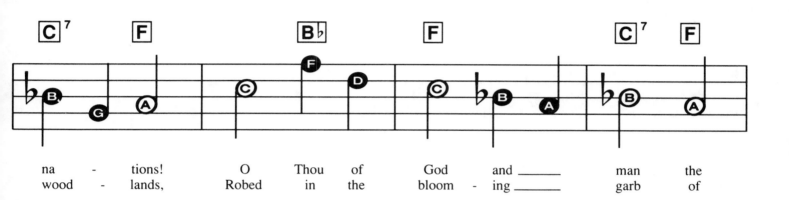

na - tions! O Thou of God and _____ man the
wood - lands, Robed in the bloom - ing _____ garb of

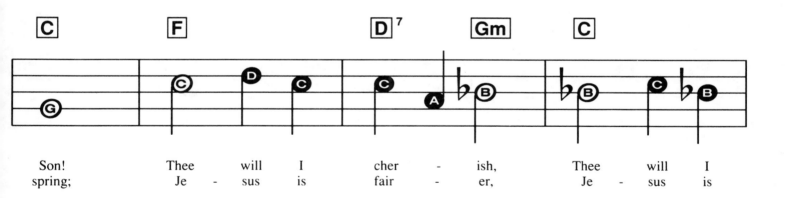

Son! Thee will I cher - ish, Thee will I
spring; Je - sus is fair - er, Je - sus is

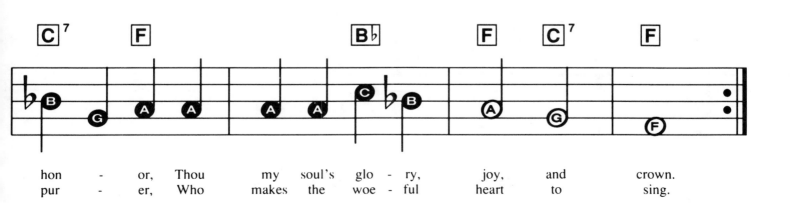

hon - or, Thou my soul's glo - ry, joy, and crown.
pur - er, Who makes the woe - ful heart to sing.

OH HAPPY DAY

Registration 1
Rhythm: Waltz

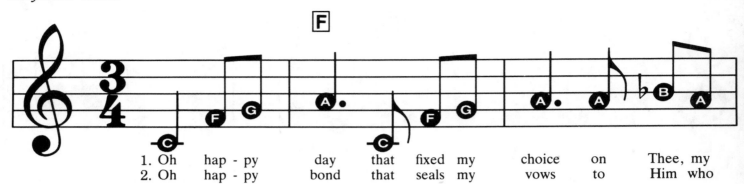

1. Oh hap - py day that fixed my choice on Thee, my
2. Oh hap - py bond that seals my vows to Him who

Sav - ior and my God! Well may this glow - ing heart re -
mer - its all my love! Let cheer - ful an - thems fill His

Chorus

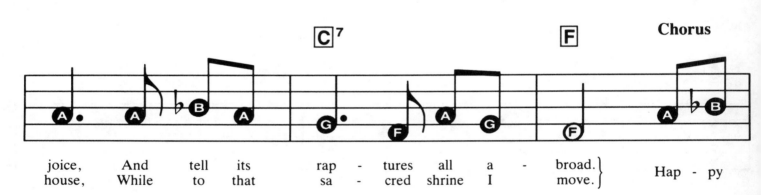

joice, And tell its rap - tures all a - broad.⎫ Hap - py
house, While tell to that sa - cred shrine I move.⎭

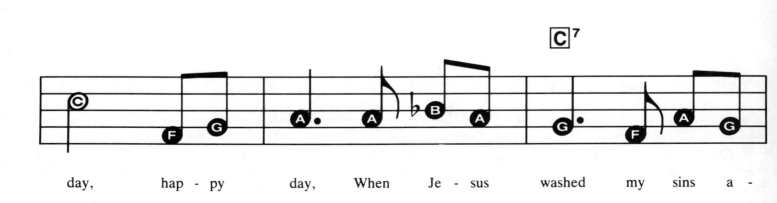

day, hap - py day, When Je - sus washed my sins a -

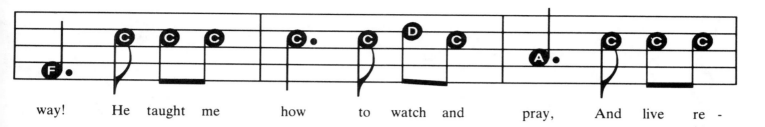

way! He taught me how to watch and pray, And live re -

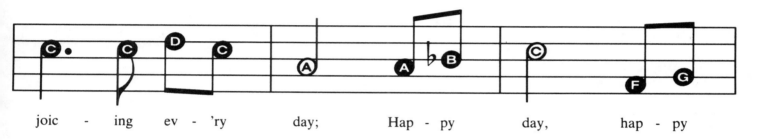

joic - ing ev - 'ry day; Hap - py day, hap - py

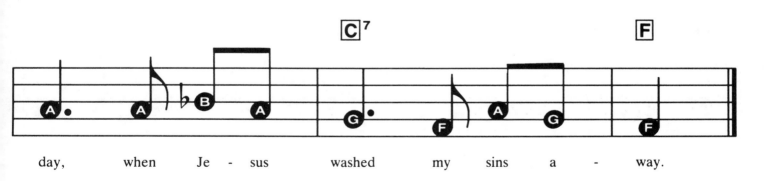

day, when Je - sus washed my sins a - way.

3. 'Tis done: the great transaction's done:
   I am my Lord's, and He is mine;
   He drew me, and I followed on,
   Charmed to confess the voice divine.
   Chorus

4. Now rest my long divided heart;
   Fixed on this blissful center rest;
   Nor ever from my Lord depart,
   With Him of ev'ry good possessed.
   Chorus

THE OLD RUGGED CROSS

Registration 10
Rhythm: Waltz

Words and Music by
REV. GEORGE BENNARD

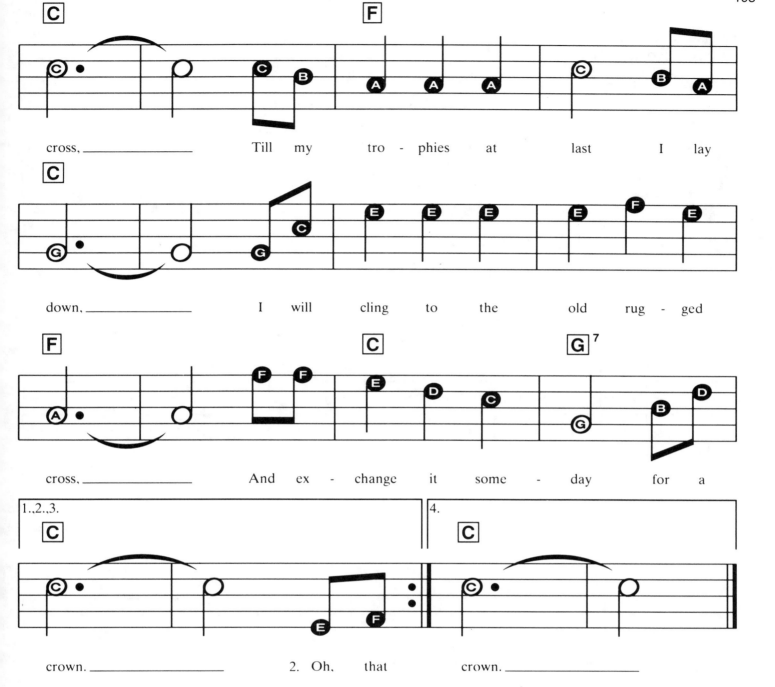

cross, _____ Till my tro - phies at last I lay

down, _____ I will cling to the old rug - ged

cross, _____ And ex - change it some - day for a

1.,2.,3.

crown. _____ 2. Oh, that

4.

crown. _____

Additional Lyrics

2. Oh, that old rugged cross, so despised by the world,
   Has a wondrous attraction to me,
   For the dear Lamb of God left His glory above,
   To bear it to dark Calvary.
   To Chorus

3. In the old rugged cross, stained with blood so divine,
   A wondrous beauty I see.
   For 'twas on that old cross Jesus suffered and died
   To pardon and sanctify me.
   To Chorus

4. To the old rugged cross I will ever be true,
   Its shame and reproach gladly bear,
   Then He'll call me some day to my home far away,
   Where His glory forever I'll share.
   To Chorus

ONWARD CHRISTIAN SOLDIERS

Registration 4
Rhythm: Rock or 8 Beat

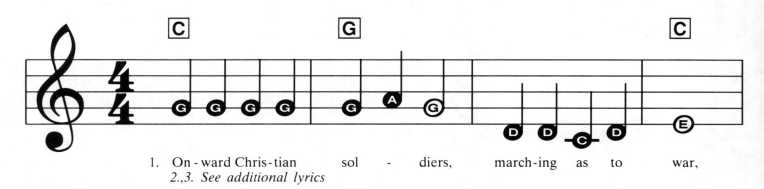

1. On - ward Chris - tian sol - diers, march-ing as to war,
   2.,3. See additional lyrics

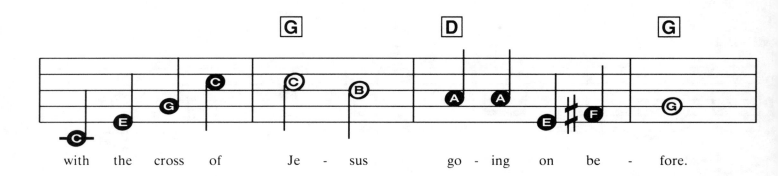

with the cross of Je - sus go - ing on be - fore.

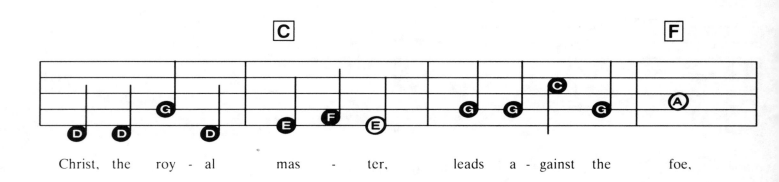

Christ, the roy - al mas - ter, leads a - gainst the foe,

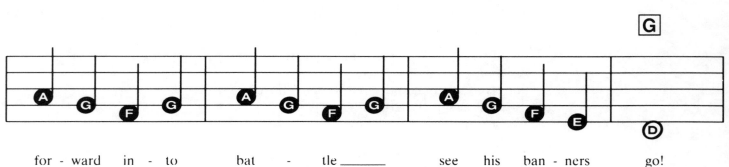

for - ward in - to bat - tle _____ see his ban - ners go!

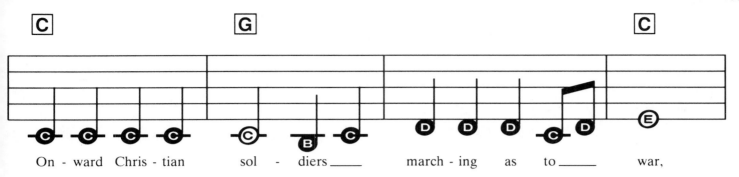

On - ward Chris - tian sol - diers____ march - ing as to____ war,

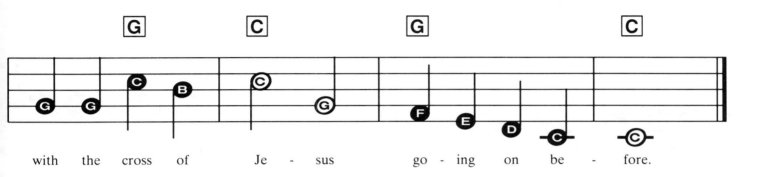

with the cross of Je - sus go - ing on be - fore.

Additional lyrics

2. Crowns and thrones may perish,
Kingdoms rise and wane,
But the church of Jesus
Constant will remain.
Gates of hell can never
'Gainst that church prevail.
We have Christ's own promise,
And that cannot fail.
To Chorus

3. Onward, then, ye people!
Join our happy throng.
Blend with ours your voices
In the triumph song.
Glory, laud and honor
Unto Christ the King.
This thro' countless ages
Men and angels sing.
To Chorus

ONE DAY AT A TIME

Words and Music by
MARIJOHN WILKIN and
KRIS KRISTOFFERSON

Registration 2
Rhythm: Waltz

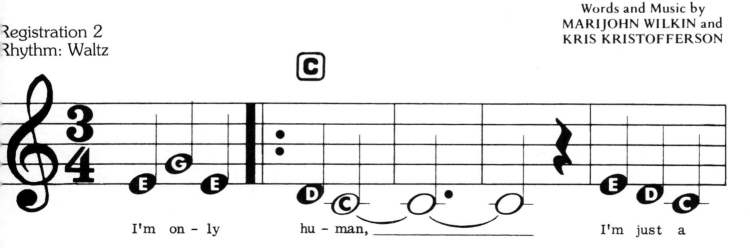

I'm on - ly hu - man,_____ I'm just a

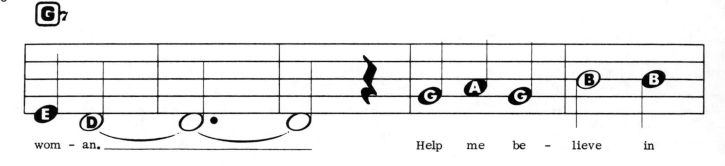

wom - an. _____ Help me be - lieve in

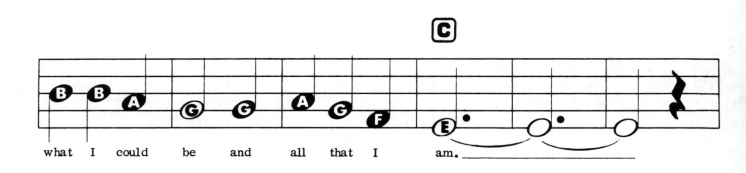

what I could be and all that I am. _____

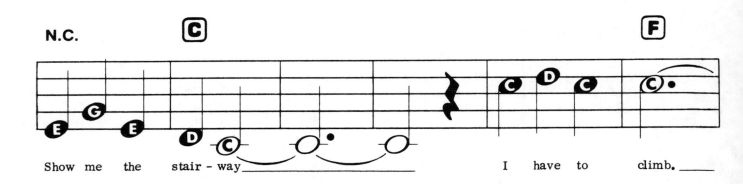

Show me the stair - way _____ I have to climb. _____

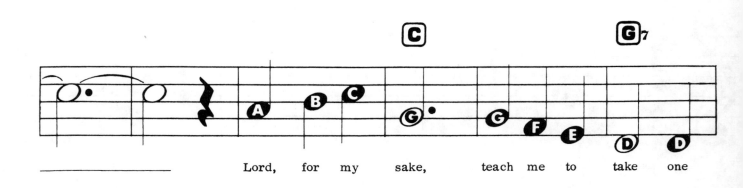

_____ Lord, for my sake, teach me to take one

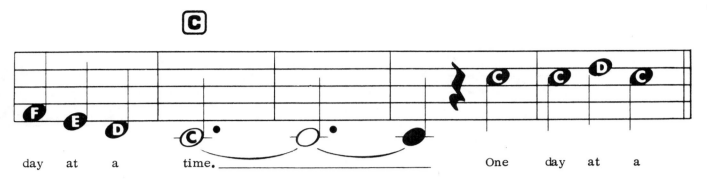

day at a time._____ One day at a

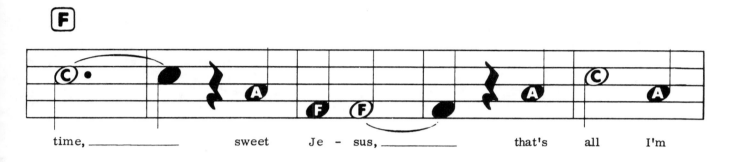

time,_____ sweet Je - sus,_____ that's all I'm

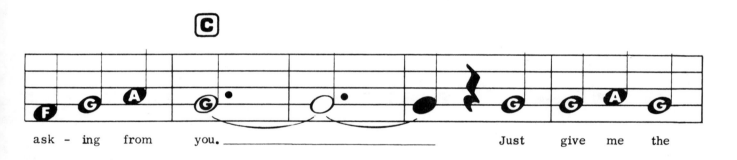

ask - ing from you._____ Just give me the

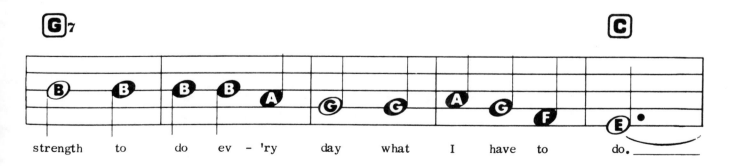

strength to do ev - 'ry day what I have to do._____

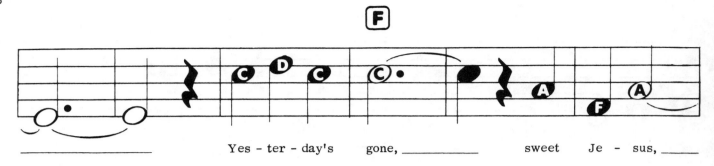

Yes - ter - day's gone, _____ sweet Je - sus, _____

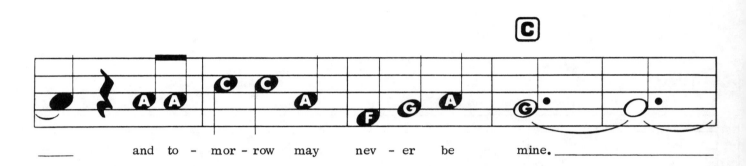

_____ and to - mor - row may nev - er be mine. _____

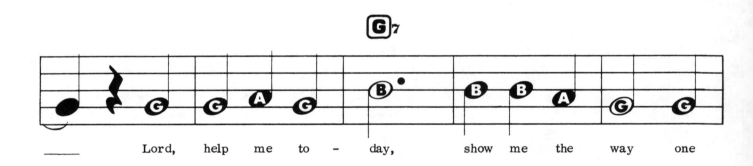

_____ Lord, help me to - day, show me the way one

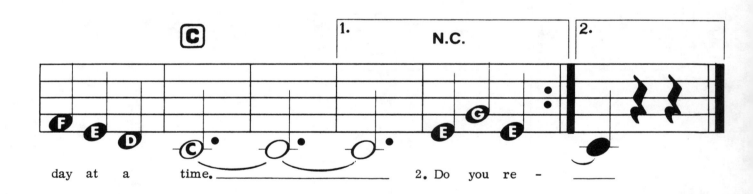

day at a time. _____ 2. Do you re - _____

2. Do you remember when you walked among men?
   Well, Jesus, you know if you're looking below that it's worse now than then.
   Pushin' and shovin', crowding my mind,
   So for my sake, Lord, teach me to take ONE DAY AT A TIME.

PRAISE TO THE LORD

Registration 9

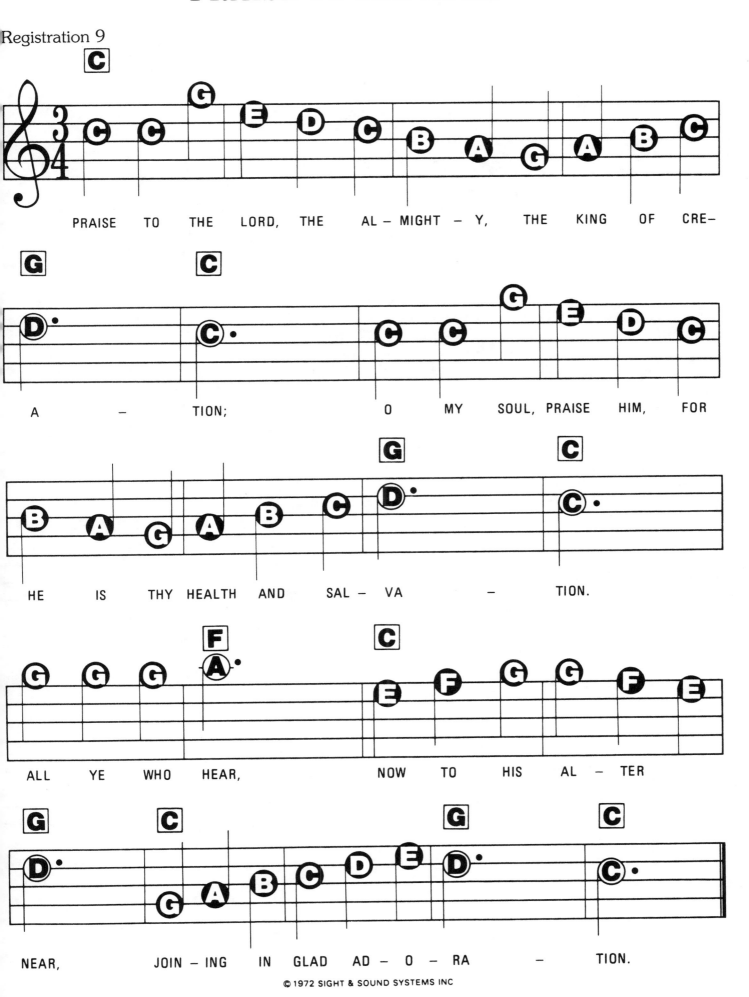

Recorded by JACKIE DeSHANNON

PUT A LITTLE LOVE IN YOUR HEART

Registration 2
Rhythm: Rock or 8 Beat

Words and Music by JIMMY HOLIDAY
RANDY MYERS and JACKI DE SHANNON

Think of your fel - low man, lend him a help - ing hand,
An - oth - er day goes by, and still the chil - dren cry,

Put a lit - tle love in your heart. _____
Put a lit - tle love in your heart. _____ If

You see, it's get - ting late, oh, please don't hes - i - tate, ___
You want the world to know, we won't let ha - tred grow, ___

Put a lit - tle love in your heart. _____
Put a lit - tle love in your heart. _____ And the
and the

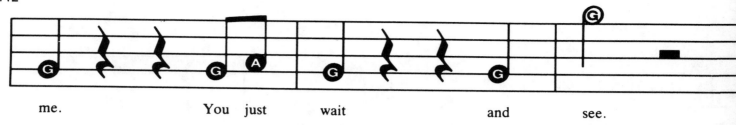

me.　　　You just　wait　　　　and　see.

F　　　　　　　　　　　　　　　　**C**　　　　　　*Repeat and fade*

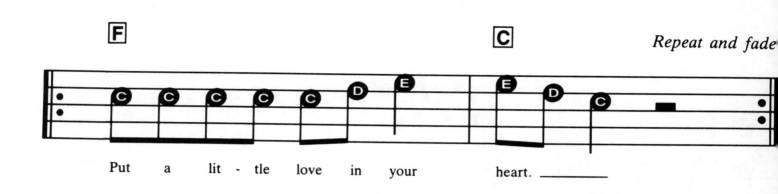

Put　a　lit - tle　love　in　your　　　heart. _____

REVIVE US AGAIN

Registration 8
Rhythm: Waltz

G

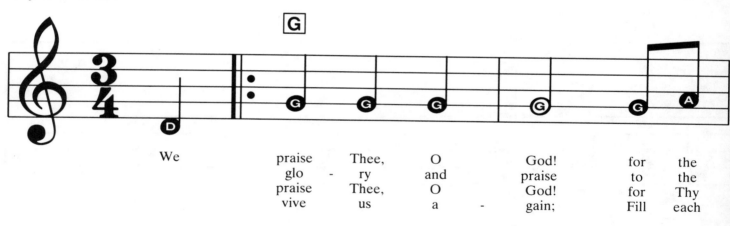

	We	praise	Thee,	O	God!	for	the
		glo - ry	and		praise	to	the
		praise	Thee,	O	God!	for	Thy
		vive	us	a -	gain;	Fill	each

Son	of	Thy	love	For _____	Je -	sus	who
Lamb	that	was	slain,	Who	has	borne	all	our
Spir -	it	of	light,	Who	has	shown	us	our
heart	with	Thy	love;	May	each	soul	be	re -

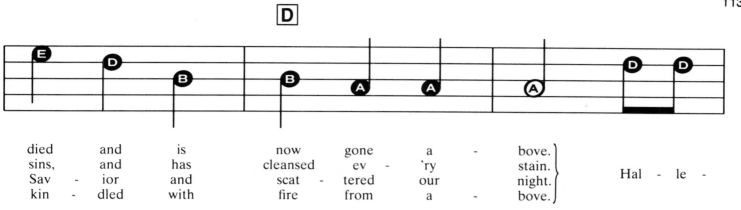

died and is now gone a - bove.
sins, and has cleansed ev - 'ry stain.
Sav - ior and scat - tered our night.
kin - dled with fire from a - bove.

Hal - le -

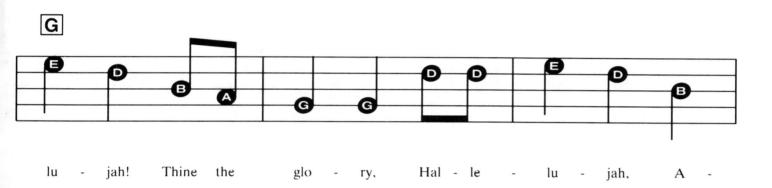

lu - jah! Thine the glo - ry, Hal - le - lu - jah, A -

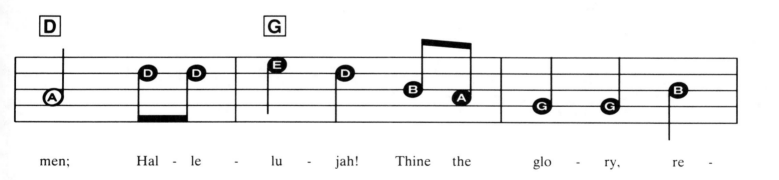

men; Hal - le - lu - jah! Thine the glo - ry, re -

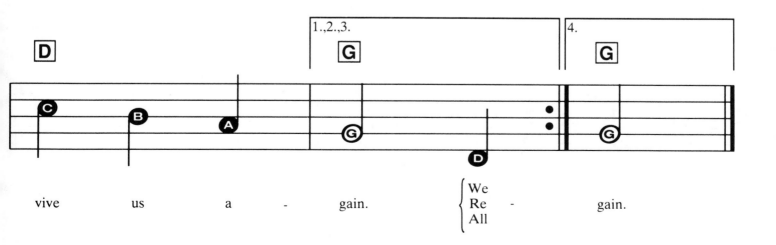

vive us a - gain.

We
Re - gain.
All

PRAYER OF THANKSGIVING

114

Registration 1
Rhythm: Waltz

RISE UP, O MEN OF GOD

Registration 6

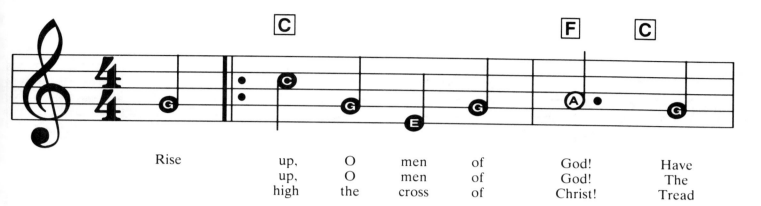

Rise   up,   O   men   of   God!   Have
up,   O   men   of   God!   The
high   the   cross   of   Christ!   Tread

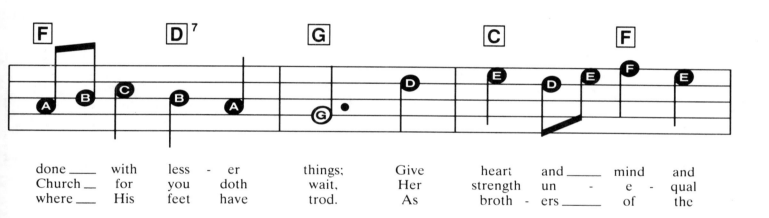

done with less - er things; Give heart and mind and
Church for you doth wait, Her strength un - e - qual
where His feet have trod. As broth - ers of the

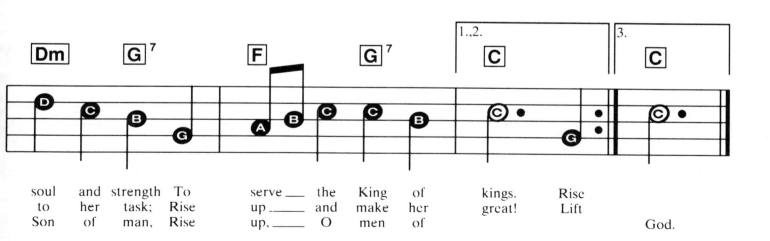

soul and strength To serve the King of kings. Rise
to her task; Rise up and make her great! Lift
Son of man, Rise up, O men of

God.

SAVIOR, LIKE A SHEPHERD LEAD US

Registration 1
Rhythm: Swing

Sav	-	ior,	like	a	shep - herd	lead	us,	
We		are	Thine,	do thou be -	friend	us,	
Thou	hast	prom - ised	to	re -	ceive	us,	
Ear	-	ly	let us seek Thy	fa -	vor,	

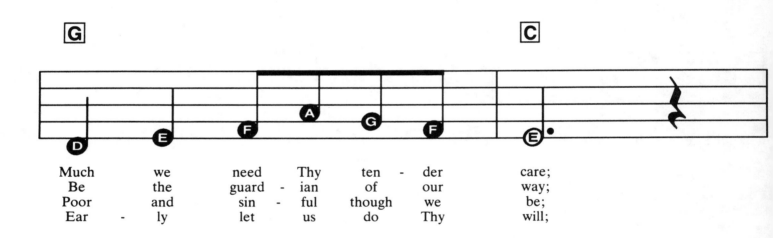

Much	we	need	Thy ten - der	care;
Be	the	guard - ian	of our	way;
Poor	and	sin - ful	though we	be;
Ear	- ly	let	us do Thy	will;

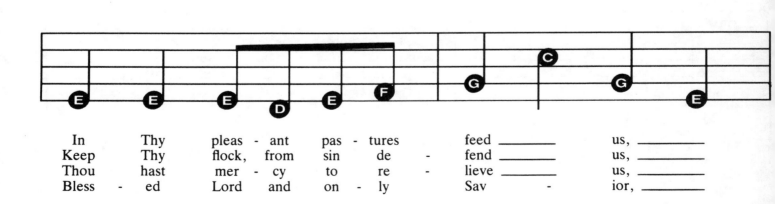

In	Thy	pleas - ant	pas - tures	feed	us,	
Keep	Thy	flock,	from sin de -	fend	us,	
Thou	hast	mer - cy	to re -	lieve	us,	
Bless	- ed	Lord	and on - ly	Sav	-	ior,

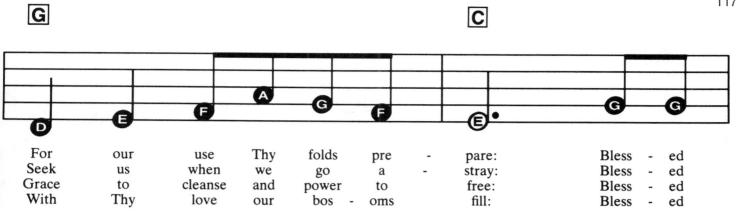

G   **C**

For	our	use	Thy	folds	pre	-	pare:	Bless - ed
Seek	us	when	we	go	a	-	stray:	Bless - ed
Grace	to	cleanse	and	power	to		free:	Bless - ed
With	Thy	love	our	bos - oms			fill:	Bless - ed

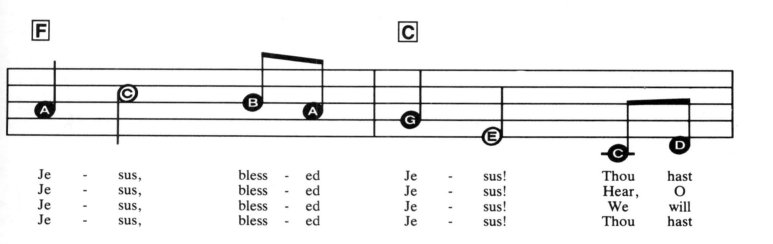

F   **C**

Je	-	sus,	bless - ed	Je	-	sus!	Thou	hast
Je	-	sus,	bless - ed	Je	-	sus!	Hear,	O
Je	-	sus,	bless - ed	Je	-	sus!	We	will
Je	-	sus,	bless - ed	Je	-	sus!	Thou	hast

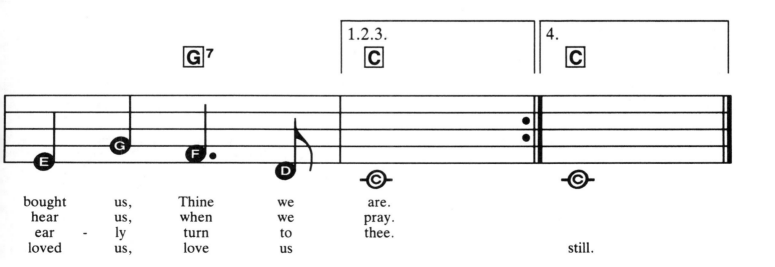

G⁷   **1.2.3.** **C**   **4.** **C**

bought	us,	Thine	we	are.
hear	us,	when	we	pray.
ear	- ly	turn	to	thee.
loved	us,	love	us	still.

ROCK OF AGES

Registration 6

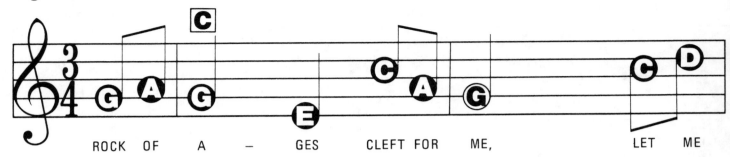

ROCK OF A — GES CLEFT FOR ME, LET ME

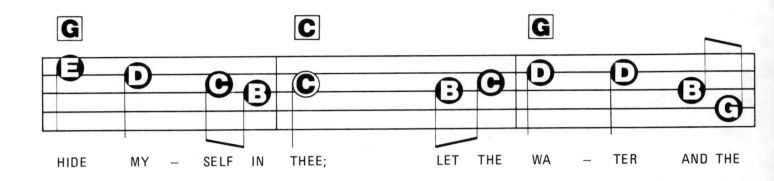

HIDE MY — SELF IN THEE; LET THE WA — TER AND THE

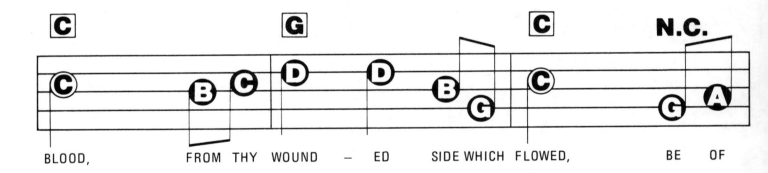

BLOOD, FROM THY WOUND — ED SIDE WHICH FLOWED, BE OF

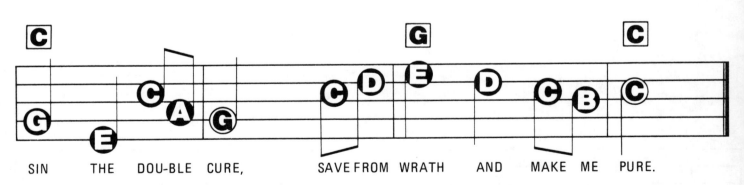

SIN THE DOU-BLE CURE, SAVE FROM WRATH AND MAKE ME PURE.

2.) COULD MY TEARS FOREVER FLOW,
COULD MY ZEAL NO LANGUOR KNOW,
THESE FOR SIN COULD NOT ATONE;
THOU MUST SAVE, AND THOU ALONE:
IN MY HAND NO PRICE I BRING,
SIMPLY TO THY CROSS I CLING.

3.) WHILE I DRAW THIS FLEETING BREATH,
WHEN MY EYES SHALL CLOSE IN DEATH,
WHEN I RISE TO WORLDS UNKNOWN,
AND BEHOLD THEE ON THY THRONE
ROCK OF AGES, CLEFT FOR ME,
LET ME HIDE MYSELF IN THEE.

SHALL WE GATHER AT THE RIVER?

Registration 2
Rhythm: Swing

OH, HOW I LOVE JESUS

Registration 4
Rhythm: Waltz

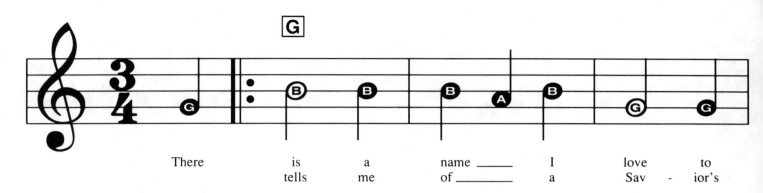

There is a name ____ I love to
tells me of _____ a Sav - ior's

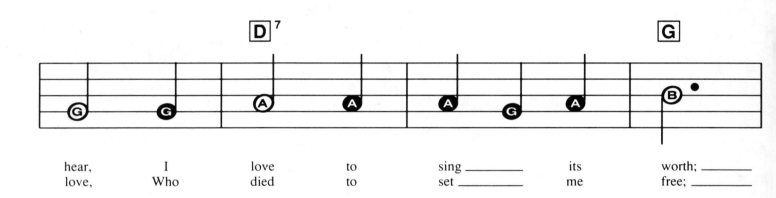

hear, I love to sing _____ its worth; _____
love, Who died to set _____ me free; _____

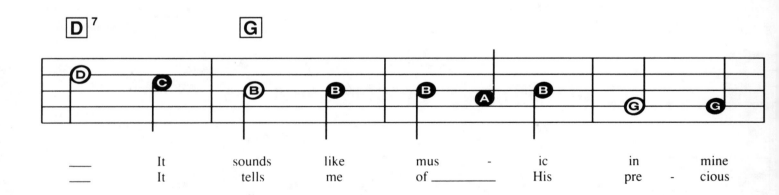

____ It sounds like mus - ic in mine
____ It tells me of _____ His pre - cious

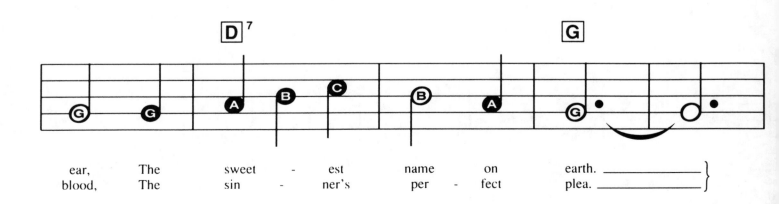

ear, The sweet - est name on earth. _____ }
blood, The sin - ner's per - fect plea. _____ }

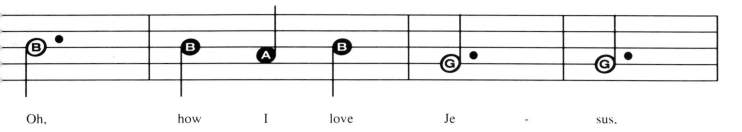

Oh,   how   I   love   Je - sus.

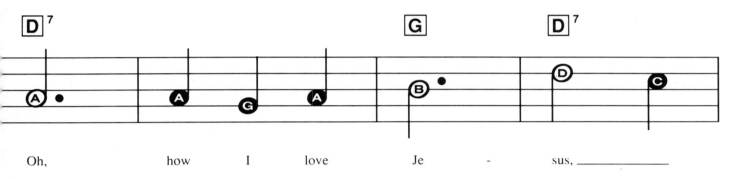

Oh,   how   I   love   Je - sus, _____

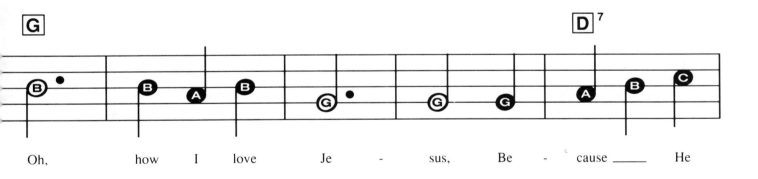

Oh,   how   I   love   Je - sus,   Be - cause _____ He

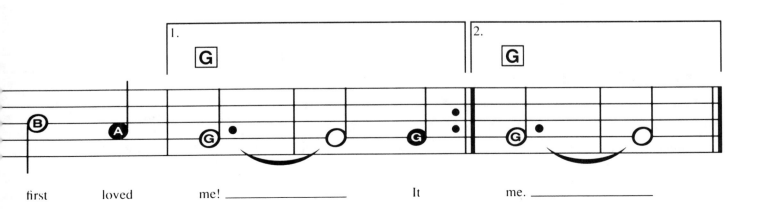

first   loved   me! _____   It   me. _____

THAT OLD-TIME RELIGION

Registration 7
Rhythm: Swing

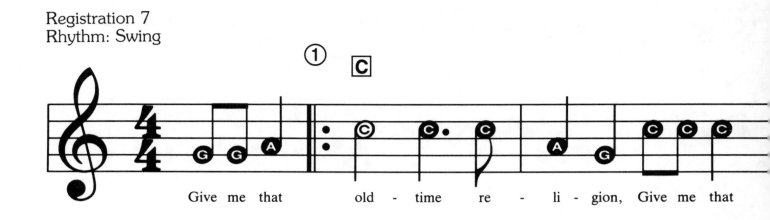

Give me that old - time re - li - gion, Give me that

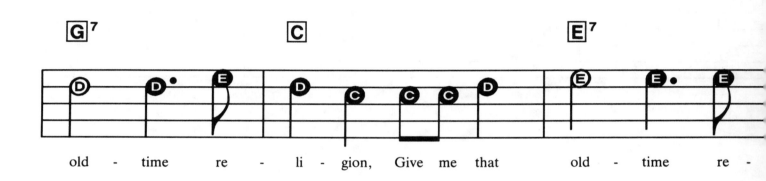

old - time re - li - gion, Give me that old - time re -

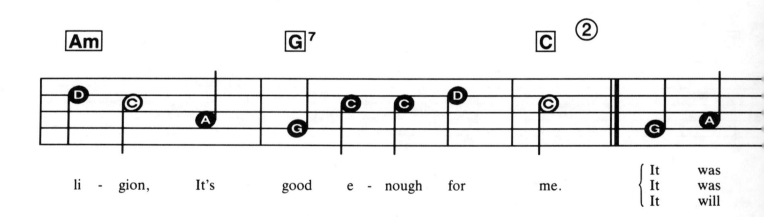

li - gion, It's good e - nough for me.

It was
It was
It will

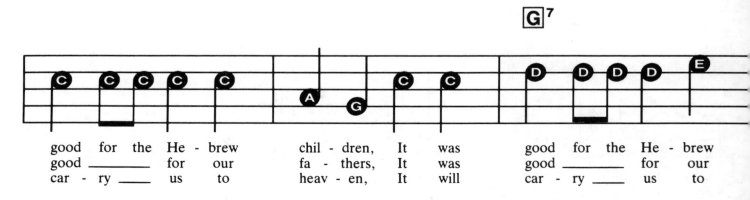

good for the He - brew chil - dren, It was good for the He - brew
good _____ for our fa - thers, It was good _____ for our
car - ry _____ us to heav - en, It will car - ry _____ us to

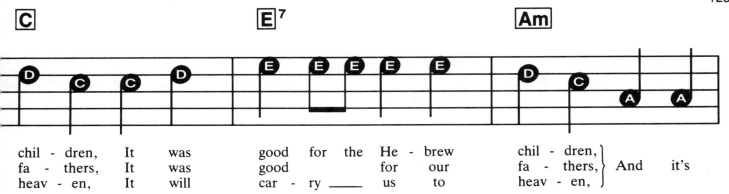

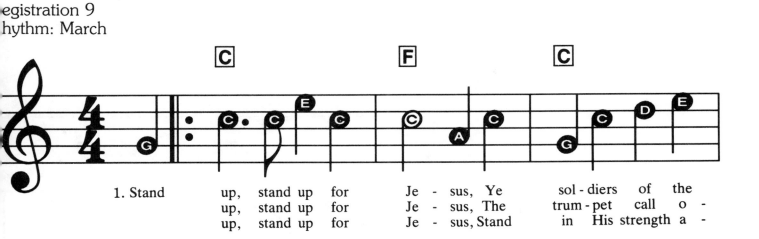

STAND UP, STAND UP FOR JESUS

Registration 9
Rhythm: March

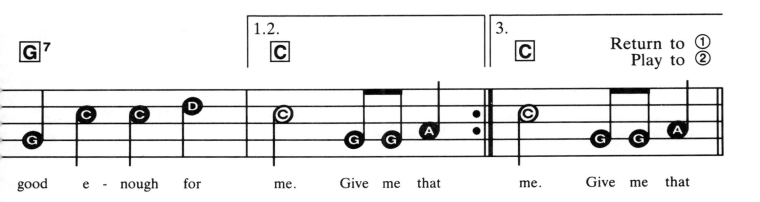

124

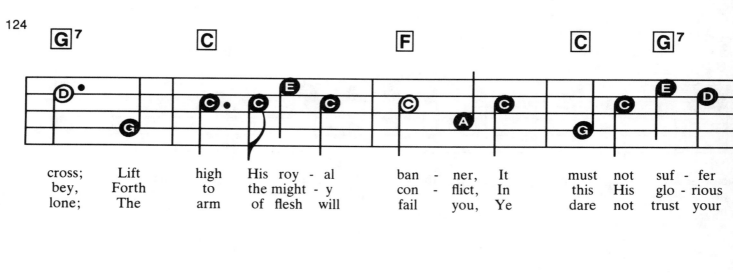

cross; Lift high His roy - al | ban - ner, It | must not suf - fer
bey, Forth to the might - y | con - flict, In | this His glo - rious
lone; The arm of flesh will | fail you, Ye | dare not trust your

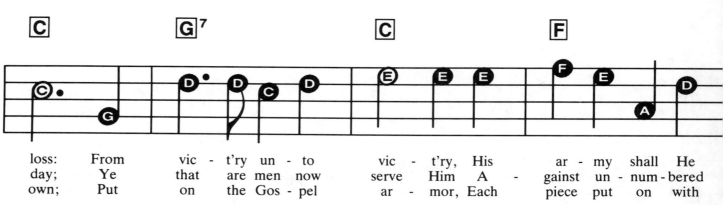

loss: From vic - t'ry un - to | vic - t'ry, His | ar - my shall He
day; Ye that are men now | serve Him A - | gainst un - num - bered
own; Put on the Gos - pel | ar - mor, Each | piece put on with

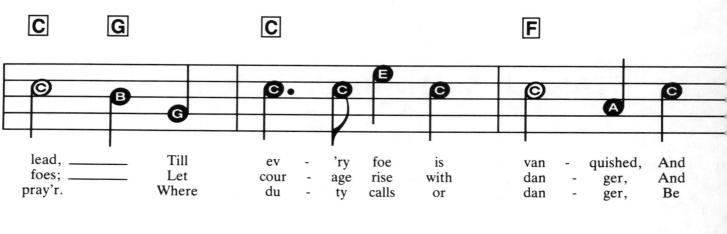

lead, _____ Till | ev - 'ry foe is | van - quished, And
foes; _____ Let | cour - age rise with | dan - ger, And
pray'r. Where | du - ty calls or | dan - ger, Be

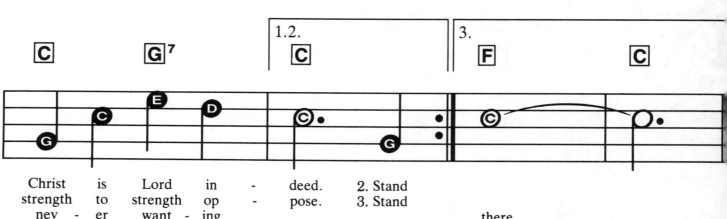

Christ is Lord in - | deed. 2. Stand
strength to strength op - | pose. 3. Stand
nev - er want - ing | | there. _____

SWING LOW, SWEET CHARIOT

Registration 7
Rhythm: Swing

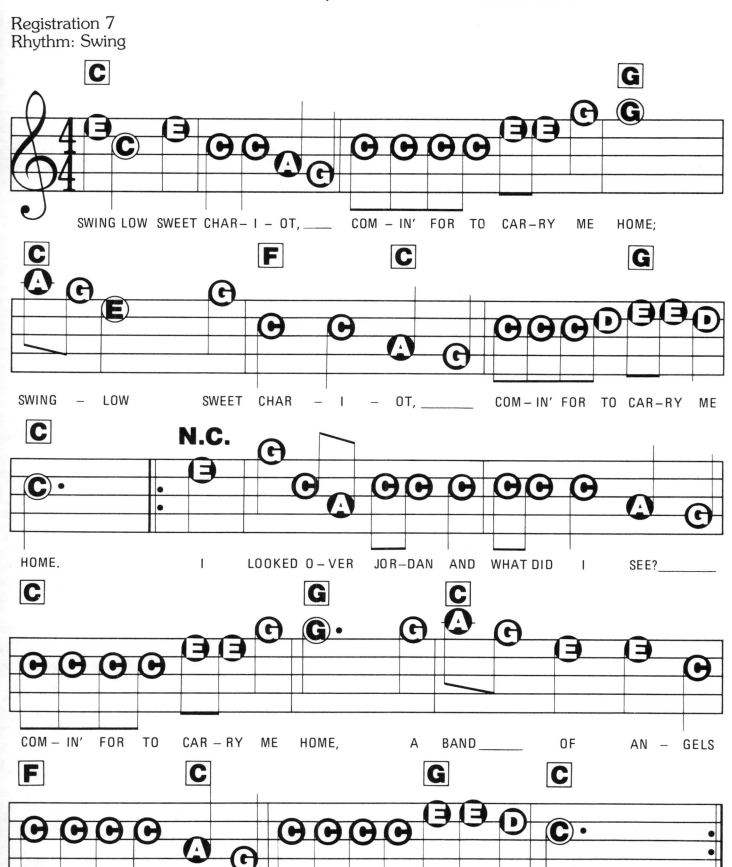

THE STRIFE IS O'ER, THE BATTLE DONE

Registration 6

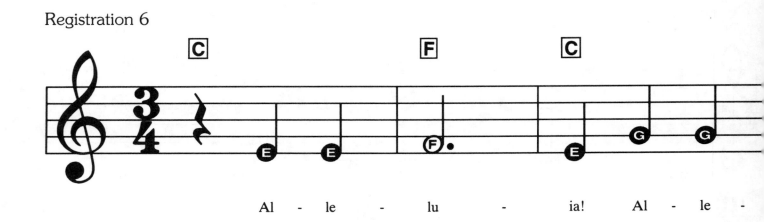

Al - le - lu - ia! Al - le -

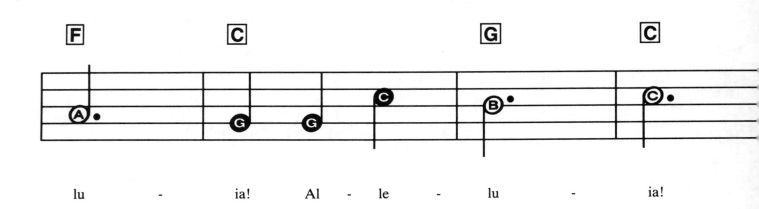

lu - ia! Al - le - lu - ia!

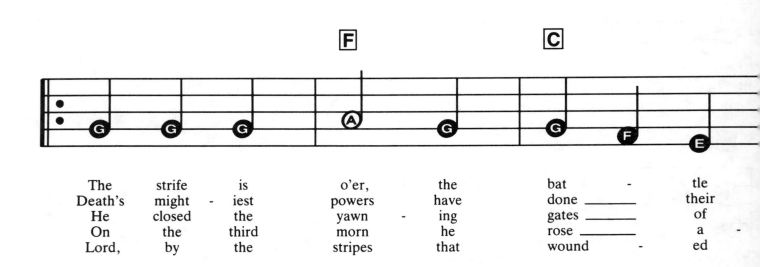

The	strife	is	o'er,	the	bat	-	tle
Death's	might	- iest	powers	have	done ____		their
He	closed	the	yawn	- ing	gates ____		of
On	the	third	morn	he	rose ____		a -
Lord,	by	the	stripes	that	wound	- ed	

done; | Now | is | the | Vic | - | tor's | tri | - | umph
worst, | And | Je | - | sus | has | his | foes ___ | dis | -
hell; | The | bars | of | heaven's | high | por | - | tal's
gain | Glo | - | rious | in | maj | es | - | ty ___ | to
thee | From | death's | dread | string | es | thy | ser | - | vants

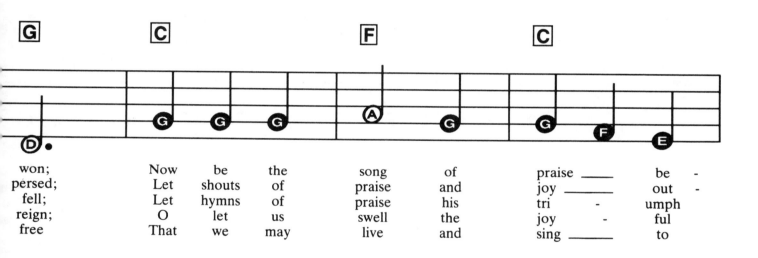

won; | Now | be | the | song | of | praise ___ | be | -
persed; | Let | be | shouts | of | praise | and | joy ___ | out | -
fell; | Let | hymns | of | praise | his | tri | - | umph
reign; | O | let | us | swell | the | joy | - | ful
free | That | we | may | live | and | sing ___ | to

1.2.3.4. | 5.

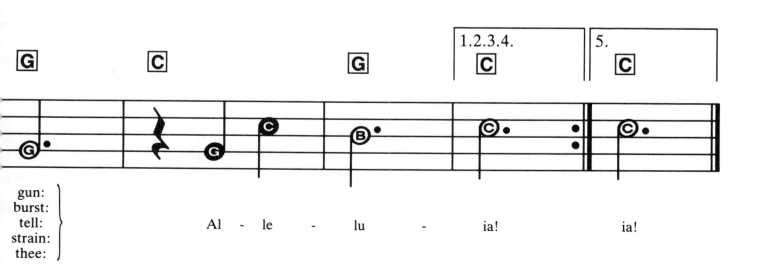

gun:
burst:
tell:
strain:
thee:

Al - le - lu - ia! ia!

SOFTLY AND TENDERLY

Registration 10
Rhythm: Swing

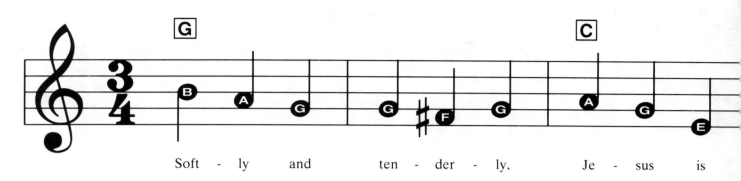

Soft - ly and ten - der - ly, Je - sus is

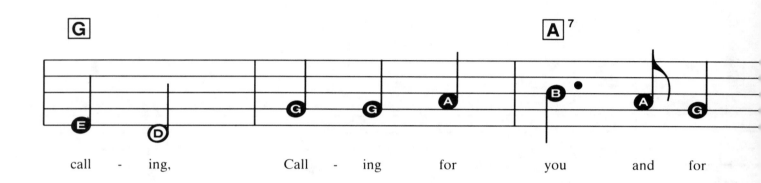

call - ing, Call - ing for you and for

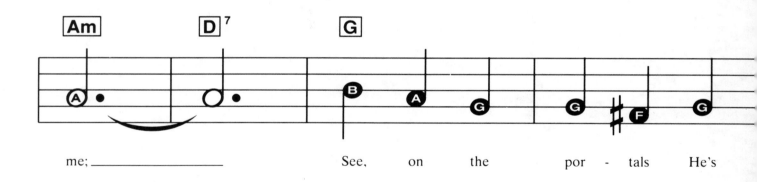

me;_____ See, on the por - tals He's

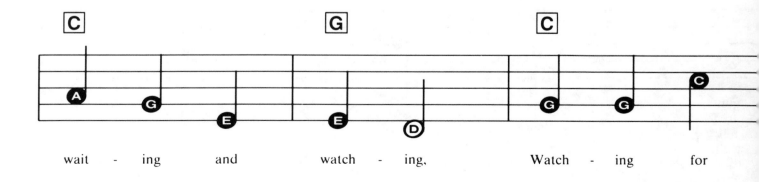

wait - ing and watch - ing, Watch - ing for

THERE IS POWER IN THE BLOOD

Registration 9
Rhythm: Rock or 8 Beat

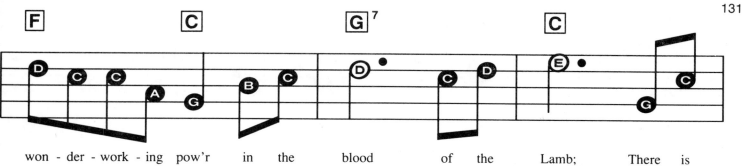

won - der - work -ing pow'r in the blood of the Lamb; There is

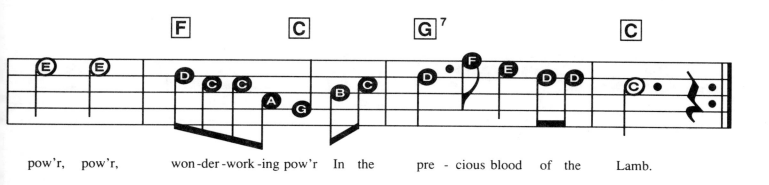

pow'r, pow'r, won-der-work -ing pow'r In the pre - cious blood of the Lamb.

STANDING ON THE PROMISES

Registration 7
Rhythm: Swing

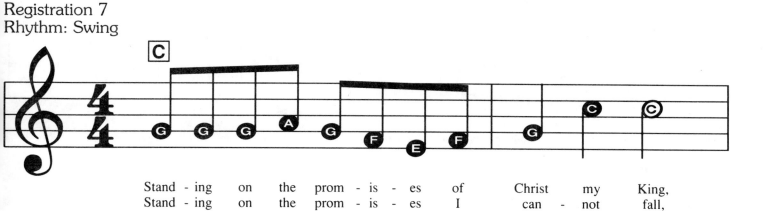

Stand - ing on the prom - is - es of Christ my King,
Stand - ing on the prom - is - es I can - not fall,

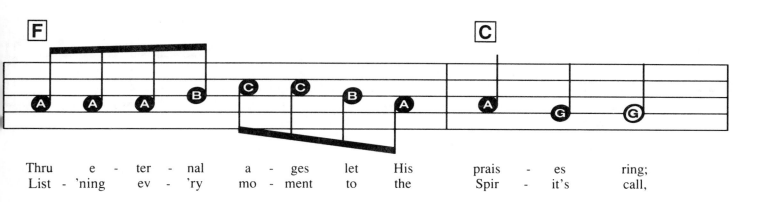

Thru e - ter - nal a - ges let His prais - es ring;
List - 'ning ev - 'ry mo - ment to the Spir - it's call,

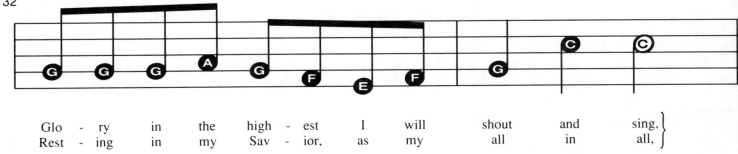

Glo - ry in the high - est I will shout and sing,
Rest - ing in my Sav - ior, as my all in all, }

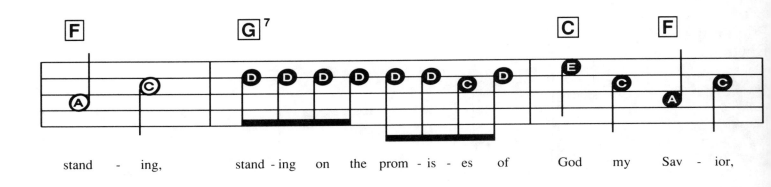

Stand - ing on the prom - is - es of God. Stand - ing,

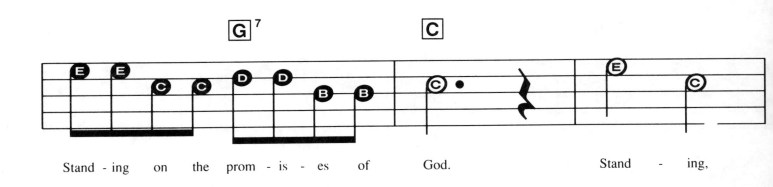

stand - ing, stand - ing on the prom - is - es of God my Sav - ior,

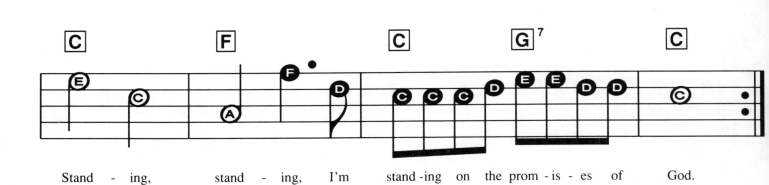

Stand - ing, stand - ing, I'm stand - ing on the prom - is - es of God.

THEE WE ADORE, ETERNAL LORD!

Registration 4
Rhythm: Waltz

THERE'S A WIDENESS IN GOD'S MERCY

Registration 1
Rhythm: Swing

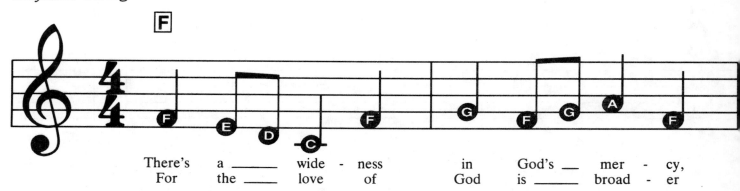

There's a ____ wide - ness in God's ____ mer - cy,
For the ____ love of God is ____ broad - er

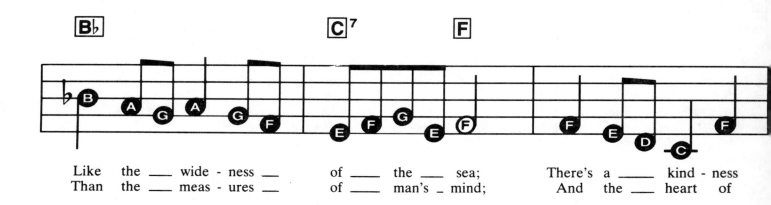

Like the ____ wide - ness ____ of ____ the ____ sea; There's a ____ kind - ness
Than the ____ meas - ures ____ of ____ man's _ mind; And the ____ heart of

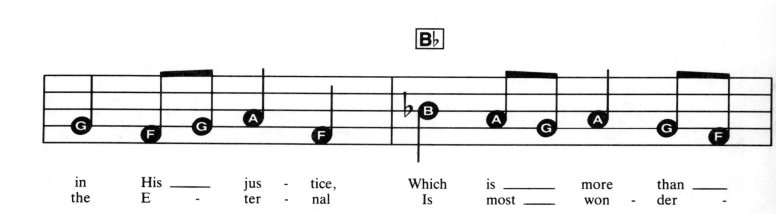

in His ____ jus - tice, Which is ____ more than ____
the E - ter - nal Is most ____ won - der -

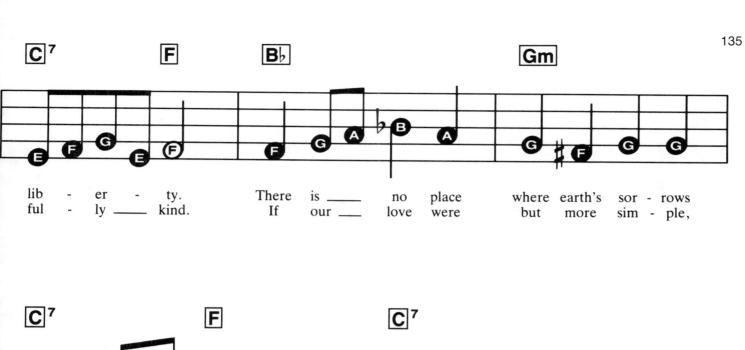

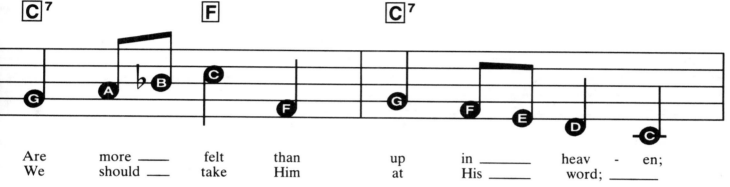

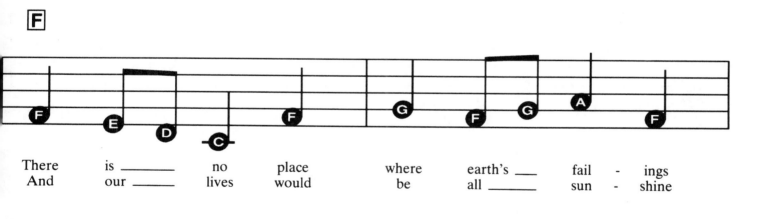

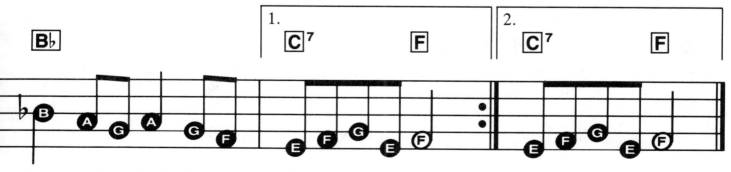

SWEET HOUR OF PRAYER

Registration 10
Rhythm: Waltz

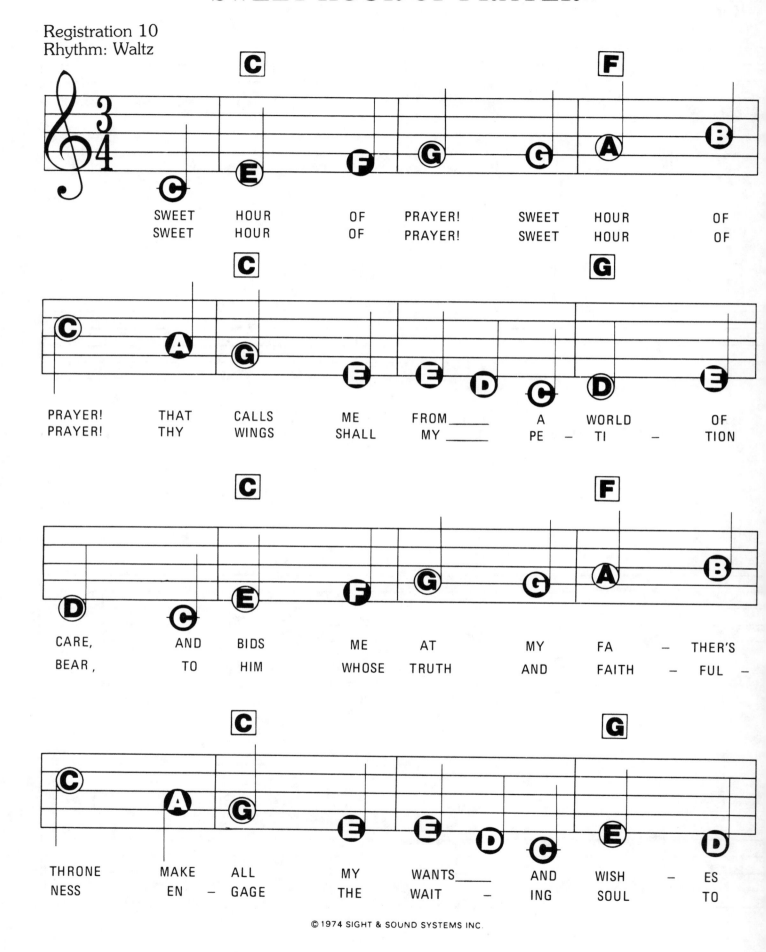

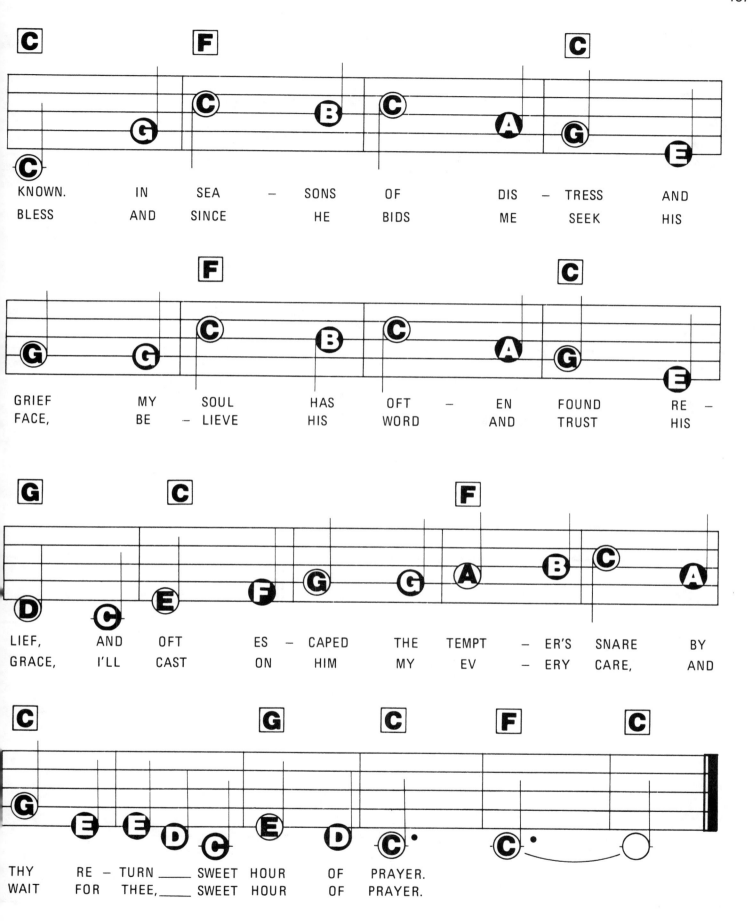

WAYFARING STRANGER

Registration 8
Rhythm: Swing

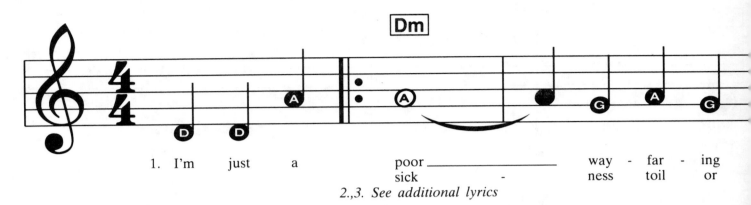

1. I'm just a poor _____ way - far - ing
sick - ness toil or
2.,3. See additional lyrics

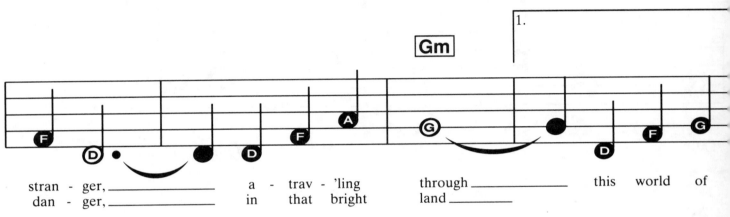

stran - ger, _____ a - trav - 'ling through _____ this world of
dan - ger, _____ in that bright land _____

woe. _____ But there's no _____ to which I

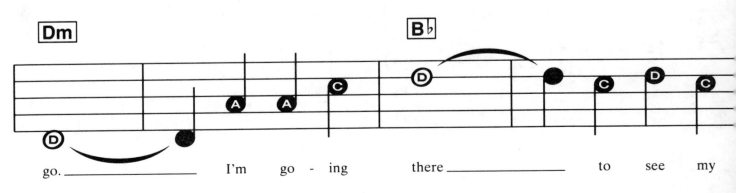

go. _____ I'm go - ing there _____ to see my

Additional Lyrics

2. I know dark clouds will gather 'round me,
   I know my way is steep and rough,
   But beauteous fields lie just beyond me
   Where souls redeemed their vigil keep.
   I'm going there to meet my mother,
   She said she'd meet me when I come . . .

3. I want to wear a crown of glory
   When I get home to that bright land.
   I want to shout Salvation's story,
   In concert with that bloodwashed band.
   I'm going there to meet my Saviour,
   To sing His praise forever more . . .

WHEN THE SAINTS GO MARCHING IN

Registration 7
Rhythm: Swing

ODE TO JOY

Registration 7
Rhythm: Rock or 8 Beat

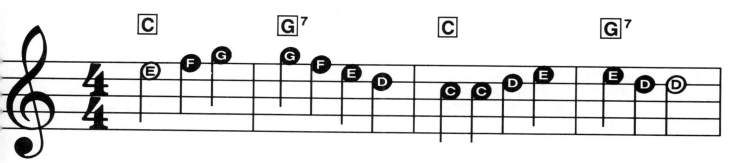

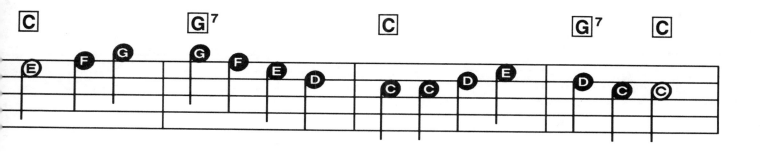

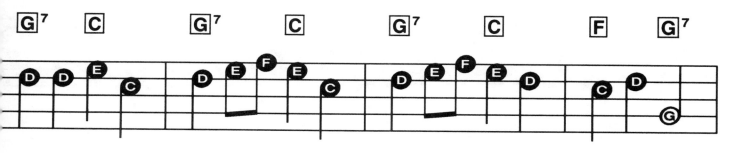

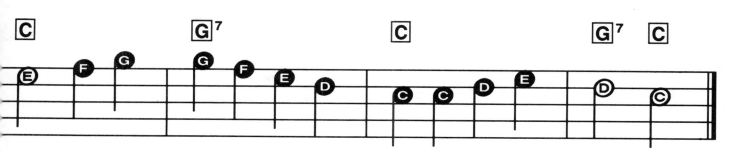

YOU LIGHT UP MY LIFE

Registration 1
Rhythm: Waltz

Words and Music
JOE BROOKS

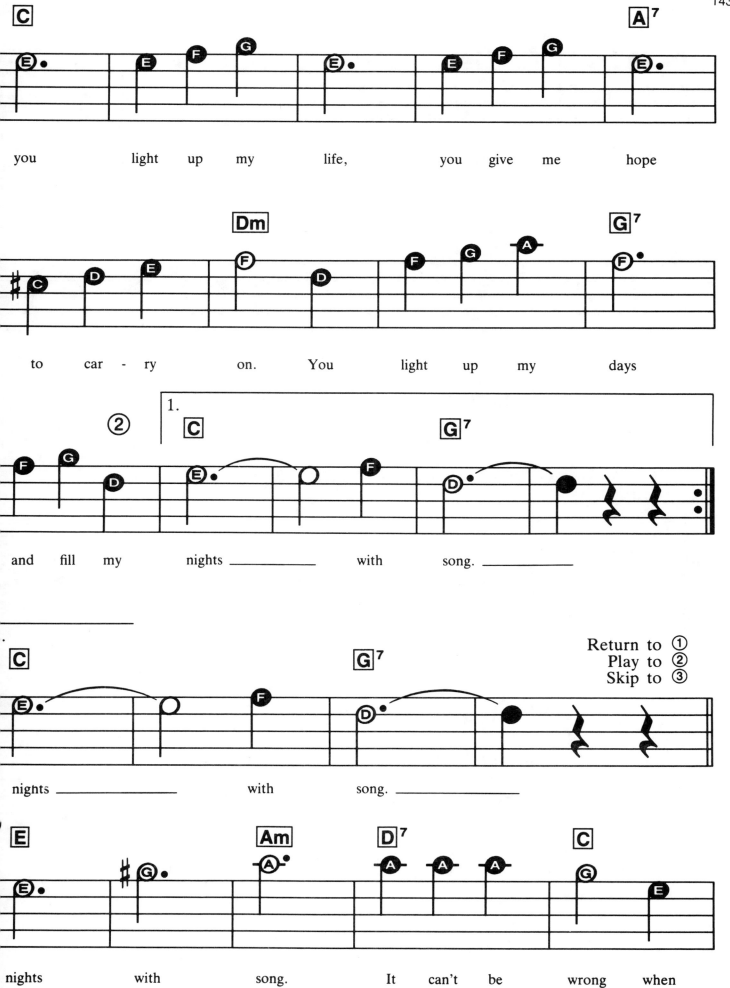

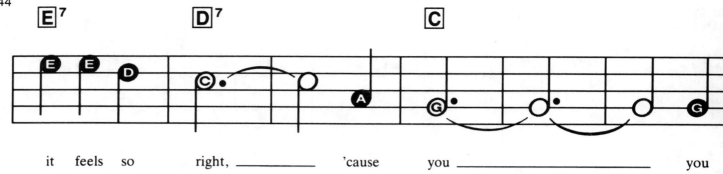

it feels so right, _____ 'cause you _____ you

light up my life. _____

THIS IS MY FATHER'S WORLD

Registration 8

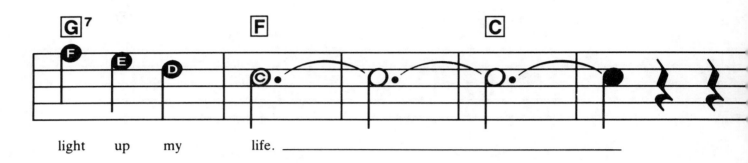

This _____   is   my   Fa - ther's   world,   And _____
                 is   my   Fa - ther's   world,   The _____
                 is   my   Fa - ther's   world,   O _____

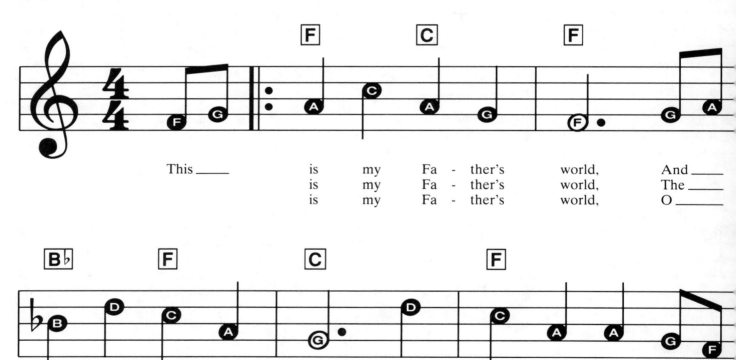

to   my   lis - t'ning   ears   All   na - ture   sings   and _____
birds their car - ols   raise,   The   morn - ing   light,   the _____
let   me   ne'er   for - get   That   tho' the   wrong   seems _____

145

'TIS SO SWEET TO TRUST IN JESUS

Registration 9

WERE YOU THERE?

Registration 2

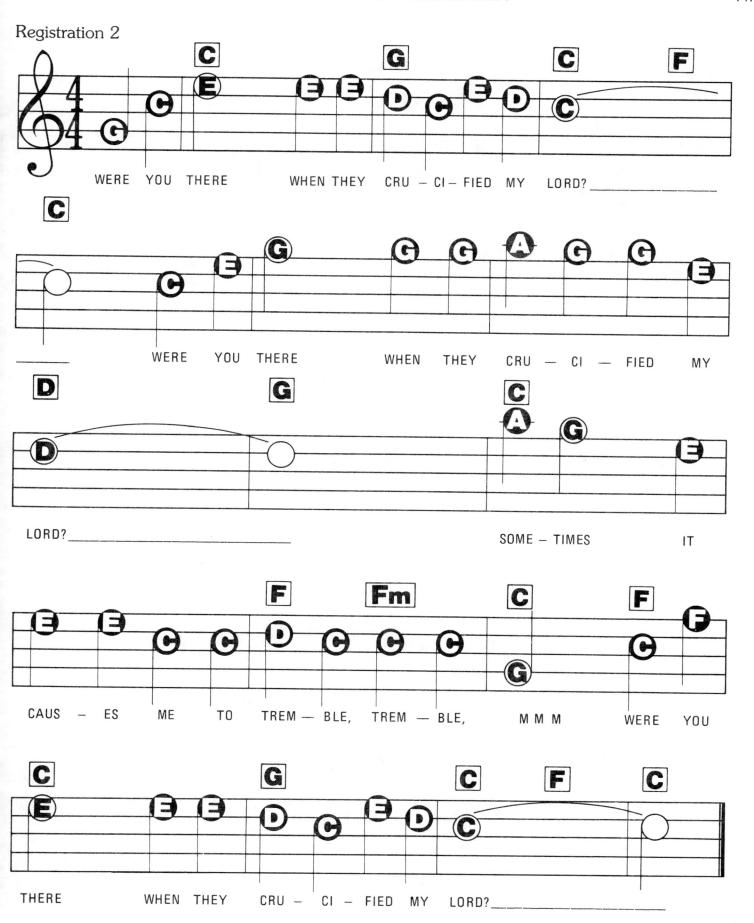

THIS TRAIN

Registration 4
Rhythm: Swing

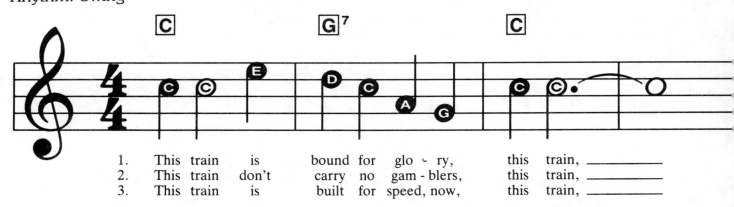

1. This train is bound for glo - ry, this train, _____
2. This train don't carry no gam - blers, this train, _____
3. This train is built for speed, now, this train, _____

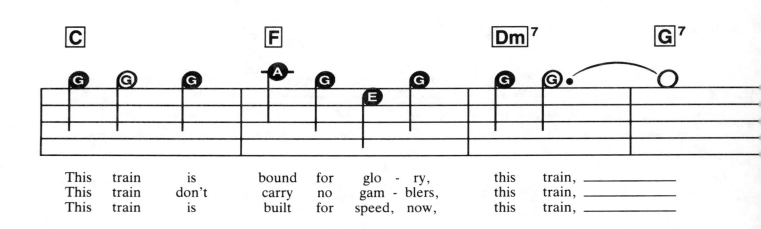

This train is bound for glo - ry, this train, _____
This train don't carry no gam - blers, this train, _____
This train is built for speed, now, this train, _____

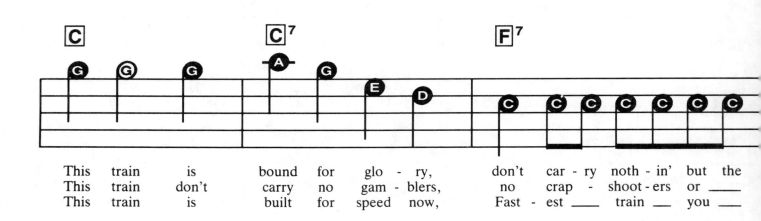

This train is bound for glo - ry, don't car - ry noth - in' but the
This train don't carry no gam - blers, no crap - shoot - ers or _____
This train is built for speed now, Fast - est _____ train _____ you

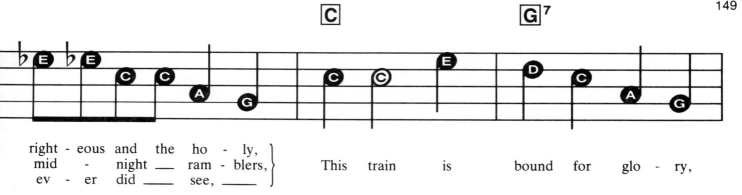

right - eous and the ho - ly,
mid - night __ ram - blers,
ev - er did __ see, __

This train is bound for glo - ry,

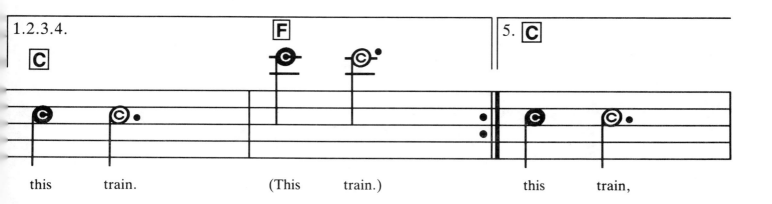

1.2.3.4.

this train.

(This train.)

5.

this train,

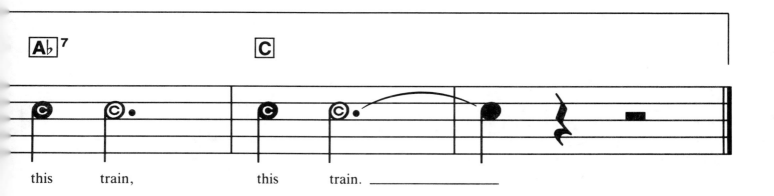

this train,

this train. ___

4. This train don't carry no liars, *etc.*
No hypocrites and no high flyers.
This train is bound for glory, this train.

5. This train don't carry no rustlers, *etc.*
Side-street walkers, two-bit hustlers.
This train is bound for glory, this train . . . this train . . . this train.

WHAT A FRIEND WE HAVE IN JESUS

Registration 7
Rhythm: Swing

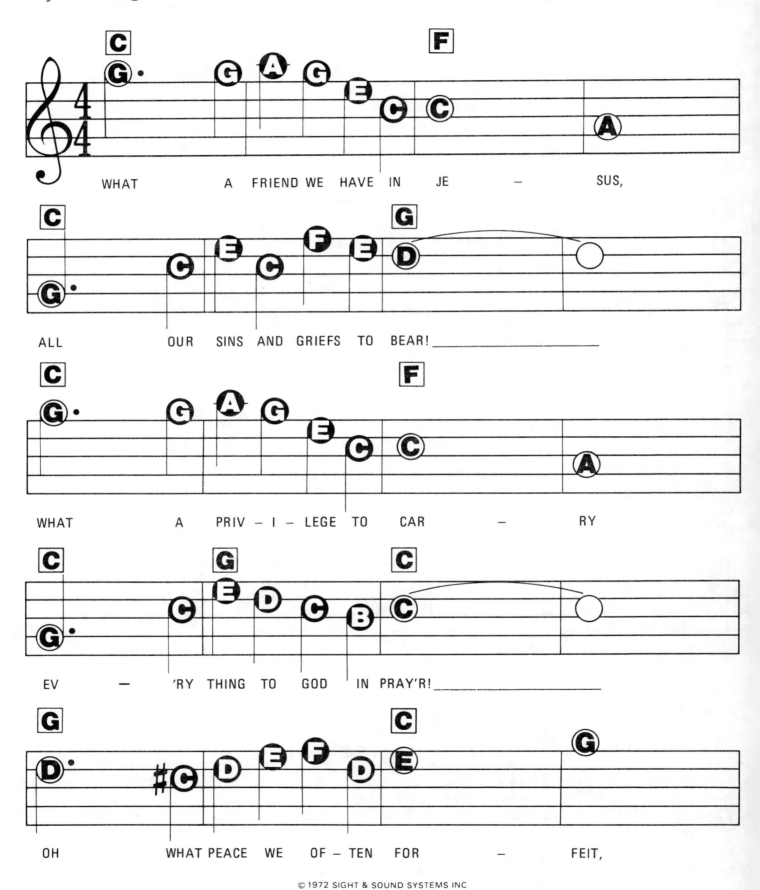

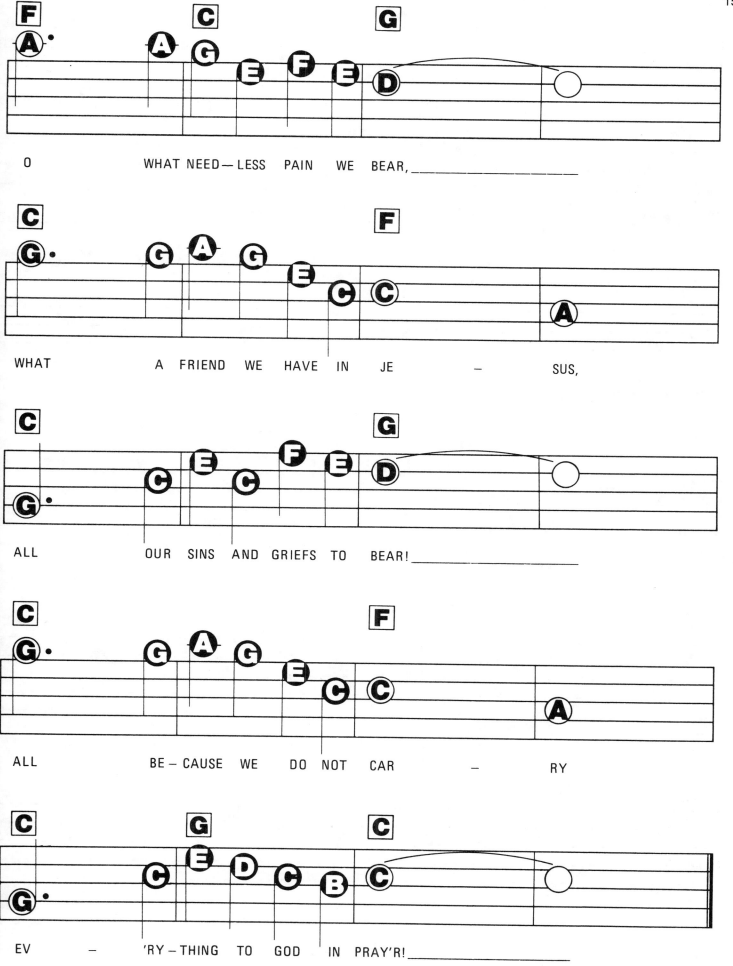

WHAT THE WORLD
NEEDS NOW IS LOVE

Lyric by HAL DAVID
Music by BURT BACHARACH

Registration 8
Rhythm: Waltz

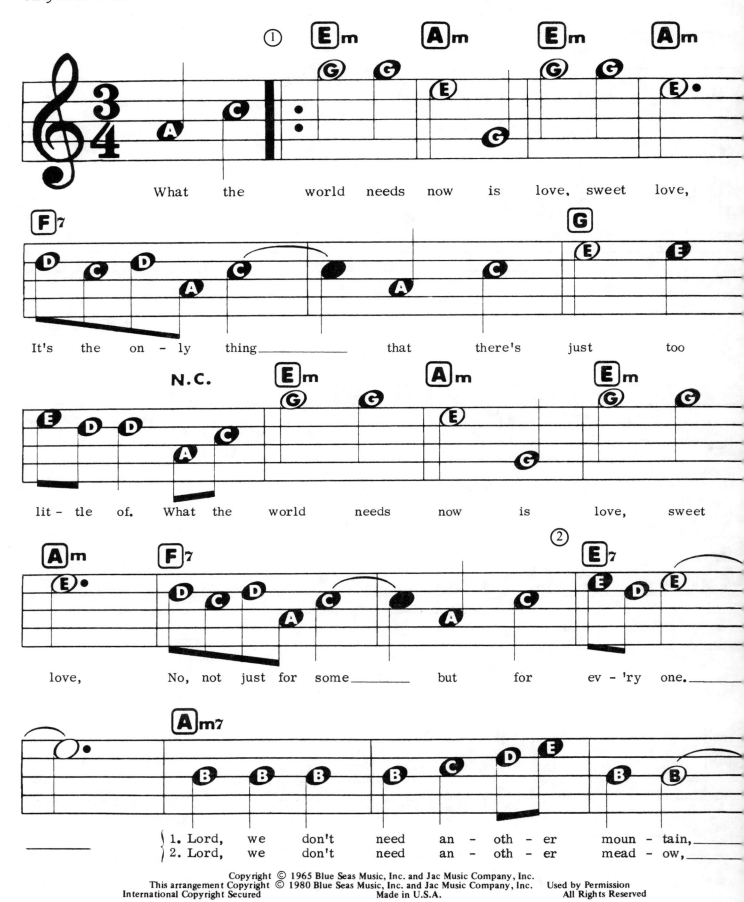

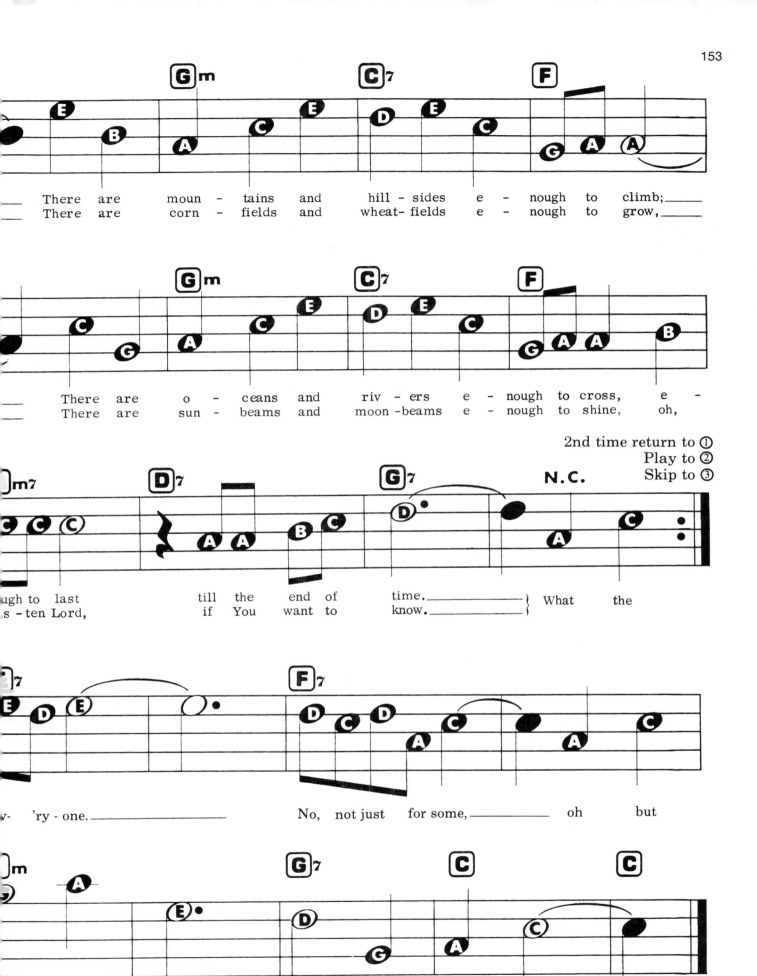

There are moun - tains and hill - sides e - nough to climb;____
There are corn - fields and wheat- fields e - nough to grow,____

There are o - ceans and riv - ers e - nough to cross, e -
There are sun - beams and moon - beams e - nough to shine, oh,

2nd time return to ①
Play to ②
Skip to ③

N.C.

..ugh to last till the end of time._____ } What the
..s - ten Lord, if You want to know._____

..v - 'ry - one._____ No, not just for some,_____ oh but

..st for ev - 'ry - one._____

WHEN I SURVEY THE WONDROUS CROSS

Registration 6

When   I   sur - vey   the _____   won - drous _____   cross,
For - bid   it,   Lord,   that _____   I   should _____   boast,
Were   the   whole   realm   of _____   na - ture _____   mine,

On   which   the   Prince   of _____   Glo - ry _____   died,
Save   in   the   death   of _____   Christ,   my _____   God;
That   were   a   pres - ent _____   far   too _____   small;

My   rich - est   gain   I _____   count   but _____   loss,
All   the   vain   things   that _____   charm   me _____   most,
Love   so   a -   maz - ing _____   so   di -   vine,

And   pour   con - tempt   on   all   my _____   pride.
I   sac - ri - fice   them   to   His _____   blood.
De - mands   my   soul,   my   life,   my _____   all.

WHEN MORNING GILDS THE SKIES

istration 4

When morn-ing gilds the skies, ___ My heart a-wak-ing
The night be-comes as day, ___ When from the heart we
Ye na-tions of man - kind, ___ In this you con-cord
Be this, while life is mine, ___ My can-ti-cle di -

cries, May Je - sus Christ be praised! A -
say, May Je - sus Christ be praised! The
find, May Je - sus Christ be praised! Let
vine, May Je - sus Christ be praised! Be

like at work and prayer, To Je - sus I re -
owers of work dark - ness fear, When this sweet chant they
all the earth a - round Ring joy - ous with the
this th'e - ter - nal song Through all the a - ges

pair;
hear; May Je - sus Christ be praised!
ound,
long,

WHISPERING HOPE

Registration 10
Rhythm: Waltz

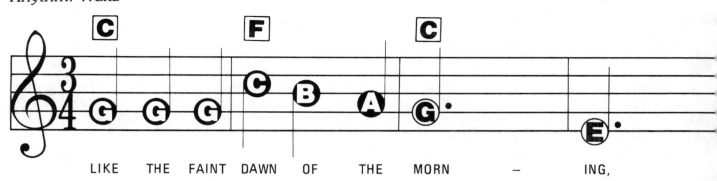

LIKE THE FAINT DAWN OF THE MORN — ING,

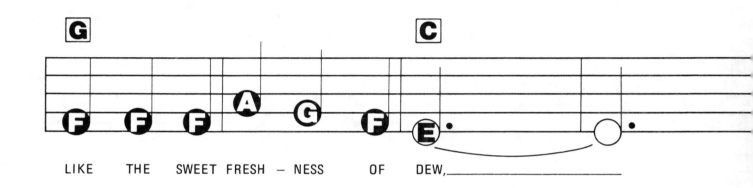

LIKE THE SWEET FRESH — NESS OF DEW,_____

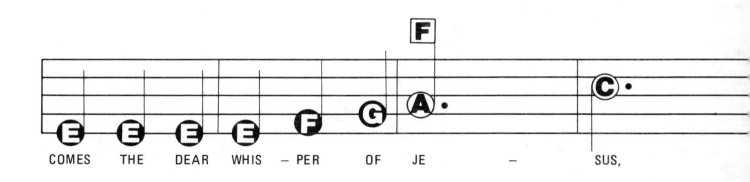

COMES THE DEAR WHIS — PER OF JE — SUS,

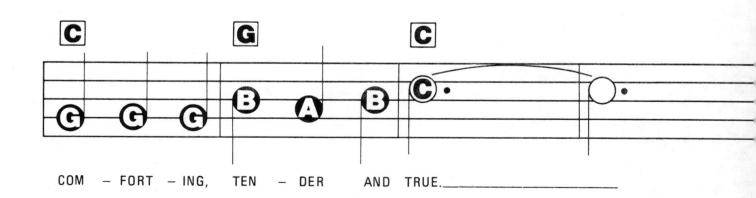

COM — FORT — ING, TEN — DER AND TRUE._____

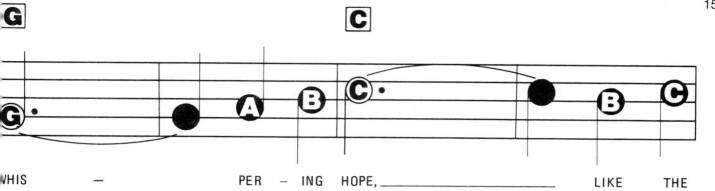

WHIS — PER — ING HOPE, _____ LIKE THE

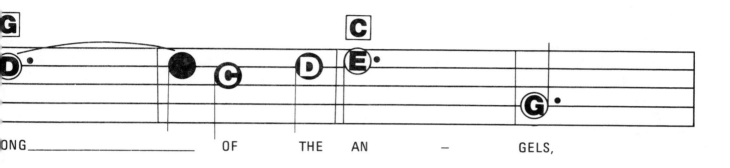

ONG _____ OF THE AN — GELS,

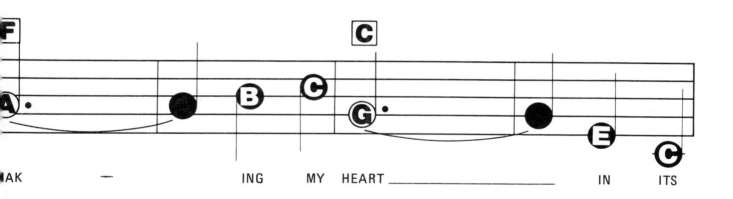

AK — ING MY HEART _____ IN ITS

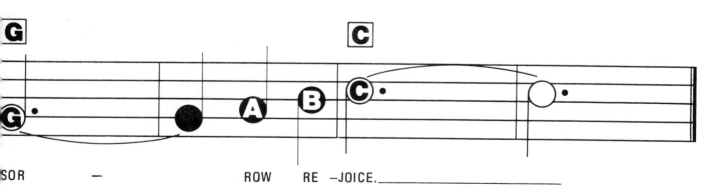

SOR — ROW RE —JOICE. _____

INGING THE SONG OF FORGIVENESS,
OFTLY I HEAR IN MY SOUL,
ESUS HAS CONQUERED FOREVER
IN WITH ITS FEARFUL CONTROL

3. HOPE IS AN ANCHOR TO KEEP US,
   HOLDING BOTH STEADFAST AND SURE:
   HOPE BRINGS A WONDERFUL CLEANSING,
   THRO' HIS BLOOD, MAKING US PURE.

Registration Guide

- Match the Registration number on the song to the corresponding numbered category bel Select and activate an instrumental sound available on your instrument.
- Choose an automatic rhythm appropriate to the mood and style of the song. (Consult you Owner's Guide for proper operation of automatic rhythm features.)
- Adjust the tempo and volume controls to comfortable settings.

Registration

1	Flute, Pan Flute, Jazz Flute
2	Clarinet, Organ
3	Violin, Strings
4	Brass, Trumpet
5	Synth Ensemble, Accordion, Brass
6	Pipe Organ, Harpsichord
7	Jazz Organ, Vibraphone, Vibes, Electric Piano, Jazz Guit
8	Piano, Electric Piano
9	Trumpet, Trombone, Clarinet, Saxophone, Oboe
10	Violin, Cello, Strings